"*I LOVED THE BOOK! Why didn't I have this book two months ago! . . . a valuable guide . . . very helpful for the first time traveler in Asia . . . worth packing in the suitcase for a return visit.*" – Editor, **Unique & Exotic Travel Reporter**

"*VERY USEFUL, PERFECTLY ORGANIZED. Finally a guide that combines Asian shopping opportunities with the tips and know-how to really get the best buys.*" – **National Motorist**

"*INFORMATION-PACKED PAGES point out where the best shops are located, how to save time when shopping, and where and when to deal . . . You'll be a smarter travel shopper if you follow the advice of this new book.*" – **AAA World**

"*DETAILED, AND RELEVANT, EVEN ABSORBING in places . . . The authors know their subject thoroughly, and the reader can benefit greatly from their advice and tips. They go a long way to removing any mystery or uneasiness about shopping in Asia by the neophyte.*" – **The Small Press Book Review**

WHAT SEASONED TRAVELERS SAY

"*IMMENSELY USEFUL . . . thanks for sharing the fruits of your incredibly thorough research. You saved me hours of time and put me in touch with the best.*" – **C.N.**, DeKalb, Illinois

"*FABULOUS! I've just returned from my third shopping trip to Southeast Asia in three years. This book, which is now wrinkled, torn, and looking much abused, has been my bible for the past three years. All your suggestions (pre-trip) and information was so great. When I get ready to go again, my 'bible,' even though tattered and torn, will accompany me again! Thanks again for all your wonderful knowledge, and for sharing it!*" – **D.P.**, Havertown, Pennsylvania

"*I LOVE IT. I've read a lot of travel books, and of all the books of this nature, this is the best I've ever read. Especially for first timers, the how-to information is invaluable.*" – **A.K.**, Portland, Oregon

"*THE BEST TRAVEL BOOK I'VE EVER READ. Believe me, I know my travel books!*" – **S.T.**, Washington, DC

"*MANY MANY THANKS for your wonderful, useful travel guide! You have done a tremendous job. It is so complete and precise and full of neat info.*" – **K.H.**, Seattle, Washington

"*FABULOUS BOOK! I just came back from Hong Kong, Thailand, and Singapore and found your book invaluable. Every place you recommended I found wonderful quality shopping. Send me another copy for my friend in Singapore who was fascinated with it.*" – **M.G.**, Escondido, California

"*THIS IS MY FIRST FAN LETTER . . . you made our trip more special than I can ever say.*" – **N.H.**, New York, New York

THE TREASURES AND PLEASURES
OF EGYPT: BEST OF THE BEST

By Drs. Ron and Caryl Krannich

TRAVEL AND INTERNATIONAL BOOKS

International Jobs Directory
Jobs For People Who Love to Travel
Mayors and Managers in Thailand
Politics of Family Planning Policy in Thailand
Shopping and Traveling in Exotic Asia
Shopping in Exotic Places
Shopping the Exotic South Pacific
Travel Planning on the Internet
Treasures and Pleasures of Australia
Treasures and Pleasures of China
Treasures and Pleasures of Egypt
Treasures and Pleasures of Hong Kong
Treasures and Pleasures of India
Treasures and Pleasures of Indonesia
Treasures and Pleasures of Israel and Jordan
Treasures and Pleasures of Italy
Treasures and Pleasures of Morocco
Treasures and Pleasures of Paris and the French Riviera
Treasures and Pleasures of the Philippines
Treasures and Pleasures of Rio and São Paulo
Treasures and Pleasures of Singapore and Bali
Treasures and Pleasures of Singapore and Malaysia
Treasures and Pleasures of Thailand
Treasures and Pleasures of Vietnam

BUSINESS AND CAREER BOOKS AND SOFTWARE

101 Dynamite Answers to Interview Questions
101 Secrets of Highly Effective Speakers
201 Dynamite Job Search Letters
America's Top Internet Job Sites
Best Jobs For the 21st Century
Change Your Job, Change Your Life
The Complete Guide to International Jobs and Careers
The Complete Guide to Public Employment
The Directory of Federal Jobs and Employers
Discover the Best Jobs For You!
Dynamite Cover Letters
Dynamite Networking For Dynamite Jobs
Dynamite Resumes
Dynamite Salary Negotiations
Dynamite Tele-Search
The Educator's Guide to Alternative Jobs and Careers
Find a Federal Job Fast!
From Air Force Blue to Corporate Gray
From Army Green to Corporate Gray
From Navy Blue to Corporate Gray
Get a Raise in Seven Days
High Impact Resumes and Letters
Interview For Success
Job-Power Source CD-ROM
Jobs and Careers With Nonprofit Organizations
Moving Out of Education
Moving Out of Government
Re-Careering in Turbulent Times
Resumes & Job Search Letters For Transitioning Military Personnel
Savvy Interviewing
Savvy Networker
Savvy Resume Writer
Ultimate Job Source CD-ROM

IMPACT GUIDES

THE TREASURES
AND PLEASURES OF

Egypt

BEST OF THE BEST

RON AND CARYL KRANNICH, PH.DS

IMPACT PUBLICATIONS
MANASSAS PARK, VA

Library of Congress Cataloguing-in-Publication Data

Krannich, Ronald L.
   The treasures and pleasures of Egypt: best of the best /
      Ronald L. Krannich, Caryl Rae Krannich
      p. cm. – (Impact guides)
   Includes bibliographical references and index.
   ISBN 1-57023-149-4
   1. Shopping – Egypt – Guidebooks. 2. Egypt – Guidebooks.
   I. Krannich, Caryl Rae. II. Title. III. Series.

TX337.E3 K73 2000
380.1'45'0002562 – dc21   00-057561

Publisher: For information on Impact Publications, including current and forthcoming publications, authors, press kits, websites online bookstores, and submission requirements, visit Impact's main website: *www.impactpublications.com*.

Publicity/Rights: For information on publicity, author interviews, and subsidiary rights, contact the Media Relations Department: Tel. 703-361-7300, Fax 703-361-7300, or email: *egypt@impactpub lications.com*.

Sales/Distribution: All bookstore sales are handled through Impact's trade distributor: National Book Network, 15200 NBN Way, Blue Ridge Summit, PA 17214, Tel. 1-800-462-6420. All other sales and distribution inquiries should be directed to the publisher: Sales Department, IMPACT PUBLICATIONS, 9104 Manassas Drive, Suite N, Manassas Park, VA 20111-5211, Tel. 703-361-7300, Fax 703-335-9486, or email: *sales@impactpub lications.com*.

Contents

Part II
Great Destinations

Preface

WELCOME TO ANOTHER IMPACT GUIDE that explores the many unique treasures and pleasures of shopping and traveling in one of the world's most fascinating places – Egypt. Join us as we explore this country from a very different perspective than found in other travel books. We'll take you on an unforgettable journey up the Nile River and into the Sinai Peninsula that will put you in touch with the best quality shops, hotels, and restaurants in Egypt. If you follow us to the end, you'll discover a whole new dimension to both Egypt and travel. Indeed, as the following pages unfold, you'll learn there is a lot more to Egypt, and travel in general, than taking tours, visiting popular tourist sites, and acquiring an unwelcome weight gain attendant with new on-the-road dining habits.

Exciting Egypt offers a wonderful travel experience for those who know what to look for, where to go, and how to properly travel and shop its major destinations. We discovered there is a lot more to "doing" Egypt than the pyramids, tombs, temples, mosques, desert, sun, and beaches that often characterize Egypt's travel image. For us, Egypt is an important shopping destination that yields unique arts, crafts, and jewelry as well as good restaurants, hotels, entertainment, and outdoor sports.

Egypt remains one of our favorite destinations. Its people, products, sights, and sounds continue to enrich our lives.

If you are familiar with our other Impact Guides, you know this will not be another standard travel guide to history, culture, and sightseeing in Egypt. Our approach to travel is very different from most guidebooks. We operate from a particular perspective, and we frequently show our attitude rather than just present you with the sterile "travel facts." While we seek good travel value, we're not budget travelers who are interested in taking you along the low road to Egypt. We've been there, done that at one stage in our lives. If that's the way you want to go, you'll find lots of guidebooks on budget travel to Egypt as well as a whole travel industry geared toward servicing budget travelers and backpackers with everything from hostels to Internet cafés. At the same time, we're not obsessed with local history, culture, and sightseeing. We get just enough history and sightseeing to make our travels interesting rather than obsessive. Accordingly, we include very little on history and sightseeing because they are not our main focus; we also assume you have that information covered from other resources. When we discuss history and sightseeing, we do so in abbreviated form, highlighting what we consider to be the essentials. As you'll quickly discover, we're very focused – we're in search of quality shopping and travel. Rather than spend eight hours a day sightseeing, we may only devote two hours to sightseeing and another six hours learning about the local shopping scene from artisans and shopkeepers. As such, we're very people- and product-oriented when we travel. Through shopping, we meet many interesting and talented people and learn a great deal about their country.

> ❏ Our approach to travel is very different from most guidebooks.
>
> ❏ We're not obsessed with local history, culture, and sightseeing. We get just enough history and sightseeing to make our travels interesting rather than obsessive.
>
> ❏ Through shopping, we meet many interesting and talented people and learn a great deal about their country.
>
> ❏ We're street people who love "the chase" and the serendipity that comes with our style of travel.

What we really enjoy doing, and think we do it well, is shop. For us, shopping makes for great travel adventure. Indeed, we're street people who love "the chase" and the serendipity that comes with our style of travel. We especially enjoy discovering quality products; meeting local artists and craftspeople; unraveling new travel and shopping rules; making new friendships with local business people; staying in fine places; and dining in the best restaurants where we often meet the talented chefs and visit their fascinating kitchens. In the case of Egypt, we want to find the best quality arts, crafts, antiques, jewelry, and apparel as well as discover the best artists and craftspeople. In so doing, we learn a great deal about present Egypt and its talented population.

The chapters that follow represent a particular perspective on Egypt. We purposefully decided to write more than just another travel guide with a few pages on shopping. Since one of our travel passions is shopping, we wanted to share our discoveries with many other travelers who share a similar passion. While some travel guides include a brief and usually dated section on the "whats" and "wheres" of shopping, we saw a need to also explain the "how-tos" of shopping in Egypt. Such a book would both educate and guide you through Egypt's shopping maze – from haggling in bazaars to handling touts and commissioned tour guides – as well as put you in contact with the best of the best in accommodations, restaurants, and sightseeing. It would be a combination travel and shopping guide designed for people in search of quality travel experiences.

The perspective we develop throughout this book is based on our belief that traveling should be more than just another adventure in eating, sleeping, sightseeing, and taking pictures of unfamiliar places. Whenever possible, we attempt to bring to life the fact that Egypt has real people and interesting products that you, the visitor, will find exciting. This is a country of very talented artists, craftspeople, traders, and entrepreneurs. When you leave Egypt, you will take with you not only some unique experiences and memories but also quality products that you will certainly appreciate for years to come.

We have not hesitated to make qualitative judgments about the best of the best in Egypt. If we just presented you with travel and shopping information, we would do you a disservice by not sharing our discoveries, both good and bad. While we know that our judgments may not be valid for everyone, we offer them as **reference points** from which you can make your own decisions. Our major emphasis is on quality shopping, dining, accommodations, sightseeing, and entertainment, and in that order. We look for shops which offer excellent quality and styles. If you share our concern for quality shopping, as well as fine restaurants and hotels, you will find many of our recommendations useful to planning and implementing your Egyptian adventure. Best of all, you'll engage in what has become a favorite pastime for many of today's discerning travelers – lifestyle shopping!

Throughout this book we have included "tried and tested" shopping information. We make judgments based upon our experience – not on judgments or sales pitches from others. Our research method was quite simple: we did a great deal of shopping and we looked for quality products. We acquired some fabulous items, and gained valuable knowledge in the process. However, we could not make purchases in every shop nor do we have any guarantee that your experiences will be the same as ours. Shops close, ownership or management changes, and the shop you visit may not be the same as the one we shopped. So use this information as a start, but ask questions and make your own judgments before you buy.

Whatever you do, enjoy Egypt. While you need not *"shop 'til you drop,"* at least shop it well and with the confidence that you are getting good quality and value for your money. Don't just limit yourself to small items that will fit into your suitcase. Be adventuresome and consider acquiring larger items that can be safely and conveniently shipped back home. As we note in the section on shipping, don't pass up something you love because of shipping concerns. Shipping is something that needs to be *arranged* rather than lamented or avoided.

We wish to thank the many people who contributed to this book. These include the Egyptian Tourist Authority which provided assistance throughout our stay in Egypt. We especially want to thank Neveen El Halawany Mohamed and Aiten Fouad who variously served as expediters and guides. They ensured that we traveled safely and as closely to our independent schedule as possible. Helene Zartarian graciously shared her time and insights on Cairo. We also want to thank Egypt Air, Abercrombie and Kent, and numerous hotels and their personnel for making our stay very special and informative. Last, but not least, we appreciated the time many shopkeepers and artisans spent with us in educating us on the living treasures of Egypt – the ones you can buy and take home with you!

We wish you well as you prepare for Egypt's many treasures and pleasures. The book is designed to be used on the streets and waters of five major destinations. If you **plan** your journey according to the first four chapters and **navigate** our five major destinations based on the next five chapters, you should have an absolutely marvelous time. You'll discover some exciting places, acquire some choice items, and return home with many fond memories of a terrific adventure. You, too, may go home fat, happy, and broke as well as experience that unexplained urge to return to Egypt next year. If you put this book to use, it will indeed become your best friend – and passport – to the many unique treasures and pleasures of Egypt. Enjoy!

Ron and Caryl Krannich
krannich@impactpublications.com

Liabilities and Warranties

WHILE THE AUTHORS HAVE ATTEMPTED to provide accurate information, please remember that names, addresses, phone and fax numbers, and email addresses do change and shops, restaurants, and hotels do move, go out of business, or change ownership and management. Such changes are a constant fact of life in ever-changing Egypt. We regret any inconvenience such changes may cause to your travel and shopping plans.

Inclusion of shops, restaurants, hotels, and other hospitality providers in this book in no way implies guarantees nor endorsements by either the authors or publisher. The information and recommendations appearing in this book are provided solely for your reference. The honesty and reliability of shops can best be ensured by you – always ask the right questions, request proper receipts and documents, and observe the many shopping rules outlined in Chapter 4, especially pages 81-87.

The Treasures and Pleasures of Egypt provides numerous tips on how you can best experience a trouble-free adventure. As in any unfamiliar place or situation, and regardless of how trusting strangers may appear, the watch-words are always the same – *"watch your wallet!"* If it's too good to be true, it probably is. Any *"unbelievable deals"* should be treated as such. In Egypt, as elsewhere in the world, there simply is no such thing as a free lunch. Everything has a cost. Just make sure you don't pay dearly by making unnecessary shopping mistakes!

THE TREASURES AND PLEASURES
OF EGYPT: BEST OF THE BEST

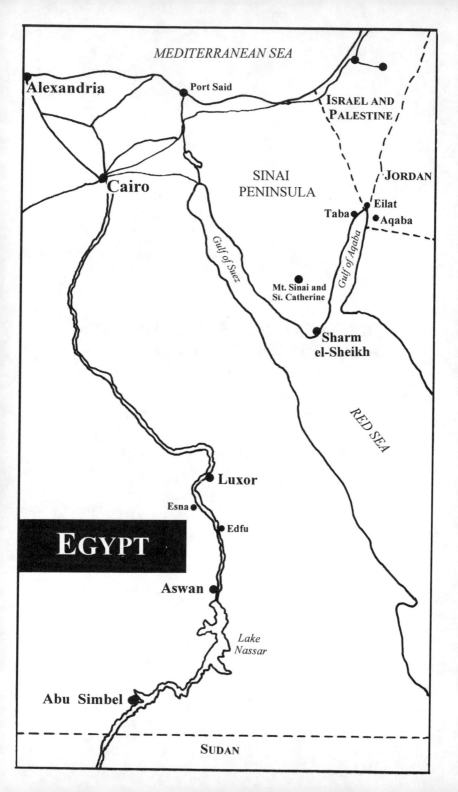

Welcome to
Surprising Egypt

I
T'S AN ANCIENT CIVILIZATION CARVED OUT OF a formidable desert and clinging to a narrow strip of fertile land along the banks of the legendary Nile River. A country with a living history of over 5,000 years, accented with massive monuments, tombs, and ruins to testify to its once grand and glorious past, this fabled North African and Middle Eastern nation of 62 million people still fascinates our imagination and lures millions of visitors each year to its many cities along the Nile, Red Sea, and the Mediterranean.

Welcome to beautiful and intriguing Egypt, land of the pharaohs and home to the very proud and hospitable Egyptians. You're in for one of the most fascinating adventures of a lifetime. You'll marvel at its history, great architectural wonders, and well preserved antiquities, as well as enjoy throbbing streets and lanes that lead to colorful mosques, churches, markets, and shops. You'll meet very friendly and curious people who are genuinely concerned about you. There's never a dull moment here as you discover a thoroughly ancient, traditional, and modern society that seems to span centuries in a single moment. If you approach this place right, it may well become one of your favorite travel destinations as you explore its many delightful treasures and pleasures.

Getting to Know You

It's as old as it gets and has as splendid a history and folklore you'll find anywhere. This is a country of great historical accomplishments that continues to amaze today's curious visitors who pack Egypt's awesome museums and historical sites. There is a fascination with ancient Egypt that is hard to explain – it's best experienced within the physical context of Cairo, Luxor, Aswan, Abu Simbel, and Alexandria, the places where most visitors head when traveling to Egypt.

The convergence of science, astrology, religion, architecture, and engineering left in its aftermath the signs of a determined people who settled and resettled along the banks of the powerful Nile River. When Alexander the Great invaded the Nile Delta in the 3rd century BC, he was actually a latecomer; Egypt already had a glorious history, grandly painted, sculptured, and carved in stone, of nearly 3,000 years. The Romans were just one of many people who passed through, stayed a while, built more stone monuments, lost interest, but still left captivated by this place. Egypt always managed to become someone else's crown jewel. Indeed, the Romans were followed by Muslim invaders, Christian Crusaders, and more Muslim rule. Nearly 2,000 years after Alexander the Great came Napoleon, who also tried his hand at conquest, became fascinated by the awesome architecture and antiquities, etched lots of graffiti on ancient stone monuments, soon discovered he had taken on more than he could really handle, declared victory (he lied), and then returned to Paris to further advance his controversial military and political career. Later came the British with their cement and steel Suez Canal, followed by a bloody period of independence and turmoil with neighboring Israel and Muslim states.

Egypt's long parade of rulers and wannabees, who worked primarily in stone in the near absence of less durable wood,

- ❑ There's never a dull moment here as you discover a thoroughly ancient, traditional, and modern society that seems to span centuries in a single moment.

- ❑ Most visitors to Egypt head for Cairo, Luxor, Aswan, Abu Simbel, and Alexandria.

- ❑ It's as old as it gets and has as splendid a history and folklore you'll find anywhere. When Alexander the Great invaded the Nile Delta in the 3rd century BC, he was actually a latecomer – Egypt already had a glorious history of nearly 3,000 years!

- ❑ There's a lot more to Egypt than ancient history and its attendant monuments and museums. Above all, it's a country of 62 million people who live on less than 4 percent of the land.

forged many different layers of history and monuments on the Egyptian landscape. From pyramids, tombs, and temples to mosques, churches, and fortresses, they have survived remarkably intact in Egypt's dry desert climate. In fact, the desert grounds continue to yield new discoveries as archeologists uncover more and more tombs, mummies, and artifacts within and beyond the Nile Valley. The result is a multi-faceted country that displays its remarkable history well.

Egypt is many different things to many different people. But it has always captivated the imagination of armchair travelers and visitors alike with its many unique physical and ancient monumental features, accented by colorful theories and folklore, that seem to bring to life noted individuals and events of a few thousand years ago. Not surprisingly, the pyramids of Giza, the treasures of Tutankhamun, the tombs of Luxor, the silted Nile, the inspiring minarets and mosques of Cairo, and the Greco-Roman ruins of Alexandria all conjure images of a once grand and tumultuous history that is the stuff of legends and folklore. Indeed, for many outsiders, Egypt is best known for its pyramids, tombs, and ancient history centered on the Nile and the gold encrusted and bejeweled mummified pharaohs. Most recently it also has been known for periodic outbursts of terrorism related to Muslim groups bent on overthrowing the government; some terrorism has been dramatically aimed at foreign tourists.

For first-time visitors to Egypt, their trip confirms popular images of Egypt, and then some – an intense journey into ancient history accented by the ubiquitous pyramids of Giza and numerous ruins, underground tombs, mummies, museums, mosques, and churches. It's an often exhausting journey into an ancient past where history comes alive as you walk and walk and walk the routes of the ancients, marvel at their architectural and engineering achievements, and delight in the unexpected beauty of the desert landscapes, dusty Third World villages clinging to the spotty green banks of the Nile River, and the colorful traffic plying the fast-flowing river. It's an unusual journey that juxtaposes the ancient past with a charming and chaotic present. It's a living history where many things you see and touch are at least 3,000 years old. You also quickly discover that Egypt is a place of friendly and intriguing people, vast stretches of inhospitable deserts, and lots of sun, heat, and humidity. After a while the obvious problems of poverty, sanitation, and congestion seem to disappear as you become absorbed by this intriguing country.

For frequent visitors to Egypt, who have gone beyond first impressions, this is a place they enjoy returning to again and again to explore its many treasures and pleasures. For them, Egypt also is very Mediterranean, at least in Alexandria; it's a first-class resort destination along the Red Sea, Sinai Peninsula, and Mediterranean coast west of Alexandria; and it's an important center for Christianity in both Cairo and the Sinai Peninsula. At least in Cairo, Egypt is a bustling place of fine restaurants, hotels, and entertainment. It's a place of intriguing shops and markets that yield many unique discoveries. Beyond Cairo, Egypt is a work in progress despite its impressive packaging of ancient history to plane, bus, and boat loads of tourists who are primarily drawn here to witness Egypt's ancient history and monuments.

MORE THAN JUST ANTIQUITIES

But there's a lot more to Egypt than ancient history and its attendant monuments and museums. Indeed, as many visitors quickly discover, you can easily get templed- and tombed-out after a few exhausting days of visiting one ancient site after another, and especially if those are hot and humid days. After a while, it all starts looking and sounding the same – only the names, cast of characters, and folklore seem to change.

For history buffs, Egypt has several distinct historical periods. Within Cairo itself, these culminate in three separate tours of the city: Pharaonic (Ancient) Egypt, Islamic Egypt, and Coptic (Christian) Egypt. Throughout the rest of Egypt you'll also discover Greco-Roman Egypt, especially in Alexandria, and Resort Egypt along the country's Mediterranean and Red Sea coasts. In fact, Egypt is quickly become a major, and relatively inexpensive, resort location boasting fabulous beaches, scuba diving, restaurants, and hotels.

Most important of all, Egypt is a 386,000 square mile country of 62 million people who live on less than 4 percent of the land which is primarily concentrated along the Nile Valley and delta regions. Nearly 370,000 square miles – 96 percent of the country – belong to a largely uninhabitable desert. The Egyptian portion of the Nile River, with its adjacent fertile valley areas, cities, and towns, runs 760 miles south of the Mediterranean to the Sudanese border. This is where both ancient and modern Egypt meet in many different ways. One moment you're touring an elaborate temple or tomb, and the next moment you're sailing peacefully along the Nile River or haggling in a colorful market for clothes, crafts, jewelry, instant coffee, or a carriage ride.

And it's the people and their places that you will remember

long after trudging through Egypt's many pyramids, tombs, and museums. This is a very poor and religious country where a disproportionate number of people migrate to densely populated Cairo, a city of nearly 18 million people. It's a throbbing and often maddening Third World city with too many people and a great deal of pollution. If it weren't for the interesting juxtaposing of the old and new, you might also consider it an ugly and inhospitable city determined to brutalize the unsuspecting visitor. Yet, there's a certain beauty to Cairo reflected in the sights and sounds of this east-meets-west Middle Eastern and African city. After a while, you begin experiencing Cairo on several different levels, from the highly touristed Pyramids, of Giza, Egyptian Antiquities Museum, mosques, and churches to the crowded bazaars of the Khan el-Khalili and the charming boats and restaurants along the river. It's a city of slums, living graveyards, active mosques, and buses overcrowded with commuters. Around the tourist areas, it's a city of pesky touts, five-star hotels, fine restaurants, casinos, belly dancers, bars, and nightclubs – a seemingly endless stream of travel pleasures for both the business and leisure crowds. Unlike many Third World cities, this is a city of hope rather than one of despair. For many Egyptians, Cairo is the center of the universe.

Given the sheer volume of antiquities and the well organized tourist routes, you'll undoubtedly spend a great deal of time becoming acquainted with the monuments and artifacts that now represent ancient Egypt. But be sure to experience as much of contemporary Egypt as possible. This is an enormously interesting country of fascinating people and products. Whenever possible, take to the streets and explore the many markets and shops that represent the best of contemporary Egypt.

A UNIQUE PERSPECTIVE

The pages that follow are not your typical treatment of travel to Egypt. Indeed, there are numerous guidebooks available on Egypt that basically focus on the same enduring theme – ancient Egypt. Most of these books are heavy on history, monuments, tombs, and museums to the near exclusion of contemporary Egypt, which is often viewed as an irritating impediment to visiting the country's treasure-trove of antiquities – too much traffic, too many touts, too much heat, excessive crowds, and not enough time! Many guidebooks go into amazing detail, accompanied by maps, including every nook and cranny of each major, and sometimes minor, temple, tomb, and museum. The result is a kind of self-guided history book for people who want to do Egypt on their own or who have difficulty hearing their tour guide at each stop along the way. Numerous budget guides touting the oft repeated *"I'm a traveler not a tourist"* philosophy outline how to experience inexpensive Egypt on your own as they provide a generous offering of cheap restaurants, hotels, and transportation. If this is your primary interest and style of travel, you'll find lots of guidebooks that offer this approach to Egypt; they are consistent with Egypt's primary tourist image – a destination for exploring ancient Egyptian history. However, if this is not your primary travel passion (you get anxious after hours in a museum or at a historic site) and you prefer a different level (class) of travel experience (you're not opposed to five-star hotels, ships, and restaurants, as well as prefer a car and driver to a crowded bus), you may find such guidebooks less than welcome additions to your luggage.

Like other volumes in the Impact Guides series, this book focuses on quality travel and shopping in Egypt. Yes, shopping. We learned long ago that one of the most enjoyable aspects of travel, and one of the best ways to meet the local people and experience another culture, is to shop its many shops, markets, factories, and galleries. In so doing, we explore the fascinating worlds of artisans, craftspeople, and shopkeepers where we discover quality products, outstanding buys, and talented, interesting, and friendly people as well as help support the continuing development of local arts and crafts.

A SHOPPING EMPHASIS

Much of *The Treasures and Pleasures of Egypt* is designed to provide you with the necessary **knowledge and skills** to become an effective shopper. We especially designed the book with two major considerations in mind:

- Focus on quality shopping
- Emphasis on finding unique items

Throughout this book we attempt to identify the **best quality shopping** in Egypt. This does not mean we have discovered the cheapest shopping or best bargains, although we have attempted to do so when opportunities for comparative shopping arose within and between communities. Our focus is primarily on shopping for **unique and quality items** that will retain their value in the long run and can be appreciated for years to come. This means many of our recommended shops may initially appear expensive. But they offer top value that you will not find in many other shops. For example, when we discover unique jewelers in Cairo, we acknowledge the fact that their work is expensive, but it is very beautiful and unique, so much so that you quickly forget their prices after you acquire and continue to admire their outstanding work. At the same time, we identify what we consider to be the best buys for various items, especially gold jewelry, textiles, and handicrafts.

APPROACHING THE SUBJECT

The chapters that follow take you on a whirlwind travel adventure of Egypt with a decided emphasis on quality shopping, dining, and sightseeing. We literally put a shopping face on Egypt, one that we believe you will thoroughly enjoy as you explore Egypt's many other pleasures.

Our **choice of cities** should not come as a surprise given the fact that most quality shopping and travel amenities tend to gravitate to Egypt's major cities and resorts: Cairo, Alexandria, Luxor, Aswan, and Sharm el-Sheikh. These are the places most tourists and business people travel to and thus where you will find the best of the best Egypt has to offer travelers and shoppers.

We've given a great deal of attention to constructing a complete **user-friendly book** that focuses on the shopping process, offers extensive details on the "how," "what," and "where" of shopping, and includes a sufficient level of redundancy to be informative, useful, and usable. The chapters, for example, are organized like one would organize and implement a travel and shopping adventure. Each chapter incorporates sufficient details, including names and addresses, to get you started in some of the best shopping areas and shops in each city or town.

Indexes and table of contents are especially important to us and others who believe a travel book is first and foremost a guide to unfamiliar places. Therefore, our index includes both subjects and shops, with shops printed in bold for ease of reference; the table of contents is elaborated in detail so it, too, can be used as another handy reference index for subjects and products. If, for example, you are interested in "what to buy" or "where to shop" in Cairo, the best reference will be the table of contents. If you are interested in jewelry shops in Cairo, look under "Jewelry" in the index. And if you are interested in learning where you can find good quality cartouches, then look under "cartouches" in the index. By using the table of contents and index together, you can access most any information from this book.

The remainder of this book is divided into two parts and eight additional chapters which look at both the process and content of traveling and shopping in Egypt. Part I – "**Smart Traveling and Shopping**" – assists you in preparing for your Egyptian adventure by focusing on the how-to of traveling and shopping. Chapter 2, "**Know Before You Go,**" takes you through the basics of getting to and enjoying your stay throughout Egypt. It includes advice on when to go, what to pack, required documents, currency, business hours, international and domestic transportation, tipping, tourist offices, useful websites, and local customs. Chapter 3, "**The Shopping Treasures,**" examines Egypt's major shopping strengths, from jewelry and antiques to clothes and handicrafts. Chapter 4, "**Shopping By the Rules,**" includes lots of advice on comparative shopping, shopping tips, bargaining rules, and shipping strategies for shopping in Egypt at its very best.

The five chapters in Part II – "**Great Destinations**" – examine the how, what, and where of traveling and shopping in and around several of Egypt's major destinations: Cairo, Alexandria, Luxor, Aswan, and Sharm el-Sheikh. Here we identify major shopping strengths of each place; detail the how, what, and where of shopping; and share information on some of the best hotels, restaurants, and sightseeing for each community and surrounding area.

OUR RECOMMENDATIONS

We hesitate to recommend specific shops, restaurants, hotels, and sites since we know the pitfalls of doing so. Shops that offered excellent products and service during one of our visits, for example, may change ownership, personnel, and policies from one year to another or they may suddenly move to another location or go out of business. In addition, our shopping preferences may not be the same as your preferences. The same is true for restaurants, hotels, and sites: they do change.

Since we put shopping up front in our travels to Egypt, our major concern is to outline your Egyptian shopping options, show you where to locate the best shopping areas, and share some useful shopping strategies that you can use anywhere in Egypt, regardless of particular shops or markets we or others may recommend. Armed with this knowledge and some basic shopping skills, you will be better prepared to locate your own shops and determine which ones offer the best products and service in relation to your own shopping and travel goals.

However, we also recognize the "need to know" when shopping in unfamiliar places. Therefore, throughout this book we list the names and locations of various shops we have found to offer good quality products. In some cases we have purchased items in these shops and can also recommend them for service and reliability. But in most cases we surveyed shops to determine the quality of products offered without making purchases. To buy in every shop would be beyond our budget, as well as our home storage capabilities! Whatever you do, treat our names and addresses as **orientation points** from which to identify your own products and shops. If you rely solely on our listings, you will miss out on one of the great adventures of shopping in Egypt – discovering your own special shops that offer unique items and exceptional value and service.

The same holds true for our recommendations for hotels, restaurants, sites, and entertainment. We sought out the best of the best in these major "travel pleasure" areas. You should find most of our recommendations useful in organizing your own special Egyptian adventure.

EXPECT A REWARDING ADVENTURE

Whatever you do, enjoy your Egyptian adventure as you open yourself to a whole new world of shopping and traveling. We're confident you'll discover some very special treasures and pleasures that will also make Egypt one of your favorite destinations.

So arrange your flights and accommodations, pack your credit cards and traveler's checks, and head for one of North Africa's and the Middle East's most delightful destinations. Two to three weeks later you should return home with much more than a set of photos and travel brochures. You will have some wonderful purchases and travel tales that can be enjoyed and relived for a lifetime.

Shopping and traveling in Egypt only takes time, money, and a sense of adventure. Take the time, be willing to part with some of your money, and open yourself to a whole new world of travel. If you are like us, the treasures and pleasures outlined in this book will introduce you to an exciting world of quality products, friendly people, and interesting places that you might have otherwise missed had you just passed through Egypt to eat, sleep, see sites, and take pictures. When you travel our Egypt, you are not just another tourist. You are a special kind of international traveler who discovers quality and learns about these places through the people and products that continue to define their culture.

kilometers (386,000 square miles), this is primarily a vast desert country with a few redeeming habitable features: the fertile Nile Valley and Delta where 96 percent of the population lives, nearly equally split between rural and urban areas.

Egypt shares a 1,000-kilometer border with the Sudan in the south and a 1,300-kilometer border with Libya in the west. At the same time, it has a 230-kilometer border with Israel in the northeast section of the Sinai Peninsula. For the most part, the border areas are desolate desert outposts, with the exception of the resort city of Taba on the Gulf of Aqaba which borders Israel in the Sinai at the resort city of Eilat. Occasional disputes with neighboring Libya and Sudan result in periodic tensions in these areas. Since the return of the Sinai Peninsula to Egypt, all has been relatively quiet along the northeast border with Israel.

❑ Egypt is the largest and most influential Arab state with 62 million people.

❑ Egypt is primarily a desolate desert country with a few redeeming habitable features – the fertile Nile Valley and Delta where 96 percent of the population live.

❑ Egypt's portion of the Nile consists of the final 750-mile run from Lake Nassar in the south to the Mediterranean Sea in the north.

❑ The tallest mountain in Egypt is the Sinai's 8,652-foot Gebel Katherina.

The world's longest river (4,022 miles or 6,435 kilometers), the **Nile**, flows south to north, from Lake Victoria in Uganda (White Nile) and the Ethiopian Highlands (Blue Nile) to the Mediterranean Sea. Egypt's portion of the Nile consists of the final 750-mile run from Lake Nassar and the Sudanese border in the south to the Mediterranean Sea in the north.

Accurately portrayed more than 2,500 years ago by Herodotus as "the gift of the Nile," the Nile River remains Egypt's lifeline. Indeed, over 90 percent of the Egyptian population is settled along the banks of the Nile which represent less than 5 percent of the country's land mass. Likened to a lotus flower, with its stem dipped into Lake Nassar in the far south and its budding flower spreading from Cairo into the lush Delta and Mediterranean Sea in the north, Egypt's share of the Nile River is historically the most significant. Forming a large fertile delta in the north as it empties its silted waters into the Mediterranean Sea, for centuries the navigable Nile linked Upper, Middle, and Lower Egypt to the outside world. The ritual of annual floods provided much needed water and silt to farm a narrow strip of land on both banks of the Nile River which at its widest point is only 12 miles wide. And it is within this fertile valley area where most of ancient Egyptian civilization evolved and prospered and left monuments to its once glorious past. With the construction of the Aswan Dam in 1970 and the subsequent creation of the world's largest man-made reservoir, Lake Nassar, today this river generates electricity and the dam regulates irrigation for expanded agricultural produc- tion. A massive new project is underway to reclaim huge tracts of desert and transform them into irrigated agricultural lands fed by the waters of Lake Nassar. The Aswan Dam also has created numerous environmental problems, from erosion and the depletion of soil nutrients to insidious water-borne diseases.

To the west of the Nile River is the vast **Western Desert** which borders the Libyan Desert. Dotted by a series of lush oases (Bahariyya, Farafra, Dakhla and Kharga in the central region and Siwa in the northwest), this rugged area with its Great Sand Sea in the northwest is largely uninhabitable. To the east of the Nile lies the **Eastern** or **Arabian Desert** which borders the Red Sea. This area represents the final stretch of North Africa's Sahara Desert. From here Egypt transitions into Asia.

On the east bank of the Red Sea is the **Sinai Peninsula** with its rugged mountains in the south and its rolling sand dunes in the north. An important and often contentious land link between Africa and Asia, as well as an up and coming resort area boasting great diving and sightseeing opportunities, the Sinai is a fascinating and adventuresome area for those who have the opportunity to go beyond the well traveled tourist paths of the Nile River.

Completed in the 1860s, the **Suez Canal** once functioned as Britain's strategic link between the Mediterranean Sea and the Red Sea for operating its far-flung Asian empire centered in India. Today the canal continues to play an important transpor- tation role, albeit much diminished, in linking Asia to the Middle East and Europe.

More and more visitors to Egypt are discovering the coun- try's delightful **Mediterranean coast** with its wonderful beaches and resort amenities. This is a very different area from the rest of Egypt. Indeed, on weekends and holidays many Egyptians from Cairo flock to the beaches west of Alexandria where they can enjoy the sun, surf, and outdoor ambience of the Mediterranean lifestyle.

Contrary to popular perceptions of a predominantly flat area with lots of rolling sand dunes, Egypt also is very mountainous along the Arabian Desert and the southern section of the Sinai Peninsula. The tallest mountain in Egypt is the Sinai's 8,652- foot Gebel Katherina.

Given Egypt's primary desert location and climate, it seldom rains here except in the northern Delta and Mediterranean region. The lack of water and the critical need to preserve scarce water resources are a constant fact of life throughout much of Egypt. Consequently, much of the country has a dusty tan desert look to it, and bathing and washing are not daily rituals as found in more water-rich areas of the world. Many cars have a battle-worn look to them, constantly battling the harsh desert elements of sun, heat, sand, and stones. Lacking bathing facilities and practices, camels, horses, and donkeys often cut an odorous path as you pass them along the road. Indeed, the so-called charming carriage ride in Luxor can literally catch your breath!

CLIMATE AND WHEN TO GO

When planning a trip to Egypt, always remember this is a desert country where the climate is usually hot and dry. The Mediterranean coast is somewhat of an anomaly in that it gets some modicum of rain. Alexandria, for example, which faces the Mediterranean Sea, is usually a few degrees cooler and more humid than Cairo. Temperature extremes tend to become more pronounced as you travel south in Egypt.

Egypt has four seasons with some temperature variations worth noting. **Summer** is from June to August. During this time the days are usually hot and dry, although humidity increases during August. Nights are often pleasant due to the cool northerly breezes.

Autumn is from September to November. During this season temperatures tend to be pleasant and evenings can be cool. November tends to be a very pleasant month.

Winter takes place from December to February. The days tend to be sunny and cool with evenings often on the cold side. Given the lack of central heating, many buildings can be chilly and damp during the winter. If you travel to Egypt at this time of the year, you may want to take some warm clothes, especially a sweater or a light jacket or coat.

Spring is from March to May. Days tend to be warm and evenings can be cool. This also is the "khamsin" season, a 50-day period of discomforting desert sand and dust storms during the months of April and May.

The overall best time to visit Egypt is between November and February. However, this is not the best time for Alexandria and the northern Mediterranean where early autumn would be an ideal time to visit.

WHAT TO PACK AND WEAR

Given Egypt's hot and sunny days and cool evenings, we recommend taking light-weight and loose-fitting cotton clothes for daytime touring. If you will be in Egypt during the winter, it's advisable to take a light jacket or coat for the cool evenings and mornings.

If you plan to visit Egypt's many ancient sites, museums, and resorts, you are well advised to take the following items:

Essentials:
- comfortable walking shoes
- hat or cap
- sunglasses

Optional:
- umbrella
- camera
- water bottle
- flashlight
- compass
- swim gear

Most visitors are surprised to discover how much walking is involved in seeing the highlights of Egypt. Given the combination of sun, heat, distances, and rough sand and stone terrain, you'll find comfortable walking shoes, a hat, sunglasses, umbrella, and water to come in very handy. If you forget to pack any of these things, you can easily pick them up in the many shops of Cairo, Alexandria, Luxor, Aswan, and Sharm el-Sheikh. While Egypt produces tons of shoes – in Cairo you may conclude Egyptians are obsessed with shoes, given the thousands of shoe stores throughout the city – you may not find the most comfortable ones for your feet. Bring with you the most comfortable pair of walking shoes you can find and break them in before using them in Egypt. If you don't wear a hat or cap, you may want to carry an umbrella to keep the sun off your head. Alternatively, many vendors will sell you the traditional Bedouin head dress (a cloth with a head band) at the various tourist sites. Since you probably won't look good in one, you may want to stick with a hat or umbrella!

It's not necessary to bring a water bottle with you since bottled water is readily available everywhere you travel. Given the heat and accompanying dehydration, you'll want to keep yourself well stocked with drinking water. If you plan to visit the coastal areas, be sure to bring your swim gear. Egypt has wonderful beaches along the Mediterranean Sea as well as beautiful beaches and coral reefs along the east coast of the Sinai Peninsula. Resorts along the Red Sea offer a full range of water sports, from diving to wind surfing and waterskiing.

Pack your camera and plenty of film. Egypt is a photographer's paradise. You'll probably shoot more film in Egypt than you initially anticipated. Film is readily available in Egypt, but you may want to stock your own brand which should be cheaper than what's available on the Egyptian market.

REQUIRED DOCUMENTS

All visitors to Egypt need a valid passport and most need a visa. The passport must be good for at least another six months after arriving in Egypt. Tourist visas, both single and multiple entry, are issued for stays of up to three months. Citizens of the United States, Canada, Australia, the United Kingdom, and most countries of Europe and East Asia can obtain a visa upon arrival in Egypt. Citizens of all African countries plus nearly 30 other countries need to acquire a visa prior to arriving in Egypt. Visas can be obtained prior to arriving in Egypt by completing an application through an Egyptian consulate nearest you. For qualifying nationals, visas are issued upon arrival at any of these major ports of entry:

Airports:	Cairo International (2 terminals)
	Alexandria Nozha
	Luxor, Upper Egypt
	Aswan, Upper Egypt
	Hurghaga, Red Sea
	Sharm el-Sheikh, South Sinai
Marine Harbors:	Alexandria, Mediterranean
	Port Said, Mediterranean
	Damietta, Mediterranean
	Suez, Gulf of Suez
	Nuweiba, Gulf of Aqaba
	Hurghada, Red Sea
	Safaga, Red Sea
	Sharm el-Sheikh, Red Sea
Overland Entry Posts:	Salloum (northwest border with Libya)
	Rafah (northeast border with Israel)
	Taba (eastern border with Israel)

A few national groups, such as citizens of Jordan, Kuwait, Libya, Saudi Arabia, Syria, and the United Arab Emirates, do not need a visa for entry into Egypt. Another visa exception situation is the border crossing at Taba, the eastern Sinai exit point from Israel. Visitors coming from the Israeli side via Taba to visit the Gulf of Aqaba coast and St. Catherine do not need visas. Instead, they are given a free residence permit for stays of up to 14 days. Transit visas are issued at international airports and ports for visits of 24 hours – just enough time to do some quick shopping and sightseeing.

The cost of a visa varies depending on your citizenship. U.S. citizens, for example, pay US$15 for a single entry visa. For more information on obtaining a visa, including an application form, visit the website of the official Egyptian government tourist office:

www.touregypt.net/visa.htm

THE PEOPLES

For many visitors to Egypt, the best aspect of this country is its people. Whatever you do, make sure you have a chance to meet Egyptians and learn about Egypt from their perspective. They are a wonderfully warm, hospitable, and proud people who often go out of their way to be helpful. Unlike many other countries, Egyptians are generally pleased to have tourists visit their country, and they will often let you know how happy they are you came to see them. They will tend to personalize your visit by saying *"It's an honor to greet you."* Indeed, some will instantly extend an invitation to a stranger to visit their home for dinner (don't accept the first time unless they insist).

Egyptians also are a very religious people but by no means religious fanatics. Predominantly a Muslim country, Egypt also has a large Christian population, the Coptics. You'll find numerous mosques and churches in the major cities, and the locals tend to be very observant of religious rituals.

Egyptians are generally divided into four groups: fellahins, urbanites, Bedouins, and Nubians. Nearly half of the popula-tion is referred to as the **fellahins**, or rural peasants. Most of these people live in mud-brick homes in villages along the Nile River, at Oases, and on the Red Sea coast; they farm nearby fields where they grow wheat, sugar cane, and vegetables. Many of the house exteriors are plastered in mud and trimmed in blue (to avoid the evil eye). Homes of those who have made the pilgrimage to Mecca are usually painted with distinctive designs that chronicle their journey to Islam's most holy city. Many homes still lack electricity and running water. Village life tends to center around family, religion, and local traditions.

Urbanites constitute the second major population group. Consisting of 46 percent of the population, they are primarily found in the large cities of Cairo (18 million) and Alexandria (5 million). Other large cities include Aswan, Assiut, Port Said, Ismailia, Luxor, Suez, and Tanta. The cities tend to be large amalgams of ethnic groups and social classes with a large concentration of poor fellahins who have migrated to the cities in search of wage labor. Like cities elsewhere in the world, Egyptian cities are centers for government, commerce, education, arts, and culture. They showcase the best of the best in shopping, restaurants, accommodations, entertainment, and sightseeing. Indeed, most of Egypt's major antiquities and thus sightseeing are found within close proximity of Cairo, Alexandria, Luxor, and Aswan. Most visitors in Egypt will spend most of their time in and around these four major cities.

The **Bedouin**, or Bedu, constitute the third group, representing nearly 2 percent of the population. Primarily a nomadic desert people in constant search of water and new grazing areas for their camels and goats, they have their own distinctive language, customs, and dress. Living in tents made of goat and camel hair panels, they reside in the desert areas and are often found camped near major transportation arteries. However, this lifestyle is changing as more and more Bedouins send their sons to schools in the big cities, acquire land, build homes, and transport 100-gallon barrels of water and their goats in the back of their Toyota pickup trucks rather than on the backs of camels. While the Bedouins are the least assimilated into Egyptian society, they also are a very gracious people, inviting strangers into their tents for tea or coffee and asking them to stay for a few days. You'll probably be most tempted to take photos of the colorful Bedouins with their camels, goats, tents, and families.

The distinctive **Nubians** are a dark-skinned people who live in a valley just south of Aswan. This is a very interesting population that is neither African nor Egyptian. Primarily carrying Caucasian genes and seldom intermarrying, their ancestry remains a mystery. Historically known as the traders and elite military forces of the Pharaohs, they have maintained a unique culture over the centuries. Once mostly living in villages along the Nile River and cultivating date palms, they had to relocate when their mosques, homes, and fertile lands were submerged by the construction of dams and the reservoir. Displaced by the British with the construction of the first

Aswan dam in 1902 and again in 1970 with the second Aswan dam and Lake Nasser, nonetheless, the Nubians continue to live around the Aswan area. Many of the Nubian men live and work several hundred kilometers north of Aswan, including Cairo, and return to their villages once or twice a year to visit their families. Others now find work in nearby towns and cities as taxi drivers, shopkeepers, and felucca sailors. You can't miss the Nubian villages with their colorful buildings and distinctive architecture that includes vaulted domes rather than flat roofs. When you visit Aswan, you'll have a chance to become well acquainted with this fascinating population group and marvel at their architecture and historic role in Upper Egypt.

LANGUAGE

The official language of Egypt is Arabic. Although sometimes difficult to understand, English is widely spoken in the major tourist areas. Most educated Egyptians speak English and/or French. You should have little difficulty getting around with English, although it's always a good idea to learn some basic Arabic words. "Misr," for example, means "Egypt" in Arabic. When you see Misr Travel, it means Egypt Travel, the largest travel group in Egypt. Egyptians appreciate efforts to speak their language, as they make a special effort to assist you.

TIME

Egyptian time is two hours ahead of Greenwich Mean Time (GMT) or seven standard time zones ahead of Eastern Standard Time (EST). When it's 12noon in Egypt, it's 5am in New York City. If you have difficulty with the time differences, you'll want to refresh your memory by visiting these useful websites: *www.timezoneconverter.com* or *www.worldtimeserver.com*.

SAFETY AND SECURITY

Contrary to what you may have heard, Egypt is one of the safest places in the world to travel. You can travel most everywhere without fear of being assaulted or robbed. The crime rate is very low and, except for an occasional pickpocket in a crowded bazaar, tourists rarely become targets of crime. Indeed, Cairo was recently ranked as the second safest city in the world, after Tokyo. You can walk almost anywhere in the city, including many poor areas, without fear of being assaulted by anything other than warm Egyptian hospitality!

Unfortunately, Egypt developed a reputation for being a dangerous place to visit because of terrorist attacks and the massacre of over 65 European tourists at the Mortuary Temple of Hatshepsut (Deir al-Bahri) in Luxor in November 1997. After that incident, tourism to Egypt plummeted and Egyptian security increased dramatically at all major tourist areas. There is no reason to believe that such terrorism will be repeated in Egypt since the country does not accommodate such terrorist groups and does not have a religious extremist problem. Although there are no guarantees, today Egypt remains perhaps one of the safest and most secure countries for tourists.

But do take care in two situations that can get you into trouble. First, watch when you cross streets. The traffic in Cairo, for example, can be dangerous if you try to cross in the middle of the streets with on-coming traffic. The same is true with horse carriages in Luxor. Be sure to look both ways when crossing streets. Pedestrians occasionally do get hit by cars, buses, and horse carriages because they either try to outrun the vehicles or carelessly cross streets. Second, watch your wallet or purse when shopping in the bazaars. Pickpockets are known to frequent these places. As the same time, take normal precautions concerning your valuables – use hotel deposit boxes and don't wear or leave valuables out that might tempt unscrupulous individuals to engage in a crime.

Getting There

Egypt is serviced by several international airlines. For North Americans, the most convenient way to get to Egypt is to take the non-stop flight from New York's JFK to Cairo on the national carrier, Egypt Air. The 11-hour flight departs JFK at 11pm and arrives in Cairo at 3:30pm the following day. Egypt Air flies the New York - Cairo route five days a week: departing JFK on Tuesday, Thursday, Friday, Saturday and Sunday. The non-stop return flights from Cairo to New York depart Cairo on Sunday and Friday at 9am and arrive in New York at 3:30pm the same day. The Tuesday, Thursday and Saturday flights depart Cairo at 1:30am and arrive in New York at 8am the same day. Egypt Air's non-stop flights are convenient. Other carriers' flights connect through European hubs in such cities as London, Amsterdam, Paris or Frankfurt.

We flew Egypt Air on our recent flights to and from – as well as within – Egypt. Our plane, a Boeing 777 on both international flights, was configured so that seating was comfortable in all classes of service. Egypt Air uses both Boeing 777's and 767's on the New York/Cairo flights. Since both are double-aisle planes with only two seats across between the window and aisle on either side of the airplane, it is possible for two people traveling together to have their own "space" and privacy that nearly rivals Business Class. Of course, if you want greater space and comfort, Egypt Air offers both Business and First Class cabins on its 767's and 777's. Service was on a par with the best of international airlines. In deference to Muslim dictates, Egypt Air does not serve alcoholic beverages on board which may dismay some passengers. However, they do serve a non-alcoholic beer. In these days of frequent "air-rage," a policy of no alcoholic beverages may actually make some passengers feel more comfortable.

We also flew Egypt Air on all our domestic flights within Egypt: Cairo to Aswan, Aswan to Luxor, Aswan to Abu Simbel, Abu Simbel back to Cairo, and Cairo to Sharm el-Sheikh. All the flights were comfortable and on time. Since these flights carry lots of tourists between major sightseeing centers, most flights used large planes – Boeing 757's or 767's. We also flew Egypt Air back to Cairo after visiting nearby Amman, Jordan. This route uses a Boeing 737 and again we found everything to be first class. One word of caution: as with most infrastructure in Egypt, Egypt Air is used to handling lots of group travelers. Every airline overbooks its flights, and Egypt Air is no exception. If a flight is oversold and more people show up than there are seats on the plane, as an individual traveler you have the greatest chance of being "bumped." We cannot emphasize enough how important it is that you reconfirm every flight and get a confirmation number from the airline. Get to the airport in plenty of time; last-minute arrivals are the most likely to be bumped. Missing your flight can be more than an inconvenience if you are on a tight schedule.

Most visitors arrive in Egypt by **air**. While a few flights, (mainly charters from Europe and the Middle East) go directly to Alexandria, Luxor, Harghada, and Sharm el-Sheikh (15-20 a day), most regularly scheduled international flights go directly into Cairo International Airport, which is the major arrival and departure point for Egypt.

Some visitors arrive by **sea** on ferries that operate daily with Aqaba, Jordan and Jeddah, Saudi Arabia. Ferries from Aqaba connect to Nuweiba, and ferries from Jeddah go to both Suez and Port Safaga.

You can also reach Egypt by **land** via two border crossings with Israel in the Sinai. If you are going from Cairo to Israel, or vise versa, the closest border crossing is at Rafah. If you are going to or from the South Sinai (St. Catherine or Sharm el-Sheikh), you'll want to use the border crossing at Taba. If you are going from Israel into Egypt at Taba for visiting St. Catherine and Sharm el-Sheikh, you will be issued a special visa at the border. However, if you plan to visit the rest of Egypt, you'll need a regular tourist visa. Although it is possible to cross to or from the Sudanese and Libyan borders, it's not recommended except for very adventuresome travelers who are used to experiencing border problems.

GETTING AROUND WITH EASE

You can easily travel to and around Egypt on your own. In fact, many independent travelers prefer to see Egypt on their own rather than with a group. Setting their own pace and selecting their own unique mix of sights and activities, they can easily use public transportation, hire a car and driver, or join a half-day or full-day tour. Cars and drivers, which are relatively inexpensive (US$35-US$60 a day), can be arranged through hotel tour desks or directly with taxi drivers. Travel agencies are happy to arrange tours and guides for independent travelers, including three- to four-day boat trips along the Nile River.

However, be forewarned that Egypt's tourism infrastructure is set up for group travel. Unlike many other countries, including nearby Israel and Jordan, independent travelers in Egypt tend to be given low priority on the travel pecking order. The bias is toward group travel, from airline seats and hotel rooms to tour guides (independent travelers are often given the worst tour guides since the best ones need to be reserved for groups). Consequently, make sure you reconfirm your flights on Egypt Air and get a confirmation number. Get to the airport in plenty of time to check in. If you encounter any problems with your reservation, keep showing them the confirmation number. As with any airline, flights are often overbooked, and independent travelers complain they are bumped and tour groups given boarding preference, which is often true.

If you have advance hotel reservations, carry a copy of the booking confirmation with you.

The easiest way to get around in Egypt is by air. **Egypt Air** and its subsidiary **Air Sinai** operate all domestic air routes. Planes regularly fly between the major tourist destinations. For example, during the high season Egypt Air operates six daily flights between Cairo and Luxor. Depending on the day of the week, Egypt Air may have four to nine daily flights operating between Aswan and Abu Simbel. Be sure to book your flights well in advance of your arrival in Egypt. Especially during the high season, many of the flights on the popular routes are fully booked days in advance.

Trains operate between Alexandria and Aswan and between Marsa Matrouh and the Suez Canal. Many visitors who don't mind taking the time enjoy traveling through the Nile Valley by train. The train trip from Cairo to Aswan takes nearly 16 hours. Be sure to purchase train tickets at least one or two days before departure. It may be best to have your hotel or a travel agent purchase the tickets for you (5-10 percent commission) rather than hassle with purchasing them at the train station.

You can **rent cars** in Egypt as long as you have an international driver's license or equivalent. Hertz, Avis, and other international car rental companies operate in most major cities of Egypt. If you are from the United States, Canada, or the United Kingdom, your national driver's license will be accepted as valid for up to six months of driving in Egypt. However, you may want to forego driving in Egypt except in the Sinai Peninsula. It's much more convenient, and cheaper, to take taxis or hire a car and driver for the day than to do your own driving in Cairo, Alexandria, Luxor, and Aswan. Street signs and maps in these cities can be very confusing to the uninitiated. You may spend most of your time trying to figure out where you are located and how to get to a destination than actually being at your destination. Parking may also be difficult. The Sinai, especially the southern portion, is another story. It's very easy to drive within Sharm el-Sheikh as well as the long stretches of desolate and sometimes mountainous highway between Sharm el-Sheikh, St. Catherine, and Taba.

Within cities, you may wish to hire a car and driver or take **taxis**. Taxis are relatively inexpensive and convenient for short distances. However, you need to know the approximate fare before starting off, since meters do not play a role in determining the cost. Ask at a hotel, restaurant, or shop how much a taxi ride should be to your desired destination and then agree on the price with the taxi driver before departing. Most taxi drivers also will hire out for several hours or a full day, depending on what you can negotiate.

Most cities have **buses**, which are relatively inexpensive. However, they are often overcrowded and uncomfortable.

A few cities, such as Luxor and Aswan, have **horse carriages**. This is a relatively inexpensive (if you bargain hard) and charming way of seeing these cities. The drivers constantly hassle visitors to take their carriages, inflate prices, and then intimidate their customers with new financial demands.

INTERNATIONAL GROUP TOURS

Most visitors to Egypt come with a group. Numerous companies offer a wide variety of interesting package tours that include everything from visiting museums, pyramids, and tombs to taking Nile cruises and desert treks and visiting seaside resorts for sand, surf, and scuba diving. Some of the major tour operators in North America include:

SUPER-DELUXE

- **Abercrombie and Kent:** 1520 Kensington Road, Oak Brook, IL Tel. 1-800-323-7308 or Fax 630-954-3324. Website: *www.abercrombiekent.com*

- **Travcoa:** 2350 SE Bristol, Newport Beach, CA 92660, Tel. 1-800-992-2003 or Fax 949-487-2800. Website: *www.travcoa.com*

DELUXE

- **Globus:** 5301 S. Federal Circle, Littleton, CO 80123-2980, Tel. 1-800-221-0090, Fax 303-347-2080. Website: *www.cosmostours.com*

- **Maupintour:** 1515 St. Andrews Drive, Lawrence, KS 66047, Tel. 1-800-255-4266, Fax 785-843-8351. Website: *www.maupintour.com*

FIRST-CLASS

- **Brendan Tours:** 15137 Califa Street, Van Nuys, CA 91411, Tel. 1-800-421-8446 or Fax 818-902-9876. Website: *www.brendantours.com*

- **Collette Tours:** 162 Middle Street, Pawtucket, RI 02860, Tel. 1-800-340-5158 or Fax 401-728-4745. Website: *www.collettetours.com*

- **Insight International Tours:** 745 Atlantic Avenue, Suite 720, Boston, MA 02111, Tel. 1-800-582-8380 or Fax 1-800-622-5015. Website: *www.insightvacations.com*

Companies such as **Egypt Tours and Travel** (6030 N. Sheridan Road, Chicago, IL 60660, Tel. 1-800-863-4978 or Fax

773-506-9996; website: *www.egypttours.com*) primarily specialize in tours to Egypt.

If you're interested in specialty tours to Egypt, check out the monthly travel magazine *ITN* (*International Travel News*) for advertisements relating to Egypt. For subscription information or to request a sample issue, call 1-800-366-9192 or visit their website: *www.intltravelnews.com*. The following groups offer several special-interest tours, from archaeology to scuba diving:

ARCHAEOLOGY

- **Archaeological Tours:** 271 Madison Avenue, New York, NY 10016, Tel. 212-986-3054 or Fax 212-370-1561.

- **Journeys of the Mind:** 221 N. Kenilworth Ave., Suite 413, Oak Park, IL 60302, Tel. 708-383-9739 or Fax 708-254-5154.

- **Smithsonian Study Tours and Seminars:** 1100 Jefferson Drive, SW, Room 30435, MRC 702, Washington, DC 20560, Tel. 202-357-4700 or Fax 202-633-9250.

ART HISTORY AND MUSEUMS

- **Spiekermann Travel Service:** 31363 Harper Avenue, St. Clair Shores, MI 48082, Tel. 1-800-645-3233. Website: *www.mideasttrvl.com*

- **Museum Tours:** 7110 S. Old Farm Road, Littleton, CO 80128, Tel. 1-888-932-2230 or Fax 303-932-2247. Website: *www.museum-tours.com*

- **Travel With the Met:** Metropolitan Museum of Art, 1000 Fifth Avenue, New York, NY 10028, Tel. 212-570-3956 or Fax 212-396-5040.

HISTORY AND CULTURE

- **Adventures Abroad:** 2148 - 20800 Westminster Hwy., Richmond, BC Canada V6V 2W3, Tel. 604-303-1099 or Fax 604-303-1076. Website: *www.adventures-abroad.com*

- **Big Five Tours & Expeditions:** 1551 SE Palm Court, Stuart, FL 34994, Tel. 1-800-244-3483. Website: *www.big five.com*

- **Calvary Tours:** 1559 Post Road, Fairfield, CT 06430, Tel. 1-800-399-1313 or Fax 203-256-8125. Website: *www.calvarytours.com*

- **Destinations & Adventures:** 8489 Crescent Drive, Los Angeles, CA 90046, Tel. 1-800-659-4599. Website: *www.daitravel.com*

- **The Learned Pilgrim:** 2902 St. Mary's Way, Salt Lake City, UT 84108, Tel. 1-800-581-9811 or Fax 801-583-5541. Email: *MBHpilgrim@aol.com*

- **Menatours:** 181 Boulevard, Suite 2D, Hasbrouck Heights, NJ 07604, Tel. 1-800-386-87885 or Fax 201-393-9397. Website: *www.menatours.com*

- **Pyramida Tours & Cruises:** 965 Forest Avenue, Staten Island, NY 10310, Tel. 1-800-334-4330. Website: *www.pyramida-tours.com*

SCUBA DIVING

- **Rothschild Dive Safaris:** 900 West End Ave., #1B, New York, NY 10025-3525, Tel. 1-800-359-0747 or Fax 212-818-249-8877. Website: *www.sportours.com*

LOCAL TRAVEL AGENCIES

You'll have no problem arranging tours once you arrive in Egypt. Numerous travel agencies operate throughout Egypt. Most are headquartered in Cairo and they are experienced in developing customized tours for individual travelers. If you are an independent traveler who will be traveling to Egypt during the high season, you may want to contact a local travel agent before arriving in Egypt. Ask them about their services, including recommended tours and costs. Most of them can communicate with you either by fax or email. You will find an extensive list of Egypt's major local tour operators, including telephone and fax numbers, on the government's tourism website:

www.touregypt.net/travela.htm

You can find other tour operators by using what we have found to be the two best search engines for travel planning:

www.google.com
www.iwon.com

NILE CRUISES

Nearly 300 river boats now cruise the Nile River between Luxor and Aswan. While you can usually book one of the cruise ships through a travel agent once you're in Egypt, you are wise to make arrangements prior to arriving, especially if you want to cruise with the best of the lot. These two groups offer the best of the river cruises:

- **Abercrombie and Kent:** 1520 Kensington Road, Oak Brook, IL Tel. 1-800-323-7308 or Fax 630-954-3324. Website: *www.abercrombiekent.com*

- **Oberoi:** The Oberoi Sherayer/Shehrazad (Nile Cruise), c/o The Mena House Oberoi, Pyramids' Road, Giza, Cairo-12556 Egypt, Tel. 20-2-383-3444 or Fax 20-2-383-7777. Website: *www.oberoihotels.com/shehm.htm*

ON-LINE TRAVEL DEALS

If you use the Internet, you can easily make airline, hotel, and car rental reservations on-line by using several on-line booking groups. The four major reservation services are:

www.expedia.com	*www.priceline.com*
www.travelocity.com	*www.hotwire.com*

Other popular on-line reservation services, with many claiming discount pricing, include:

www.air4less.com	*www.moments-notice.com*
www.airdeals.com	*www.onetravel.com*
www.air-fare.com	*www.site59.com*
www.bestfares.com	*www.smarterliving.com*
www.biztravel.com	*www.thetrip.com*
www.cheaptickets.com	*www.travelhub.com*
www.concierge.com	*www.travelscape.com*
www.etnlinks.com	*www.travelzoo.com*
www.lowestfare.com	

However, while these on-line booking operations may appear to be convenient, we've found many of them can be more expensive than using a travel agent. This is especially true in the case of airline tickets. You'll often get the best airline rates through consolidators, which may be 30 to 40 percent less than the major on-line ticketing operations. Consolidators usually have small box ads in the Sunday travel sections of the *New York Times*, *Washington Post*, *Los Angeles Times*, and other major newspapers. Some of them, such as International Discount Travel, also provide price quotes on the Internet: *www.idt travel.com*. Other popular consolidators specializing in discount ticketing include TicketPlanet (1-800-799-8888, *www.ticket planet.com*), Airtreks.com (1-800-350-0612, *www.air-treks. com*), Air Brokers International (1-800-883-3273, *www.air brokers.com*), International Airline Consolidators (1-800-305-6536, *www.intl-air-consolidators.com*), and World Travellers' Club (1-800-693-0411). If you're in a gambling mood, try these two "reverse auction" sites that allow you to set the price in the hopes that the company will make your dream price come true: *www.priceline.com* and *www.hotwire.com*.

For more information on these and many other online resources relevant to travel planning, see our new companion volume entitled *Travel Planning on the Internet: The Click and Easy™ Guide* (see pages 231 and 233 for details).

CUSTOMS AT HOME

It's always good to know your country's Customs regulations before leaving home. If, for example, you are a U.S. citizen planning to travel abroad, the United States Customs Service provides several helpful publications which are available free of charge from your nearest U.S. Customs Office (or write P.O. Box 7407, Washington, DC 20044). Several also are available in the "Traveler Information" section of the U.S. Customs Web site, *www.customs.ustreas.gov/travel.htm*:

- *Know Before You Go* (Publication #512): Outlines facts about exemptions, mailing gifts, duty-free articles, as well as prohibited and restricted articles. Original art purchased in Egypt should enter the U.S. duty-free as should items over 100 years old with proper documentation. However, most other items, especially jewelry, will be dutiable.

- *International Mail Imports* answers many questions regarding mailing items from foreign countries back to the US. The U.S. Postal Service sends packages to Customs for examination and assessment of duty before they are delivered to the addressee. Some items are free of duty and some are dutiable. The rules have changed on mail imports, so do check on this before you leave the U.S.

- **GSP and the Traveler** itemizes goods from particular countries that can enter the U.S. duty-free. GSP regulations, which are designed to promote the economic development of certain Third World countries, permit many products, especially arts and handicrafts, to enter the United States duty-free, but only if GSP is currently in effect. If not, U.S. citizens will need to pay duty as well as complete a form that would refund the duties once GSP goes into effect again and is made retroactive – one of the U.S. Congress's annual budgetary rituals that is inconvenient to travelers and costly for taxpayers. Most items purchased in Egypt should be allowed to enter duty-free when GSP is operating. Do check on this before you leave the U.S. so you won't be surprised after you make your purchases in Egypt.

U.S. citizens may bring in U.S. $400 worth of goods free of U.S. taxes every 30 days; the next $1,000 is subject to a flat 10 percent tax. Goods beyond $1,400 are assessed duty at varying rates applied to different classes of goods. Original works of art may enter the U.S. duty-free as do items over 100 years old. You may be asked to provide documentation as to the age of an item you claim is an antique. If you are in Cairo and uncertain about U.S. duties on particular items, contact the U.S. Embassy and ask for local U.S. Customs assistance.

CURRENCY AND EXCHANGE RATES

Egyptian currency is based on the Egyptian pound (L.E. or E£). It consists of 100 piasters (PT) or E£1 = 100 Piastres. Banknotes come in 100, 50, 20, 10, 5, and 1 E£ denominations. Piaster coins are issued in 25, 10, and 5 denominations. Be sure to carry plenty of small change with you since taxi drivers, shopkeepers, and others always seem short of change.

The Egyptian pound is relatively stable in relation to the U.S. dollar with US$1 = E£3.77 as of November 2000.

Since the exchange rate is fixed in Egypt, you will get the same rate wherever you officially exchange your money. Traveler's checks are accepted at most banks and *bureaux de change*; a transaction charge is added to each check, so you may want to carry US$100 rather than US$20 traveler's checks. Carry U.S. dollars to exchange for small purchases just before leaving the country when you don't want to exchange a large amount.

Major credit cards (Visa, MasterCard, and American Express) are accepted at most major hotels, restaurants, shops, and travel agencies. When using a credit card in a restaurant, the custom is to keep your card when giving you the receipt; only after you've signed the receipt and given it back to the waiter will the waiter come back with your card.

ELECTRICITY AND WATER

Electricity in Egypt is 220 volts, 50 cycles alternative current (AC). If you bring 110-volt appliances with you, be sure to use a voltage converter. Since most outlets use rounded plugs, you may need an adapter if your appliances take a flat plug.

Tap water is not safe to drink in Egypt. Hotels and restaurants usually provide bottled water. You can purchase inexpensive bottled water most places you travel. Baraka and Siwa are the most popular and trustworthy brands.

HEALTH AND INSURANCE

If you watch where and what you eat, drink plenty of fluids, and avoid excessive sun and heat, you should travel through Egypt without any health problems. However, travel illnesses frequently do occur in Egypt because of the failure to take adequate precautions against potential health problems. Forgetting about the sun and heat, many visitors experience painful sunburns and debilitating heat stroke requiring some form of rehydration therapy. Many also go through a bout of diarrhea ("the pharaoh's curse") because of the food and water. Should you experience such illnesses, local doctors, medical facilities, and pharmacies are well equipped to assist you.

It's always a good idea to make sure your personal insurance or travel insurance includes coverage for illness or accidents during your stay in Egypt. Also, consider evacuation insurance in case serious illness or injuries would require that you be evacuated home through special transportation and health care arrangements. Many companies offer evacuation insurance. One of the best kept travel secrets for acquiring inexpensive evacuation insurance is to become a member of DAN (Divers Alert Network). In the U.S., call 1-800-446-2671 (The Peter B. Bennett Center, 6 West Colony Place, Durham, NC 27705; website: *www.diversalertnetwork.org*). Without such insurance, special evacuation arrangements could cost between US$10,000 and US$20,000! If you are into adventure travel and plan to engage in physically challenging activities, health and evacuation insurance should be on your "must do" list before departing for Egypt.

FOOD AND BEVERAGES

You'll find a wide range of cuisines in Egypt, and especially in the many international restaurants of Cairo and Alexandria. Egyptian cuisine is a tempting combination of Mediterranean, Greek, Turkish, and Lebanese dishes along with several unique local dishes. The Egyptian diet tends to be high in carbohydrates, centered around bread, rice, and beans. It includes lots of brown flat breads (*aish baladi*), similar to pita bread, accompanied by several small salads (*messas*), soups, fresh vegetables, meats, and fish. Many dishes include the use of yogurt, white feta-style cheese, minced lamb (*kofta*), and grilled lamb pieces (*kebab*). Fish (sea bass, red snapper, shrimp, and lobster)is a special treat in the seafood restaurants of Alexandria and the seaside resorts but less common elsewhere in Egypt. Seasonal fruits, such as bananas, apples, strawberries, oranges, pears, guavas, mangoes, grapes, and melons, are readily available in the major cities. During the winter, look for a wide selection of dates. Egyptian desserts tend to be very sweet, sticky, and fattening. For a real treat, try the *Om Ali* (Mother of Ali), a wonderful soggy pastry covered with coconut, raisins, nuts, and milk. It quickly becomes the favorite Egyptian dish for many visitors who order and reorder the dish everywhere they dine – hoping to discover the ultimate *Om Ali*!

While you will find lots of fruits and vegetables in Egypt, don't expect to find vegetarian dishes in restaurants. If you are a vegetarian, you may want to order breads, salads, and fruits, although we generally avoid salads because of potential health problems related to the handling of ingredients.

Lunch is considered the main meal of the day and usually takes place between 2pm and 5pm. If you are used to an early and light lunch, this local dining custom may throw off both your eating and traveling habits. If you dine like the locals, you'll quickly find your afternoon preoccupied with food rather than shopping or sightseeing. Consequently, you may not want to do like the locals. Given both late and long lunches, the dinner hour gets pushed late into the evening. Restaurants become active around 10pm and close late. If you arrive before 8pm, you may be the only person in the restaurant!

You'll find plenty of soft drinks, juices, coffee, and tea in Egypt. International soft drink brands, such as Coca Cola, Pepsi, 7-Up, and Fanta, are widely available in small shops and grocery stores. The mint and cinnamon teas are good, although somewhat sweet. As you may quickly discover, tea is more than a drink in Egypt – it's an institution that greets strangers, bonds friendships, and initiates communication. Along with coffee, tea is served regularly in cafes, homes, and offices.

Alcoholic beverages are not widely available because of religious restrictions. Nonetheless, most major hotels and restaurants serve local beers and wines. The best local beer brands are Stella and Stella Export. If you are a wine drinker, you will discover some of the world's worst wines in Egypt, although they are getting better. The local wines are cheap but not worth tormenting your palate. Local beers are a much better alternative. Imported wines are very expensive and selections are limited.

If you need to buy bottled water, soft drinks, juices, or snacks, you'll find numerous small shops and stalls along the street offering such items. Many cities also have well stocked convenience stores and supermarkets from which you can periodically restock your hotel mini-bar and acquire additional provisions.

ACCOMMODATIONS

Egypt has a good selection of four- and five-star hotels, as well as budget accommodations, for a wide range of travelers. While by no means inexpensive, the cost of accommodations tends to be reasonable by international standards. Expect to pay US$150-$300 a night for a five-star hotel in Cairo. You'll also find many mid-range three- and four-star hotels for US$50-$100 a night. The level of service and hotel amenities are generally very good in the top hotels. The Hilton Hotel, for example, has a large presence in Egypt with nearly 30 properties found in the major cities and resort areas. You'll also find the Marriott, Sofitel, Sheraton, Inter-Continental, Le Meridien, Oberoi, Sonesta, Renaissance International, and Mövenpick chains well represented in Egypt. Major resort areas, such as Sharm el-Sheikh and Hurghada are experiencing a hotel building boom due to the increased influx of tourists who have discovered Egypt's wonderful resort areas. At the same time, cities such as Alexandria, Luxor, and Aswan offer some legendary old hotels (Cecil in Alexandria, Winter Palace in Luxor, and the Old Cataract in Aswan) that have played important roles in

Egypt's recent (150 years) history.

Most of Egypt's major hotels also have shopping arcades attached to their properties, as well as offer some of the best restaurants and entertainment venues in the city. Staying in one of these properties will put you in close proximity to the best shopping, restaurants, and entertainment in a city.

BUSINESS HOURS

Business hours vary depending on the season, day of the week, and the nature of the business; Friday is a holiday for both government offices and banks. Most shops are open 9am-12:30pm and 4-8pm in the summer and 9am-7pm in the winter; some will close on Friday whereas others will close on Sunday. However, shops in Sharm el-Sheikh remain open until midnight each night. Shops and bazaars in tourist areas may remain open during the afternoon in summer. Government offices are open 9am-2pm and banks are open 8:30am-2pm everyday except Friday and national holidays. Some banks in major hotels (especially those with casinos) will stay open 24 hours a day.

ANTICIPATED COSTS

Egypt is one of those wonderful destinations you can approach at many different levels. You can splurge with a fabulous suite facing the pyramids at the Mena House just outside Cairo in Giza, take a deluxe cruise along the Nile River, dine at the best restaurants, and try your luck in casinos where the house usually wins! At the same time, you can take an inexpensive tour to Egypt or organize a budget trip where you stay in very inexpensive hotels or hostels, dine at cheap eateries, and get around by bus. It just depends on how you want to experience Egypt. Like travel in many other countries, in Egypt you normally get what you pay for. Quality and service normally improve the more you pay for quality and service.

Depending on your style of travel, Egypt can be a relatively inexpensive or a very expensive destination. Backpackers, for example, have their own network of accommodations, restaurants, and transportation that makes Egypt an inexpensive travel destination. Travelers with lots of time and a limited budget often turn to these popular budget travel guides which are available in most bookstores or through our online travel bookstore (*www.ishoparoundtheworld.com*): **Lonely Planet Egypt**, **Rough Guides Egypt**, and **Let's Go Israel and Egypt**. Egypt also is a great jumping-off point for traveling to nearby Israel, Jordan, Turkey, Europe, and Africa.

However, if you follow our many "best of the best"recommendations, you'll find Egypt no more or less expensive than other major countries that offer quality travel and shopping. You should expect the top hotels and restaurants to be relatively expensive. And you also should expect them to be top quality, offering the very best Egypt has to greet its guests.

You should be aware of one unanticipated cost if you are traveling alone. Many independent travelers discover a high cost of admission fees to the various pyramids, tombs, palaces, and museums. If you travel with a group, you won't notice such costs because most are already included in your package; your guide will be responsible for paying entrance fees at each stop and handing you a paid entrance ticket. While such fees may seem irritating and expensive when totaled for the day, keep in mind that the government needs the revenue in order to maintain all the antiquities. Consider such fees as contributions to the continuing maintenance of the world's finest antiquities.

TIPPING

Tips are expected in Egypt, but for many first-time visitors the ubiquitous tipping culture can be irritating at times in airports and at various monuments. Since many people associated with the travel and hospitality industry make low wages (less than US$50 a month), they depend on tips to supplement their meager incomes. While hotels and restaurants add a 10 percent service charge to your bill, personnel in these establishments still expect to receive tips – perhaps another 5 percent of the bill. Doormen, porters, and guards at monuments expect to receive 50 piasters to a E£1 tip for either their services or the asking. Taxi drivers also expect tips – 5-10 percent of the fare. At airports and train stations, individuals may grab your bags to assist you in checking in; they expect a tip. Don't be surprised if one helpful person takes your bag from your taxi, another person then picks up your bag to put it through the security X-ray machine, and another person takes it to the check-in counter. You've unwittingly just employed three different people who all want tips from you for their "handling" services. Even when you enter a monument area, someone may come up to you and initiate a conversation with the expectation you will tip them for their "service." Others, who appear to be officials or volunteers, may ask you to take their picture, which in the end will not be free; you are expected to "tip" this person for his picture! In heavily touristed areas, you are potentially a "tip" for the local touts who either provide you with an unwanted service or simply pester you for money.

If you are not used to tipping in such a manner, you will find such behavior to be very irritating. Everyone seems to be on the "take" for *baksheesh* rather than for a tip earned by giving exceptional service.

Who and how much you tip is up to you. Again, keep in mind that most service personnel are paid very low wages. Two general rules to follow when tipping in Egypt:

1. **Carry lots of small change with you for small tips**, especially 50pt and 1-pound coins or bills. You'll constantly find yourself without adequate change and thus are faced with either over-tipping with large bills or not tipping at all and thus earning the displeasure of people who deserve a tip.

2. **If you are going to tip, be sure to tip generously to the right people at the right time.** Timing is everything when tipping. Important people should be tipped early on and generously if you want to maximize their services. For example, tip your hotel doorman, porter, and room attendant immediately upon arrival. Let them know you will be appreciating their future service. Don't decide to keep everyone guessing what you plan to give them when you leave. They may turn out to be your best friend for getting things you need, from extra service to information and advice on the city.

TOURIST OFFICES

The Egyptian Tourist Authority (E.T.A.) maintains several offices abroad as well as in Egypt. These offices provide a series of colorful and informative brochures on various locations in Egypt. Their personnel also provide travel advice. The E.T.A. offices abroad include:

USA   **New York**
                Egyptian Tourist Authority
                630 Fifth Avenue
                New York, NY 10111
                Tel. 212-246-6960
                Fax 212-956-6439

San Francisco
Egyptian Tourist Authority
232 Geary Street, Suite 303
San Francisco, CA 94102
Tel. 415-781-7676
Fax 415-781-7678

Chicago
Egyptian Tourist Authority
645 North Michigan Ave., Suite 829
Chicago, IL 60611
Tel. 312-280-4666
Tel. 312-280-4788

Canada

Montreal
Egyptian Tourist Authority
Place Bonaventure
40 Frontence, P.O. Box 304
Montreal, P.Q., Canada H5A 1B4
Tel. 514-861-4420
Fax 514-861-8071

Europe

Athens
Egyptian Tourist Authority
10 Amerikis St., 6th Floor
Athens, 10671, Greece
Tel. 360-66906
Fax 363-6681

Frankfurt
Fremdenverkehrsamt Ägypten
64 A, Kaiserstrasse, D-6000
Frankfurt/Main, W. Germany
Tel. 69-252-153
Tel. 69-239-876

Geneva
Office du Tourisme d'Egypte
9, Rue Des Alpes, Geneva
Switzerland
Tel. 22-732-9132
Fax 22-738-1727

Madrid
La Toree de Madrid Planta 5
Oficina 3

Plaza de Espana
28008 Madrid, Espana
Tel. 559-2121
Fax 5592-7121

London
Egyptian Tourist Authority
170 Piccadilly, London W1V 9DD
Tel. 441-493-5282
Fax 441-408-0295

Paris
Bureau du Tourisme
Ambassade de la R.A.E.
90 Av. Des Champs Elysees
8775008 Paris, France
Tel. 331-4562-9443
Fax 331-4289-3481

Rome
Office Turistico Egiziano
19 Via Bissolati – 00187 Rome, Italy
Tel. 396-482-7985

Stockholm
Egyptian Tourist Authority
Drottnin 99 Atan 65
S-11136 Stockholm, Sweden
Tel. 102-548
Fax 102-541

Vienna
Ägyptisches Fremdenverkehrsamt
Elisabethstrasse 4, Stiege 5/1
Opernringhof, 1010 Wien
Austria
Tel. 222-587-6683
Fax 222-587-6634

Arab Region   **Dubai**
Egyptian Tourist Authority
Reqqa St. El Otaiba Building
Flat No. 203, Dubai
United Arab Emirates
Tel. 625-955
Fax 622-906

Kuwait
Egyptian Tourist Authority
Villa 5 F Omar Ibn el Khatab Street
Kuwait
P.B. 27233 Safat, 13133 Kuwait
Tel. 240-3104
Fax 240-3103

Japan   **Tokyo**
Egyptian Tourist Authority
Embassy of Egypt
Akasaka 2-Chome
Annex, M-S Akasaka 2-Chome
Minato – Ku-Tokyo
Japan
Tel. 589-0653
Fax 589-1372

Within Egypt, look for E.T.A. offices in the following locations:

Cairo	Misr Travel Tower (Headquarters Office)	823-510
	Adly Street	391-3454
	Pyramids	385-0259
	Airport	291-4255
	Railway Station	764-214
	Manial Palace	126
Alexandria	Saad Zaghlul Street	807-985
	Nuzha Airport	425-8764
	Alexandria Port	492-5986
	Misr Station	492-5985
Port Said	Palestine Street	223-868
	Customs Area	21687-1
Suez	Canal Street	221-141
	Port Tawfeek	223-589
Hurghada	Bank Misr Street	440-513
Al Minya	Governorate Building	330-150
Luxor	Nile Street	382-215
	Airport	383-294

Aswan	Tourist Souk	323-297
New Valley	El-Khargah	901-205
	Governorate Bldg.	401-206
Marsa Matruh	Governorate Bldg.	394-3192
	City Council Building	Ext. 7
North Sinai	Al-Arish (Fouad Zikry)	341-016
	Rafah (El Mena	3000-655
South Sinai	Sharm el-Sheikh	768-385

USEFUL WEBSITES

You can find a great deal of useful information on Egypt on the Internet. Two of the most useful sites are sponsored by the Egyptian Tourist Authority:

❑ *www.touregypt.net:* Includes lots on information on travel to Egypt. Includes information on pretrip planning, sightseeing, restaurants, hotels, entertainment, and much more. Offers chat groups and message boards. If you have a question, just post it to the board. You may want to sign up for their newsletter which is emailed once a month.

❑ *www.egyptmonth.com:* A monthly magazine with many informative articles on various aspects of Egypt, from tourist attractions to hotels, restaurants, entertainment, cooking, and shopping. Also included as part of *www.touregypt.net.*

Other useful websites with numerous linkages to Egypt include the following:

www.egypttourism.org
http://ce.eng.usf.edu/pharos
www.egypt.com
www.idsc.gov.eg
www.arab.net/egypt
www.geocities.com/Pentagon/3435/
www.sas.upenn.edu/African_Studies/Country_Specific/
    Egypt.html

LOCAL CUSTOMS, TRICKS, AND TIPS

There are a few things you need to know about traveling in Egypt that will save you from surprises and possible problems that may or may not be of your own making. Some relate to local customs and official rules you should observe, whereas others deal with some of the seamier sides of tourism – from toilets to touts.

DEALING WITH PEOPLE

When visiting Egypt, keep in mind that the Egyptians are a very polite, courteous, and hospitable people. Treat them with the same courtesy and friendliness they extend to you. Avoid public displays of anger or criticism. This is not the Egyptian way of handling problems. When encountering a problem, such as a tout who demands payment for an unwanted service, be patient, firm, and persistent – and keep walking. Don't get into an argument which only further legitimizes the encounter.

RELIGION AND DRESS

Egyptians also are religious, with the majority being Muslims. When visiting mosques, you are expected to remove your shoes and dress modestly – no shorts or bare shoulders. In some religious buildings you will be required to wear shoe covers, which will be provided at the entrance (be sure to tip). If you arrive at a mosque and you are deemed to be dressed inappropriately (usually shorts), you can usually rent cover-all garments which will bring you up to an acceptable dress standard.

TAKING PHOTOS

Egypt is a photographer's paradise. Indeed, one of the real highlights of any trip to Egypt are the great photos you may take, especially of the desert sands, pyramids, people, camels, and *feluccas* (traditional river sailing boats). This is a story-book country where the lighting is often magical and the setting is frequently stunning. Be sure to pack a camera or two and lots of film appropriate for Egypt's lighting conditions and photo rules.

Be especially careful who, what, where, and how you take pictures. The rules on photography vary. For example, you are prohibited from photographing soldiers, police, bridges, military areas, airports, radio and television stations, and other public utilities. You also are prohibited from taking photos with a flash in tombs, at many museums, and of the ancient icons and books at St. Catherine Monastery. Many museums and historic sites also charge special camera fees – much higher for video cameras than for still cameras – but you will still be prohibited from using a flash inside areas with paintings and artifacts that are sensitive to light.

Unless you are shooting unobtrusively from a distance, the general rule for taking photos of people is to ask permission before taking their photo. Taking photos of women is unwise. Many people will ask for a tip (*baksheesh*) to take their photo, from children to camel drivers to maintenance workers. Others volunteer to pose for a photo – even encourage you to take their photo. These ostensibly friendly people are actually slick entrepreneurs who will then approach you for a "photo payment"; they constantly "work the tourist crowd" for photo payments. After this happens to you once, you'll get the idea of how this "pay for view" system works. Even the goat herder may ask for payment if you photograph his goats!

While Egypt is a photographer's paradise, it also can be frustrating if you are not prepared for the two photo extremes – very bright light and very little light. Because of the general prohibition on using flashes in museums and tombs, you may want to bring lots of high-speed (400 ASA) film with you for indoor (non-flash) shooting. You'll have no problem finding slower films, especially 100 ASA which is ideal for outdoor shots, in most major tourist sites throughout Egypt. Many visitors miss out on some wonderful photographic opportunities because they failed to pack high-speed film. Our advice: two-thirds of your film should be 100-200 ASA; one-third should be 400 ASA. Many people will travel with two cameras, each loaded with a different film.

If you're planning to travel with a digital camera, be sure to review your lighting options before traveling with it as your only camera. Most digital cameras will require a flash for indoor shooting. Consequently, you may need to travel with two cameras – a digital for outdoor shots and a regular film camera loaded with 400 ASA film for indoor shots.

WOMEN TRAVELING ALONE

Women traveling alone should be prepared for some male harassment, be it rude or suggestive comments or inappropriate touching. Single women traveling alone are viewed by many macho males as easy sex objects – probably women of loose morals, since they are traveling without a male companion and thus looking for sex in Egypt. If you wear skimpy shorts and revealing tops, you'll confirm the worst foreign sexual stereotypes of Hollywood. It's best to ignore such people – they are up to no good and giving them attention merely encourages them. Such behavior also emphasizes the importance of dressing modestly when in Egypt. Avoid suggestive dress that would encourage such pestering behavior. Better still, consider traveling with a companion or joining someone when you go out in public.

TOILETS

One of the major complaints tourists have is the availability and condition of toilets in Egypt – a complaint similarly leveled at many other countries that pay little attention to this very important element of travel. Travelers tend to remember their toilets and talk about their bad experiences with fellow travelers. Many even judge a country by its toilets. The condition of public toilets is usually an indicator of how well a country maintains its public areas. If you judge Egypt by its toilets, it would get very poor marks. In Egypt public toilets are generally filthy, smelly, and wet; many are the ubiquitous Third World squatting type (awkward for the uninitiated) and lack toilet paper (a bucket of water or a hose is often available as a splashing alternative). At many crowded monuments, you may need to stand in line a long time to use restroom facilities. And when your moment arrives, you may be disappointed or appalled by the experience. You are well advised to do two things in preparation for the Egyptian toilet experience. First, carry a supply of toilet paper or tissues with you for emergency purposes. Second, whenever possible, use toilets in four- and five-star hotels and restaurants, which tend to be operated according to higher standards. Shoppers should visit restrooms before spending much time in the bazaars. Looking for a toilet in a bazaar is not the type of cultural experience you'll want to remember, although it will probably make for an interesting "road story" about Egypt!

3

The Shopping Treasures

E GYPT HAS A GREAT DEAL TO OFFER SHOPPERS. Whether you enjoy the adventure of haggling in crowded bazaars, cruising through shopping arcades, visiting factories and galleries, or discovering unique out-of-the-way shops, Egypt seems to have it all. From the cluttered antique and furniture shops of Alexandria and the glittering jewelry stores and leather shops of Cairo to the intriguing alabaster and papyrus factories of Luxor and the Nubian artifact shops of Aswan, Egypt offers an interesting and serendipitous adventure in shopping that quickly energizes what is otherwise a predictable trip into the history, antiquities, monuments, and tombs of Egypt. Go shopping in Egypt and you'll discover some lovely handcrafted products that represent living traditions as well as meet many interesting and hospitable people who also are happy you have come so far to visit their shops. In the end, shopping in Egypt can be great fun that leads to acquiring some very lovely products that represent the best of the best in Egypt.

WHAT TO BUY

Few travelers think of Egypt as a shopper's paradise. And for the most part they are right – until they descend into the huge

Khan el-Khalili Bazaar in Cairo! Egypt is by no means on the shopping par with Hong Kong, Italy, Spain, Thailand, or even India. Shopping in Egypt is more comparable with shopping in Turkey, Morocco, and Israel – lots of jewelry, handcrafted items and exotic medieval bazaars. When you shop in Egypt, you come in close contact with many of Egypt's living traditions that have involved the continuing production of arts and crafts over the centuries. Indeed, Egypt offers an astonishing variety of goods, many of which seem over-produced for the amount of shopping traffic. You'll find everything here from tacky tourist junk and fake antiquities to excellent quality jewelry, ceramics, leather goods, and inlaid furniture. In Cairo, you may become overwhelmed with the many shops offering similar products in the expansive and exotic Khan el-Khalili Bazaar and the profusion of shoe stores that line the city's streets and shopping arcades. As you'll quickly discover when often urged to visit shops and haggle over prices, there's never a dull moment when shopping in Egypt. It's as much a cultural experience as an exercise in acquiring interesting items to grace your home and wardrobe.

❑ Shopping in Egypt can be great fun that leads to acquiring products that represent the best of the best in Egypt.

❑ Shopping in Egypt is comparable to shopping in Turkey, Morocco, and Israel – lots of jewelry, handcrafted items, and exotic medieval bazaars.

❑ There's never a dull moment when shopping in Egypt. It's as much a cultural experience as an exercise in acquiring interesting items to grace your home and wardrobe.

❑ Good quality shopping is often hard to find because of a decided production bias toward tourist souvenirs with antiquity themes.

Shopping in Egypt will acquaint you with a variety of interesting products of varying quality and quantity. **Jewelry** is found everywhere. Tourists especially enjoy purchasing the popular gold cartouches, personalized with one's name embossed in hieroglyphics, gold pendants with pharaonic themes, and silver tribal (Bedouin) jewelry. Serious jewelry buyers find a good range of quality rings, bracelets, pendants, and necklaces crafted in gold and precious stones. **Handicrafts** run the gambit, from truly tacky souvenirs designed for busloads of tourists making pilgrimages to historical sites and overpriced factory shops to excellent quality works. Good quality is often hard to find because of a decided production bias toward tourist souvenirs with antiquity themes. Within a day or two of sightseeing, you'll see the full range of Egyptian handicrafts: painted papyrus, soapstone carvings, brass and copper ware, baskets, pottery, alabaster bowls, mother-of-pearl inlay work, glassware, and ceramics. **Carpets**, especially camel hair rugs with local scenic designs as well as Bedouin rugs, and **appliqué work**, in

the form of tents, wall hangings, and pillow covers, are especially appealing to visitors who frequent bazaars and carpet
factories. **Clothes and fabrics**, ranging from traditional
Egyptian clothes (*galabiyyas* or long men's robes), brand name
ready-made garments, and tailored clothes to handwoven silk
and cotton fabrics, are found in abundance throughout Egyptian bazaars and shopping centers. **Leather goods** in the form
of handbags, luggage, shoes, briefcases, and belts in knock-off
Italian designs are especially appealing to visitors in Cairo and
Alexandria. While Egypt is very old, its **antiques** are not. Many
are fakes; real antiquities require government export permits.
Antique colonial furniture in Alexandria and Cairo and tribal
artifacts in both Cairo and Aswan are well worth examining.

JEWELRY AND GEMS

Jewelry is one of the most appealing buys in Egypt, and especially anything made in gold. Indeed, Egyptian jewelry shops
glitter with gold. The jewelry ranges in quality from tourist
souvenir trinkets (US$2-20 silver and gold charms) to exquisite
designer jewelry (US$1,000++). One merely needs to contrast
the jewelry shops in Luxor and Aswan (geared toward tourists)
with those in the major hotels and shopping centers in Cairo
and Alexandria (geared toward businesspeople and Egyptian
upper classes).

Egyptian jewelry shops offer a wide range of varying quality
jewelry. Much of it is 18- to 22-carat gold pieces made with
traditional Egyptian themes and pharaonic motifs, such as the
cartouche (gold pendant with one's name embossed in hieroglyphics), scarab (a beatle that stands for good luck), ankh (the
Egyptian cross that symbolizes life), and the Eye of Horus. Be
sure to do comparative shopping for such jewelry since similar
pieces appear in many jewelry and souvenir shops. Also, be sure
to bargain for jewelry which could result in a 50 percent
discount; however, some reputable shops do not bargain since
they initially set fair prices. You may discover prices varying as
much as 200 percent on an identical piece. Better still, shop in
a reputable jewelry shop (see our "best of the best" recommendations in Cairo) rather than in a shop crammed with busloads
of tourists who probably were taken to the shop by a guide who
receives a commission (30 to 60 percent) on your purchases. Be
especially careful when buying the popular cartouche. Many
shops are known for gluing on the hieroglyphic figures rather
than soldering them on permanently. Inexpensive cartouches
tend to be glued; many with fall apart within a month – shortly

after you've returned home! Many shops will tell you they solder the pieces in place but they actually glue them on; be sure to examine your purchase carefully. Cartouches can range in price from US$20 to US$500 or more, depending on the size and complexity of the pieces; the more gold content, the more expensive. Since gold is sold by the gram weight, you can check the price by weighing the piece; the cost of craftsmanship should be relatively the same from one shop to another since the designs are very simple and thus do not require special designer expertise.

Jewelry made with Islamic motifs may or may not appeal to you. Somewhat utilitarian, this jewelry usually is designed with hands and eyes inscribed with "Allah." Such designs supposedly ward off evil. Tribal (Bedouin) jewelry, which has religious (Islamic) significance, usually consists of turquoise strands and large intricate silver beaded necklaces. If attractively framed, many of the larger and older silver Bedouin necklaces make attractive displays.

The majority of Egyptian jewelry consists of 18- to 22-carat gold rings, earrings, chains, necklaces, and bracelets. Indeed, the bazaars in most cities are filled with small jewelry shops offering the same type of gold jewelry. Many of the jewelry shops found in major hotel shopping arcades and in specialty shops also carry nicely designed gold and silver jewelry as well as jewelry made with diamonds, lapis, emeralds, sapphires, rubies, and other precious stones. The trend in both Cairo and Alexandria is to offer more and more jewelry with European designs.

Egypt has long been known for its rich assortment of minerals and gems. From ancient times until the present, Egypt has had an abundance of limestone, sandstone, basalt, granite, and calcite-alabaster which have been used for grand construction projects. At the same time, numerous precious and semiprecious stones have been mined in Egypt and adorned the bodies of royalty. While not as richly endowed as Brazil with its fabulous "gem-belt," nonetheless, Egypt holds its own in the world of gem mining by producing this array of gems which are also set in Egyptian jewelry: amethyst, emerald, lapis lazuli, jade, nephrite, rhodochrosite, chrysoberyl, hematite, jasper, agate, malachite, aragonite, aquamarine, granite, topaz, turquoise, tourmaline, zircon, and many more. Occasionally even a diamond is found in Egypt. You can purchase loose gems in many jewelry shops, especially in Cairo's famous Khan el-Khalili Bazaar. However, make sure you know your gems before investing a great deal of money. While generally of good quality, Egyptian gems are not always the world's best quality and could even turn out to be glass. This is not the place to start learning about gems by purchasing from a street or market vendor. For a quick online introduction to gems and jewelry, visit *www.mondera.com*.

HANDICRAFTS AND SOUVENIRS

Souvenir shops and bazaars overflow with a wide range of locally-produced handicrafts and souvenirs. The quality varies considerably, with many items mass-produced for tourists who primarily shop at popular tourist rest stops. Some of it is simply tacky. The most ubiquitous handicrafts include papyrus paintings; alabaster vases, bowls, and carved figures; inlaid boxes; mother-of-pearl; perfume bottles; baskets; decorative plates; woven bags; embroidery; and stuffed toys (especially camels). At the pyramids, vendors hawk Arab headdresses (keeps the sun off your head, just in case you forgot your hat) and lots of stone carvings with pharaonic themes (Horus is very popular).

Some of the nicest quality handicrafts are produced by the Bedouins of the Western Desert and the Sinai and by the Nubians near Aswan. You'll fine several good-quality shops offering Bedouin arts and crafts in Cairo and Sharm el-Sheikh. Nubian arts and crafts, some of antique quality, are well represented in the street shops of Aswan.

BRASS AND COPPERWARE

Look for brass and copper plates, trays, and coffee pots. Many of the flashy plates and trays are engraved with intricate local designs. Some of the items have a decided ethnic look to them which may or may not make nice home decorative or gift items. You'll find the largest concentration of such items in the brass and copper *souk* (marketplace) along Sharia an-Nahassin (Street of the Coppersmiths) in the Khan el-Khalili in Cairo as well as the bazaars of Luxor.

CARPETS AND RUGS

Egypt produces lots of carpets, but they are not the same quality as those found in Iran, Turkey, Afghanistan, Pakistan, and India. Nonetheless, you may find a beautiful Egyptian or colorful Bedouin carpet. Some of the best and most interesting carpets are produced in the textile shops along Sakkara Road in Giza, just outside Cairo, especially the Wissa Wassef Art Center. Many of the rugs, which also make interesting wall hangings, are made from camel hair and depict rural scenes in Egypt. Also look for the very colorful red Bedouin rugs which tend to be smaller than the woven Egyptian rugs.

APPLIQUÉ WORK

Colorful appliqué work is a noteworthy Egyptian specialty. Numerous craftsmen are skilled in producing tents, pillowcases, wall hangings, and bedspreads. The smaller items, especially pillowcases and wall hangings, make nice gifts. Tent making, which is done in arabesque and calligraphy patterns for weddings and funerals, is fascinating to watch along the Tent-makers' Street (Sharia al-Khayamiyya) in Islamic Cairo.

CLOTHES

Since Egyptian cottons are world famous for their quality, it comes as no surprise to find lots of clothes available in Egypt, from the traditional *galabiyyas* (long robes for men) and *melayas* (black gowns for women) to ubiquitous T-shirts and designer label clothes from Europe. If you collect T-shirts, you'll have fun shopping in Egypt. You'll find T-shirts with all types of photos and slogans relating to Egypt's antiquities. In Luxor, look for shops that produce T-shirts with personalized car-touches (name) embroidered on the front; they make great gifts for children and some adults seem to like them too. The traditional garments and T-shirts can be found everywhere tourists stop, especially at major tourist sites and bazaars. Several shops represent fashionable lines of Egyptian clothes, from sweaters to cotton shirts and blouses. Many of these shops are found in the World Trade Center in Cairo. You'll also find numerous tailors who can produce good quality garments at very reasonable prices. Be sure to bring pictures of what you want made, since tailors are skilled at copying from photos.

TEXTILES AND FABRICS

In addition to clothes, rugs, appliqué, and wall hangings, be sure to look for fabrics, linens, and towels made from top quality Egyptian cotton. Some of the best places to buy such items will be found in the World Trade Center and hotel shopping arcades in Cairo. They're not cheap, but the quality is excellent.

ANTIQUES AND ANTIQUITIES

Genuine antiques and antiquities require an export license from the Department of Antiquities. While you will encounter many people offering antiquities for sale, most such items are fakes; indeed, many are obvious fakes. However, some of the best antiques found in Egypt consist of furniture, both Egyptian and European – tables, chairs, chests, chandeliers, and accessories. Many of the items reflect the Egyptian preference for ornate French, Spanish, and Italian style furniture. The interesting antique furniture shops are found in Alexandria's Attarine district as well as in Cairo behind the Marriott Cairo Hotel (Zamalek) and in the Khan el-Khalili Bazaar. We prefer Alexandria over Cairo for antique furniture.

ART

Egypt has a budding art community which produces quality paintings, sculptures, glassware, woodwork, and ceramics. Many of the art themes relate to Egypt's antiquities and daily life in the cities and villages. Other artists work with modern themes shared by artists elsewhere in the world. Several painters, such as Wageeh Wahba, regularly exhibit abroad and are popular with foreign art collectors (his works are occasionally on display at Espace Karim Frances Gallery in Cairo).

Most of Egypt's talented art community are well represented in several art galleries in Cairo (see the latest listings under "Galleries" in the monthly magazine *Egypt Today*) which hold monthly exhibitions as well as offer permanent displays. Many of these galleries are concentrated in the Zamalek area behind the Marriott Cairo Hotel.

Please be forewarned that the term "gallery" has broad meaning in Egypt – a practice left over from the French. While a shop that has "gallery" in its name may be strictly an art gallery with paintings and sculptures, it often is an arts and crafts shop or a shop selling furniture and antiques. You may want to call ahead to make sure the "gallery" or "art center" offers the type of art you are interested in seeing.

CERAMICS AND POTTERY

Egypt has a long tradition in producing ceramic pots, plates, bowls, and figures. Traditional pottery, especially large earthenware jars, are particularly attractive and inexpensive, although the expense of shipping such items abroad will add to the cost. You'll find several shops, galleries, and factories in and around Cairo offering a nice range of quality ceramics, from traditional to modern designs. Ceramic artists, such as the internationally renowned potter Mohammed Allam ("The Crazy Artist"), maintain their own galleries just outside Cairo. Some of our best purchases in Egypt have been ceramics and pottery. They make wonderful additions to art and home decorative collections as well as utilitarian serving dishes and tableware. After seeing so much tourist kitsch in the bazaars and at tourist shops, be sure to visit some of our recommended shops for quality ceramics and pottery. You may be pleasantly surprised by what you find.

ALABASTER

You can't miss it, especially when visiting Luxor. Egypt's rich deposits of calcite-alabaster have resulted in numerous alabaster factories which produce a large variety of vases, bowls, and statuary for the tourist trade. Many of the items have beautiful colors, patterns, and translucent quality. Others are crudely fashioned pieces designed for transient tour groups that are steered into the alabaster factories by guides and drivers who receive commissions from the factory shops.

Shopping in an alabaster factory/shop is like shopping in a rug shop – always friendly, high-pressured, and terribly overpriced. These are the places that give shopping in Egypt a bad reputation. When you visit one of these places, expect to experience three things: an outdoor demonstration area where craftspeople show how they cut, drill, and turn alabaster stone into artifacts; free drinks accompanied with aggressive service; and highly inflated prices. In fact, if you pay the asking prices, you'll probably pay three times what you should pay. An item selling for E£100 in one of these factory shops should probably sell for no more than E£30. If you find something you really like, be sure to bargain hard; better still, survey the nearby shops which do not have buses parked in front or bargain hard after everyone has left for the bus. Chances are you'll get a much better deal than the "highway robbery" prices the unsuspecting tourists pay with the help of their commissioned guides. However, if you find a unique piece you really love, bargain hard and buy it. If you procrastinate, it may be gone by the time the bus leaves!

MARQUETRY AND MOTHER-OF-PEARL

Some of the most popular tourist items are the many inlaid wood (marquetry) boxes, chests, mirrors, screens, tables, chest boards and backgammon boards that are found in Egypt's bazaars. While many are of poor quality, others exhibit excellent craftsmanship. You'll frequently find small inexpensive boxes inlaid with plastic or camel bone rather than mother-of-pearl. You'll find lots of such items in Cairo's Khan el-Khalili Bazaar. For good quality inlaid chests and tables, be sure to visit the many furniture and antique shops in Alexandria's Attarine district.

WATER PIPES (SHISHAS)

You'll see them everywhere, from sidewalk cafes to hotel restaurants. Many cafes and restaurants maintain a special section for preparing the *shishas* for their patrons – clean, fill with water, and prepare charcoal and tobacco. These big, colorful, and ornate bulbous glass water pipes are popular with men and women alike in Cairo. Ordered and served like dessert at the end of meal, patrons puff on these water pipes at the end of their meal while drinking coffee. They also are one of the reasons patrons linger so long around cafes and restaurants – a meal becomes a two-hour ritual of eating, conversation, and the obligatory *shisha*. Some visitors enjoy trying what is both a cool and sweet smoke and then decide to acquire one of these ethnic water pipes for themselves. Shops in most bazaars will offer a wide selection of *shishas* of varying colors and sizes. While they may look great in Egypt and remind you of a cultural tradition, *shishas* may look tacky or out of place back home. Nonetheless, they're exotic and will serve as a good conversation piece! If you buy one of these water pipes, make sure it's packed well because it's primarily made of glass which can easily break.

MUSKI GLASS

This popular glass is made from recycled bottles. It comes in several different colors: brown, turquoise blue, green, purple, red, blue, and translucent white. The glass is hand-blown into a variety of attractive products: pitchers, vases, drinking glasses, cups, beakers, tumblers, dishes, and red Christmas ornaments. Most of these items are very inexpensive and easily breakable. The Khan el-Khalili Bazaar in Cairo is a major center for this unique glass. Many visitors also enjoy seeing the glassblowers at work in the nearby factories. If you purchase this glass, make sure you have it packed very well against possible breakage.

PAPYRUS

For a dying art form, papyrus sure has staged a terrific comeback! Any visit to Egypt seems incomplete without a visit to a papyrus shop or factory. Papyrus is a plant or reed that was used to make paper in ancient Egypt. Revived in recent years almost single-handedly by Dr. Ragab, papyrus growing and painting now reaches all corners of the tourist trade, from Alexandria to Aswan and from Sharm el-Sheikh to Taba. The quality varies greatly from inexpensive tourist paintings and bookmarks (the really cheap stuff is made from banana leaf) to very expensive pieces produced at Dr. Ragab's Papyrus Institute. Most of the papyrus paintings depict popular scenes from ancient Egyptian wall paintings. While many tourists are attracted to this art form, others don't see it as great art; much of it might best be termed "borderline tacky souvenirs." However, to get a true appreciation for this art form, you should visit Dr. Ragab's Papyrus Institute in Cairo (located on boats in front of the Cairo Sheraton Hotel in Dokki). There you can see a demonstration of both the papyrus paper making process and papyrus painting. Here you'll also have an opportunity to purchase good quality papyrus products which can be very expensive. Just in case you miss this place, Dr. Ragab also has shops in Alexandria, Luxor, and Aswan. Most major cities in Egypt will have shops selling a wide range of papyrus products. Many of the tour guides and touts in Luxor will try to steer you into particular shops and factories that supposedly offer "good deals" on papyrus. Don't believe them. Much of this so-called papyrus is made from inexpensive banana leaves. Except for acquiring bookmarks as unique gift items, we have yet to develop a taste for this art form.

SHOES AND LEATHER GOODS

Egypt produces a great deal of leather items which are well represented in the shops of major cities and resorts. One of the first things you'll notice when shopping in Cairo is the large number of shoe stores found throughout the city. In some shopping centers, over 50 percent of the shops are shoe stores. Along some city blocks, 90 percent of the shops are shoe stores. At times the city appears to be wall-to-wall shoes! Indeed, the local joke is that the Egyptians must have a foot fetish because of the high concentration of shoe stores. At the same time, quantity does not mean quality. In fact, one of the major shopping complaints is that in a country with so many shoes, there are no good shoes to be found except in very expensive upscale shops that import shoes from Italy and France. While most Egyptian-manufactured shoes may look nice in the window, they are generally of poor quality; many deteriorate quickly on Egypt's streets and sidewalks. If you succumb to making a shoe purchase, chances are you will be very disappointed with the outcome.

Putting shoes aside, you'll find many other Egyptian leather goods to be good buys. Leather handbags tend to be very stylish – knock-offs of Italian and French designs – and good buys. Many come in unusual colors such as silver, bronze, rose, yellow, and green. While not as good as the handbag knock-offs in neighboring Israel, in Egypt these items are less expensive (US$25 in Egypt versus US$100 in Israel for a US$1200 Chanel, Fendi, or Yves St. Laurent knock-off) and very acceptable in terms of quality. Also look for leather belts, wallets, luggage, clothes, and slippers (*shibshib*). Many of the leather jackets are good quality, nicely styled, and reasonably priced. You'll find the best quality leather goods in the upscale shopping centers, department stores, and hotel shopping arcades in Cairo and Alexandria. Much of Egypt's leather production takes place in numerous factories just outside Alexandria.

PERFUMES

Perfumes and perfume bottles seem to be as prolific as shoes in Egypt. The locals, especially well dressed women, are heavy users of perfumes. The country is well known for producing pure essence used in making perfumes. You can buy pure essence and make your own perfumes or purchase perfumes diluted with alcohol. You'll also find many shops offering a large variety of colorful small glass perfume bottles which look like collector's items. The largest concentration of perfume purveyors will be found in the perfume section of Cairo's Khan el-Khalili Bazaar as well as around Midan al-Tahrir.

MUSIC AND MUSICAL INSTRUMENTS

If you enjoy the sounds of traditional and modern Egyptian music, you're in luck. Numerous shops offer locally produced CDs and cassettes featuring both Egyptian and Arab artists.

When in Aswan, look for shops offering recordings of Nubian music. If you're intrigued by traditional Egyptian and Middle Eastern instruments, such as the flute (*nay*), drums(*tabla*), violin (*kamaan*), or lute (*oud*), you'll find several shops in the bazaars offering these instruments. In Cairo, you'll find such shops along Sharia Muhammad Ali near the Citadel.

HOME DECORATIVE ITEMS

Egyptian home decorating is heavily influenced by French, Italian, and Spanish design elements. Indeed, Egyptian furniture, accessories, lighting fixtures, and fabrics tend to be very European and often flamboyant. For the latest in home decorative items, both imported and Egyptian made, visit the World Trade Center in Cairo. Here you'll find numerous shops offering everything from furniture, upholstery and drapery fabrics to chandeliers, lighting fixtures, and paintings.

SPICES

Egypt is a spice lovers paradise. Walk through most bazaars and you'll smell the aromas of spice shops. You'll find several vendors offering a wide variety of intriguing and colorful spices piled high in pans, stored in containers, or packaged in small bags. Most spices are sold by the gram weight. If you know your spices, you can get terrific buys on Egyptian spices. Saffron, for example, is less than 1/10 the price you may pay for it back home. If you are packing such purchases in your luggage, be sure to pack them well so your luggage and clothes won't smell like a spice market!

BOOKS

We normally don't shop for books when traveling abroad, because they tend to be very expensive and because we usually can get most any book back home. However, in the case of Egypt, you may find numerous books that are not readily available outside Egypt, with many focusing on the finer points of Egyptian antiquities. Many are coffee table books printed in either Egypt or Europe. Some of the best selections of such books are at museum shops. Be sure to visit the book shop at the Egyptian Antiquities Museum in Cairo as well as the bookstore at the American University in Cairo. L'Orientaliste in Cairo also has a nice selection of old books for collectors.

THE MORE YOU LOOK

The shops and markets of Egypt brim with all types of intriguing products. The more you look, the more you find. What we've outlined thus far are some of the major products you are likely to encounter throughout Egypt, but especially in Cairo, Alexandria, and Luxor. As you move farther south in Egypt along the Nile River, you'll find many more local ethnic products. When you visit resort areas such as Sharm el-Sheikh, you'll find more quality products that appeal to more upscale and independent travelers who are used to shopping in air-conditioned shops with nice window displays. In many respects, you'll find the best of the best represented in these places because the shops cater to the tastes and spending habits of this class of traveler. Here the Khan el-Khalili and other bazaars may be best remembered as a cultural experience involving lots of people, unusual sights and sounds, and a place to try out your new-found bargaining skills rather than as an exercise in quality shopping.

While much of what you'll encounter is rightfully classified as tourist kitsch and of poor quality, you'll also find many fine quality items – if you look beyond the typical tourist shops and seek out quality. Don't just head for Cairo's Khan el-Khalili Bazaar or the popular rug and alabaster factory/shops and confine your shopping to these places. If you do, you'll miss out on some of Egypt's best quality shopping. You'll come away with a very distorted view of shopping in Egypt – a place where you encountered many aggressive in-your-face merchants and touts who tried to pawn off tasteless merchandise at exorbitant prices. There's a lot more to shopping in Egypt than these well worn tourist places.

Shopping By the Rules

I F YOU WANT TO REALLY ENJOY YOUR SHOPPING experience in Egypt – meet new and interesting people, acquire great products, and get good deals – you should consider following many of the tips and rules identified in this chapter. These range from pre-trip planning to approaching shops and merchants with certain street smarts. As you'll quickly discover, shopping in Egypt is not like shopping back home. This is a buying and selling culture where bargaining plays a central role in many transactions. If you don't know how to bargain, you can easily make many shopping mistakes and end up paying two to three times the value of items. But if you know some basic rules of bargaining, which we outline in this chapter, you should do well in Egypt's many shops and bazaars. You'll have a good time shopping and get some very good deals on purchases. You'll also need to be prepared for possible scams and for packing and shipping your treasures home with ease.

TAKE KEY SHOPPING INFORMATION

Depending on what you plan to buy, you should take all the necessary information you need to make informed shopping decisions. After all, you don't want to end up purchasing an emerald ring or lapis pendant in Cairo for US$1,000 and then discover you can get the same item back home for US$600. Put this information in a separate envelope. If you are looking for home furnishings, especially carpets and furniture, include with your "wish list" room measurements to help you determine if particular items will fit into your home. You might take photographs with you of particular rooms you hope to furnish.

If you plan to shop for clothes and accessories, especially leather goods such as shoes and handbags, your homework should include taking an inventory of your closets and identifying particular colors, fabrics, and designs you wish to acquire to complement and enlarge your present wardrobe. Good quality clothes, shoes, and handbags made in Egypt can be an excellent buy – half of what you may pay back home. At the same time, many shoes and handbags come in very interesting and, at times, unusual colors. Be sure you known what colors work best for your wardrobe. Top quality imported designer-label clothes and accessories (mainly from Italy and France) will probably be more expensive than similar items found in department stores and boutiques back home. If you are from the U.S., you should look at comparable selections found at the top department stores, such as Saks Fifth Avenue, Neiman Marcus, Macy's, and Nordstrom. This means visiting their designer-label and couture sections for comparable quality and prices. Since you will see lots of shoes, handbags, and other leather goods in Egypt – many being knock-offs of Italian and French designer-labels – you may want to prepare yourself for such items.

❑ Take with you measurements and photographs of rooms that could become candidates for home decorative items.

❑ Be sure to take information on any particular clothes, accessories, or jewelry (sizes, colors, comparative prices) with you to look for or have made when in Egypt.

❑ Do comparative shopping before arriving in Egypt.

❑ Half the fun of shopping while traveling in Egypt is the serendipity of discovering the unique and exotic.

DO COMPARATIVE SHOPPING

Prices for comparable items seem to be all over the place in Egypt, from small bazaar shops to factories. Since many merchants expect visitors to haggle, their initial asking prices may have little relation to actual market value – only to the perceived size of the tourist's wallet. Indeed, one often feels the merchant's main pricing rule is *"whatever the tourist market will bear!"* It's very easy to be taken advantage of if you don't know fair market values in Egypt, especially for jewelry, alabaster, and carpets. While you should do comparison shopping before you leave home, once you arrive in Egypt, the only comparisons you can make are between various shops and products you encounter. You'll never know if you are getting a good deal unless you have done your shopping homework beforehand.

The first step in doing comparative shopping starts at home. Determine exactly what you want and need. Make lists. As you compile your list, spend some time "window shopping" in the local stores, examining catalogs, telephoning for information, and checking Internet shopping sites such as *www.novica.com* and *www.eziba.com*. Even check out the shopping section on the official Egyptian tourism website which includes a store selling items directly from Egyptian shops: *www.touregypt.net*.

Once you arrive in Egypt, your shopping plans will probably change considerably as you encounter many new items you had not planned to purchase but which attract your interest and buying attention. Indeed, half the fun of shopping while traveling in Egypt is the serendipity of discovering the unique and exotic – a gorgeous ceramic pot, a beautiful lapis pendant, an intricately woven camel's hair rug, a lovely painting of a desert scene, an unusual antique table or inlaid box, or a beautifully designed gold necklace – things you could not have anticipated encountering but which you now see, feel, and judge as possible acquisitions for your home and wardrobe. These are the great shopping moments that require local knowledge about differences in quality and pricing. Many products, such as paintings, ceramic pots, or pieces of jewelry, may be unique one-of-a-kind items that are difficult to compare. You must judge them in terms of their designs, colors, and intrinsic value. Other items, such as leather goods, carpets, and alabaster, will beg comparative shopping because the same or similar quality items are widely available in numerous shops and factories.

You'll have plenty of opportunities to do comparison shopping in Egypt. You are well advised to visit several shops immediately upon arrival in order to get some sense of market prices for various items you are likely to frequently encounter in Egypt: jewelry, gems, cartouches, scarabs, shoes, handbags, silver work, books, handicrafts, and carpets. Visit shops in the World Trade Center, Ramses Hilton Center, and the Khan el-Khalili Bazaar to get a good sense of the product range and comparative pricing. Keep in mind that you are dealing with two different shopping worlds and cultures. Most shops in Cairo's two shopping centers will probably feel familiar to you – they have nice window and store displays as well as offer fixed prices and run sales. The shops in the bazaar are definitely Third World – cluttered, exotic, aggressive, few prices displayed, and require bargaining in order to get a good deal. Make sure you understand pricing for the ubiquitous cartouches and alabaster vases, bowls, and statuary. You can easily pay twice what you should for a cartouche and five to ten times more than what you should pay in the many alabaster factories in Luxor that are located along the well traveled tourist bus stops.

Assuming you enter Egypt at Cairo, make a special effort to spot-check prices on various items you are likely to buy during your stay in Egypt. Visit a few of the shopping centers and you may get a feel for full retail prices for quality items; a comparable bazaar or factory price should be 20 percent less. However, be sure to examine the quality of items which will probably be lower in the bazaars and factories. What you don't want to do is arrive in a bazaar or in a tourist shop not knowing what the fair market rate is for an item. While you may think you are a good haggler, because you often manage to get a 20 to 40 percent discount, you're only as good as your ability to distinguish quality and know what the real value of an item is because you did comparison shopping to establish such value. Indeed, you may discover through comparison shopping that you should get a 60-75 percent discount rather than your usual 20-40 percent discount!

KEEP TRACK OF RECEIPTS

It's important to keep track of all of your purchases for making an accurate Customs declaration. Be sure to ask for receipts wherever you shop. If a shop doesn't issue receipts, ask them to create a receipt by writing the information on a piece of paper, include the shop's name and address, and sign it.

Since it's so easy to misplace receipts, you might want to organize your receipts using a form similar to the following example. Staple a sheet or two of notebook or accountant's paper to the front of a large manila envelope and number down the left side of the page. Draw one or two vertical columns down the right side. Each evening sort through that day's purchases, write a description including style and color of the purchase on the accompanying receipt, and enter that item on your receipt record. Record the receipt so later you'll know exactly which item belongs to the receipt.

CUSTOMS DECLARATION RECORD FORM

Receipt #	Item	Price (E£)	Price (US$)
1. 2398	cartouche	E£300	$88.24
2.			
3.			
4.			

Put the receipts in the manila envelope and pack the purchases away. If you're missing a receipt, make a note of it beside the appropriate entry.

22 SHOPPING RULES FOR SUCCESS

One of the great pleasures of visiting Egypt is its intriguing shopping. You'll discover lots of interesting jewelry, gems, silver, clothes, leather goods, handicrafts, and art to keep you busy shopping for several days.

As you begin shopping in Egypt, keep these basic "rules" in mind:

1. **Expect to shop in two very different shopping cultures which require different shopping skills**. The first world is the most familiar one for visitors – shopping centers, department stores, and hotel shopping arcades. Shops in this culture tend to have window displays, well organized interiors, and fixed prices which may or may not be all that fixed, depending on your ability to persuade shops to discount prices. The second shopping culture consists of traditional street shops, bazaars, vendor stalls, and touts which tend to be somewhat chaotic and involve price uncertainty and bargaining skills. You will most likely be able to directly transfer your shopping skills to the first culture, but you may have difficulty navigating in the second shopping culture which at times can be intimidating but often fun.

2. **Be prepared for "in-your-face" retailing.** Egyptian merchants, especially those found in the bazaars, can be very aggressive. Used to maintaining close personal space, many of these people will get up close to you – even breathe on you – and thus may make you feel uncomfortable as they try to persuade you to enter their shops and buy their products. If you're not interested, don't maintain eye contact nor engage in a conversation with such individuals. Doing so only encourages them to be even more aggressive!

3. **Focus your initial shopping on the major shopping areas.** Most shopping areas are very well defined – hotel shopping arcades, shopping centers, bazaars, factories, major streets, and vendor stalls and touts at tourist sites.

4. **Expect to find the best quality shopping at the best quality locations.** It should come as no surprise that the best quality shopping is usually found in the shopping arcades of top quality hotels which tend to screen the quality of shops that are allowed to rent their shop space. These shops tend to cater to the tastes of upscale visitors who stay there. And it should come as no surprise that the best quality shopping will be found in the hotel shopping arcades and shopping centers of Cairo. With the exception of a few well established shops in Cairo's famous Khan el-Khalili Bazaar, don't expect to do your best quality shopping in the bazaars. These are fun and exotic places to acquire "bargains" and encounter a variety of interesting cultural experiences. When in doubt where to shop for quality items, head for the major hotels. If the hotel does not have a shopping arcade, ask the concierge or front desk for shopping recommendations. They usually know the best places to shop based upon the experiences of their hotel guests.

5. **Look for a few out-of-the-way places for quality shopping.** Some of the best shopping will be found in studios, galleries, shops, and homes that are located outside the major shopping areas. If you learn of a shop that is excellent but located off the beaten path, it may be worth finding it – literally a diamond in the rough. Many of these places cater to an exclusive clientele rather than to walk-in traffic. Indeed, some of our best shopping in Egypt has been with shops that are difficult to find.

6. **Check out the interiors of shops where you may find some hidden treasures.** Be sure to go deep into a shop, especially ask to see the backrooms or upstairs where the "good stuff" may be found. Fronts of shops may be filled with tacky tourist trash. But the really good quality items may be found in other areas of shops, especially upstairs. This pattern is very prevalent amongst many of the small shops found in Cairo's Khan el-Khalili Bazaar.

7. **Beware of shopping recommendations.** The best shopping recommendations will usually come from the concierges and front desk managers of top hotels – they often know where their best guests shop for such popular items as jewelry, gems, clothes, art, handicrafts, and antiques. They also know which shops generate complaints because of high prices, poor quality and service, and problems with shipping. Ask for their top three recommendations in different product categories. Many of these people maintain a printed list of recommended shops by category which you should try to see. However, not all top hotels are so knowledgeable and helpful when it comes to shopping. It depends on the hotel and the services it provides for its guests. The worst people to ask for shopping recommendations are tour guides, drivers, touts, and general service personnel. They are either "on the take" or have no sense of quality shopping. You'll pay dearly for their advice!

8. **Expect to be "taken for a ride" in shops recommended by your friendly tour guide and driver.** Beware of shopping in major tourist shops and factories frequented by tour buses and taxis. Like elsewhere in the world, these places tend to be patronized by clients of tour guides who get commissions – often in the 30 to 60 percent range – on everything their clients purchase. The quality of products in these places is usually mediocre and the prices are often sky high. Expect to pay a real premium for shopping in such places that are highly recommended by tour guides and drivers. Whatever you do, don't ask your tour guide or driver to help you bargain for an item – a frequent request of naive tourists. Your guide is not your friend in these places. He or she instead is the problem – leading you to the shopping slaughter where you are likely to pay 100 percent above retail! A percentage of what you pay for each item will go directly into the pocket of your guide or driver. Few

people can knowingly afford such friendship! If taken to such a place, take advantage of the "freebies" (drinks and snacks) but be careful what you buy; it may become a lasting reminder of a bad shopping experience!

9. **Avoid "slaughter shopping" by shopping next door to where the buses and drivers stop.** Seasoned independent travelers know a little secret that can upset group travelers – tour guides make lots of money from those little shopping stops along the way. In Egypt, those carpet and alabaster factories are a gold mine for tour guides and drivers. If you are with a tour group and your guide decides it's time to "go shopping" at his or her favorite place, which is often a friendly factory offering free drinks and great one-on-one customer service, you are about to experience a form of "slaughter shopping" – you're being taken to the slaughter. We recommend that you do this in order to avoid being ripped off: follow the group by going into the shop, surveying the products, and checking the prices. Then make a quick exit. While everyone else is being treated to free drinks and great customer service, leave the shop and look around for a similar shop next door or across the road (most congregate in the same area) which does not have buses or drivers parked in front. These shops, which usually have idle and envious salespeople hanging around, either are between their scheduled tour buses or are being boycotted by tour guides for various reasons, such as not giving them as good a commission as the shop you just visited. If you visit one of these other quieter shops, you may be amazed by the prices and how willing the shop is to bargain with major discounts. Indeed, we often get items for less than half of what the other tourists are paying in the tour guide's shop; in some cases we have paid one-fifth. The fun part is getting back on the bus and comparing prices.

10. **Expect to get the best prices on locally produced items that use inexpensive labor.** Imported goods, such as designer clothes and accessories, will be expensive. But any products that use inexpensive local labor – handcrafted jewelry, carvings, brass work, woven rugs and handicrafts – are excellent buys because the cost of labor continues to go up and many of the handcrafting skills will disappear with the onslaught of inexpensive plastic materials and machine labor.

11. **Don't expect to get something for nothing.** If a price seems too good to be true, it probably is. Good quality products, especially jewelry, antiques, and art, may not seem cheap in Egypt. But they are bargains if you compare prices to similar items found in the shops of Paris, London, or New York City.

12. **Ask for assistance whenever you feel you need it.** At times, especially in bazaars, you may feel lost and have difficulty finding particular shops or products. Whenever this happens, just ask for assistance from your hotel, shopkeepers, and others. Egyptians are very friendly and will assist you if they can. Hopefully you won't accidentally meet a friendly tout who claims he's taking you to his brother's shop where prices are real cheap. This is not the friend you want to make for more than a minute!

13. **Bargain wherever possible.** Especially in bazaars, factories, and small shops and with touts, you are expected to haggle over prices. Discounts can run anywhere from 10 percent to 80 percent, depending on the seller and your ability to bargain. If you pay the asking price, chances are you have been "taken" for an exorbitant price. If you are not used to bargaining, try our bargaining scenario in the next section. It may do wonders for your confidence and your wallet!

14. **Be prepared to pay fixed prices in many places.** Not all shops engage in haggling. Some shops, which are often the best quality shops, announce that they are "fixed price" shops. Some may even show you newspaper articles and excerpts from travel guides that state they are the best quality shops. Given their excellent reputations and steady clientele, such shops usually set fair prices. Most shops in hotel shopping arcades and shopping centers also have relatively fixed prices. Many run occasional sales or they may do some discounting (10-20 percent) if you ask (*"Is it possible to do any better on this price?"*). When buying a high ticket item, such as gems and jewelry, always ask for a discount even though the shop may initially indicate they have fixed prices.

15. **Use your credit cards whenever possible.** Many shops accept major credit cards. Even small shops in bazaars often take credit cards because they are used to dealing with tourists who expect to pay with plastic. It's always

good to charge a purchase just in case you later have a problem with authenticity or shipping. Your credit card company may be able to assist you in resolving such problems. Credit card purchases usually receive the best exchange rates.

16. **Be sure to comparative shop for many items.** Many shops carry similar items, and prices can vary considerably from one shop to another on jewelry, clothes, leather goods, brass ware, alabaster, and handicrafts. Be sure to survey your shopping options by visiting various shops offering such products. You'll quickly get some idea as to how to best value these items.

17. **Be sure to ask for assistance and background information.** One of the great pleasures of shopping in Egypt is learning about various products, artists, and craftspeople. Since you may be unfamiliar with many items, such as cartouches, camel hair rugs, and alabaster pots, be sure to ask questions about the various selections. Shopkeepers tend to be very friendly and informative and many of them have workshops nearby or on their premises. They can quickly educate you about their products and artisans, from child labor to eccentric artists. In some cases you may have an opportunity to meet the artists and craftspeople. In so doing, you will probably gain a new appreciation for "Made in Egypt" products as well as the history and culture of this fascinating country.

18. **Expect most shops to arrange packing and shipping.** Don't be afraid to purchase large or delicate items that you may not want to take with you. Most shops have experience in packing and shipping since they regularly deal with international visitors. However, if you decide to have items shipped, it's always a good idea to get a receipt describing the item and stating who is doing what and for how much. If an item is considered an antique or piece of art, the receipt should specify the age or state "original work of art" – important issues with U.S. Customs and its GSP exemptions (see pages 30-31).

19. **Take photos of all items being shipped.** We always take pictures just in case we might have a problem with a shipment, which occasionally does occur. Better still, take a photo of the item with the merchant and/or

shipper standing next to it. Such visual documentation may later come in handy and it's always provides a nice memento of the interesting people you met and did business with in Egypt. The photo also helps in later clearing Customs, especially if they are not sure how to classify and assess a particular item.

20. **Take items with you whenever possible.** While many shops can pack and ship, especially tourist shops selling large and heavy carpets, alabaster, and furniture, you may want to take smaller items with you. Don't just take a shop's word that they can ship with no problem. You may discover the cost of shipping a small item can be very expensive, especially when it arrives "collect" by international courier service!

21. **Take your purchases with you as part of your carry-on or check-through luggage.** While shipping from Egypt is relatively easy to arrange, it also can be very expensive. We usually try to take our purchases with us whether they be small or large. In preparation, we usually limit ourselves to one check-through piece of luggage on our flight to Egypt. For the two of us, this allows us three more check-through pieces of luggage on our international flight back home. Our advice: take very little luggage with you on your way to Egypt in anticipation of accumulating purchases along the way that you will want to take with you. Alternatively, if two people are traveling together, take two pieces of luggage and fill the second one primarily with bubble wrap and packing materials. You still can have two boxes made for larger pieces and bring them home at no additional costs. You'll save a great deal of time and money by planning in this manner. If you purchase an item that can be checked through as luggage, such as a piece of pottery or rug, ask the shop to pack the item well so it can be checked through with your airline as a piece of luggage. Be sure to check with your airline on the dimensions of allowable check-through items. Most shops can do such packing or they can arrange for excellent packing that will protect delicate purchases. Even large pieces of pottery can be well packed (packer builds a sturdy wood box) to be shipped through as an extra piece of luggage. Make sure the size of such boxes are within the dimensions allowed by the airline.

22. **Be very careful when buying gems, jewelry, rugs, alabaster, and so-called antiquities.** If you're unfamiliar with such items, you need to get a quick education before making any serious purchases. In the case of gems and jewelry, patronize the top jewelry shops and ask lots of questions about their products. A good shop will make a special effort to educate its potential clients. For example, watch out for those popular cartouches which are produced at different levels of expertise. Beware of antiquities. They cannot be exported from Egypt without special government permission. Reproductions of antiquities, both good and bad, abound in Egypt. It's safe to assume the most antiquities in Egypt are fakes. And be especially cautious when buying rugs. They are everywhere, including the prices. If you shop around for rugs and ask lots of questions, you should be able to learn a great deal about what to look for in Egyptian rugs. Egyptian rug merchants are like rug merchants and mattress dealers elsewhere in the world – very entrepreneurial and at times creative in their story-telling. Our rule of thumb: never trust a rug merchant who appears to have fallen in love with his rugs . . . and with you!

16 BARGAINING TIPS AND SKILLS

If you're not used to bargaining when shopping, you will be at a price disadvantage in Egypt. Indeed, you'll probably be paying 100 percent above retail! And if you consider yourself a good bargainer in other countries, you may quickly discover your bargaining skills need to be upgraded for the Egyptian shopping culture. This isn't China, Indonesia, India, or Brazil.

Bargaining can be great fun and result in excellent buys. But for the uninitiated, bargaining can be very intimidating; it seems to be a waste of precious shopping and travel time. Individuals from fixed price cultures would rather see a price sticker and make a decision on whether or not to purchase without someone haggling with them over the price. But if everything were fixed prices, you would really miss out on a terrific cultural experience in Egypt. You would miss a chance to meet and interact with merchants and artisans. After you get the hang of how to bargain in Egypt, you should have a great time shopping and you'll probably make lots of new friends who will conclude you are indeed a savvy shopper who loves Egypt and the Egyptians! So let's take a look at some basic bargaining rules to put you on the road to shopper's heaven.

CULTURE SHOCK

Most North American, European, and Australian tourists come from fixed-price cultures where prices are nicely displayed on items. In such cultures, the only price uncertainty may be a sales tax added to the total amount at the cash register. Only on very large-ticket items, such as automobiles, boats, houses, furniture, carpets, and jewelry, can you expect to negotiate the price. If you want to get the best deal, you must do comparative shopping as well as wait for special discounts and sales. Bargain shopping in such cultures centers on comparative pricing of items. Shopping becomes a relatively passive activity involving the examination of advertisements in newspapers and catalogs or the use of price comparison sites on the Internet.

Expert shoppers in fixed-price cultures tend to be those skilled in carefully observing and comparing prices in the print advertising media. They clip coupons and know when the best sales are being held for particular items on certain days. They need not be concerned with cultivating personal relationships with merchants or salespeople in order to get good buys.

Like a fish out of water, expert shoppers from fixed-price cultures may feel lost when shopping in Egypt. Few of their fixed-price shopping skills are directly transferable to Egypt's shopping environments. Except for shops in shopping centers and hotel shopping arcades and some ads in the monthly tourist literature as well as local newspapers announcing special sales, few shops advertise in the print media or on TV and radio.

DEALING WITH PRICE UNCERTAINTY

Goods in Egypt fall into three pricing categories: **fixed, negotiable,** or **discounted**. While some shops have fixed prices, price uncertainty – negotiable or discounted prices – is the standard way to sell most goods and services in Egypt. The general pricing guideline is this: Unless you see a sign stating otherwise, you can expect prices of most goods in small shops to be negotiable. You can safely assume that all stated prices are the starting point from which you should receive anything from a 10 to 60 percent discount, depending on your haggling skills and level of commitment to obtain reduced prices.

Discount percentages in Egypt will vary for different items and from one shop to another. In general, however, expect to receive at least a 10 to 20 percent discount on most items in shops willing to discount. Some will discount more – up to 70 percent in some cases!

When in doubt if a price is fixed, negotiable, or subject to discounts, **always ask for a special discount**. After the salesperson indicates the price, ask one of two questions: *"What kind of discount can you give me on this item?"* or *"What is your best price?"* Better still, ask the classic *"Is it possible?"* question: *"Is it possible to do any better on this price?"* Anything is possible in Egypt! If the person indicates a discount, you can either accept it or attempt to negotiate the price further.

While skilled shoppers in fixed-price cultures primarily compare prices by reading ads and listening to special announcements, the skilled shopper in bargaining cultures is primarily engaged in face-to-face encounters with sellers. To be most successful, the shopper must use various interpersonal skills to his or her advantage. Once you know these and practice bargaining, you should become a very effective shopper in Egypt – as well as in many other countries where bargaining remains the shopping norm.

ESTABLISH VALUE AND PRICE

Not knowing the price of an item, many shoppers from fixed-price cultures face a problem. *"What is the actual value of the item? How much should I pay? At what point do I know I'm getting a fair price?"* These questions can be answered in several ways. First, you should have some idea of the **value** of the item, because you already did comparative shopping at home by using the Internet, examining catalogs and visiting discount houses, department stores, and specialty shops. If you are interested in an emerald ring, for example, you should know what comparable quality jewelry sells for back home.

Second, you have done comparative shopping among the various shops you've encountered in Egypt in order to **establish a price range** for positioning yourself in the bargaining process. You've visited shops in Cairo's major shopping centers to research how much a similar item is selling for at a fixed price. You've checked with a shop in your hotel and compared prices there. In your hotel you might ask *"How much is this item?"* and then act a little surprised that it appears so expensive. Tell them that you are a hotel guest and thus you want their *"very best price."* At this point the price may decrease by 10 to 20 percent as you are told this is *"our very special price for hotel guests."*

Once you initially receive a special price from your first price inquiry, you may get another 10 to 20 percent through further negotiation. But at this point do not negotiate any more. Take the shop's business card and record on the back the item, the original price, and the first discount price; thank the shop-keeper, and tell him or her that you may return. Repeat this same scenario in a few other shops. After doing three or four comparisons, you will establish a price range for particular items. This range will give you a fairly accurate idea of the going discount price. At this point you should be prepared to do some serious haggling, playing one shop off against another until you get the best price.

Effective shoppers in Egypt quickly learn how to comparative shop and negotiate the best deal. In learning to be effective, you don't need to be timid, aggressive, or obnoxious – extreme behaviors frequently exhibited by first-time practitioners of the art of bargaining. Although you may feel bargaining is a defensive measure to avoid being ripped-off by unscrupulous merchants, it is an acceptable way of doing business in many cultures. Merchants merely adjust their profit margins to the customer, depending on how they feel about the situation as well as their current cash flow needs. It is up to you to adapt to such a pricing culture.

One problem you may soon discover is that every situation seems to differ somewhat, and differences between items and shops can be significant. You can expect to receive larger discounts on jewelry than on home furnishings.

Our general rule on what items to bargain for is this: **bargain on ready-made items you can carry out of the shop**. If you must have an item custom-made, be very careful how you arrive at the final price. In most cases you should not bargain other than responding to the first price by asking *"Is this your best price?"* or *"Is it possible to do better on this price?"* Better still, drop a few names, agree on a mutually satisfactory price, and then insist that you want top quality for that price.

Except for custom-made items and shops displaying a "fixed prices" sign, never accept the first price offered. Rather, spend some time going through our bargaining scenario. And in some cases so-called "fixed price" shops will also give a discount – at least it doesn't hurt to try!

Once you have accepted a price and purchased the item, be sure to **get a receipt** as well as **observe the packing process**. While few merchants will try to cheat you, some tourists have had unpleasant experiences which could have been avoided by following some simple rules of shopping in unfamiliar places.

Get the Best Deal Possible

Chances are you will deal with a merchant who is a relatively seasoned businessman. As soon as you walk through the door, most merchants will want to sell you items then and there. **The best deal you will get is when you have a personal**

relationship with the merchant. Contrary to what others may tell you about bargains for tourists, you often can get as good a deal – sometimes even better – than someone from the local community. It is simply a myth that tourists can't do as well on prices as the locals. Indeed, we often do better than the locals because we have done our comparative shopping and we know well the art of bargaining – something locals are often lax in doing. In addition, some merchants may give you a better price than the locals because you are *"here today and gone tomorrow."* After all, you won't be around to tell their regular customers about your very special price.

More often than not, the pricing system operates like this: **If the shopkeeper likes you, or you are a friend of a friend or relative, you can expect to get a good price**. Whenever possible, drop names of individuals who referred you to the shop; the shopkeeper may think you are a friend and thus you are entitled to a special discount. But if you do not have such a relationship and you present yourself as a typical tourist who is here today and gone tomorrow, you need to bargain hard.

PRACTICE 16 RULES OF BARGAINING

The art of bargaining in Egypt can take on several different forms. In general, you want to achieve two goals in this haggling process: **establish the value of an item** and **get the best possible price**. The following bargaining rules work well in most negotiable shopping situations.

1. **Do your research before initiating the process.**

   Compare the prices among various shops, starting with the fixed-price items in department stores. Spot-check price ranges among shops in and around your hotel. Also, refer to your research done with catalogs and discount houses back home to determine if the discount is sufficient to warrant purchasing the item abroad.

2. **Determine the exact item you want to buy, but don't express excessive interest.**

   Select the particular item you want and then focus your bargaining around that one item without expressing excessive interest. Even though you may be excited by the item and want it very badly, once the merchant knows you are committed to buying it, you weaken your bargaining position. Express a passing interest; indicate through eye contact with other items in the shop that you are not necessarily committed to the one item. As you ask about the other items, you should get some sense concerning the willingness of the merchant to discount prices.

3. **Set a ceiling price you're willing to pay – and buy now!**

Before engaging in serious negotiations, set in your mind the maximum amount you are willing to pay, which may be 20 percent more than you figured the item should sell for based on your research. However, if you find something you love that is really unique, be prepared to pay more if you can afford it. In many situations you will find unique items not available anywhere else. Consider buying **now** since the item may be gone when you return. Bargain as hard as you can and then pay what you have to – even though it may seem painful – for the privilege of owning a unique item. Remember, it's only money and it only hurts once. You can always make more money, and after returning home you will most likely enjoy your wonderful purchase and forget how painful it seemed at the time to buy it at less than your expected discount. Above all, do not pass up an item you really love just because the bargaining process does not fall in your favor. It is very easy to be *"penny wise but pound foolish"* in Egypt simply because the bargaining process is such an ego-involved activity. You may return home forever regretting that you didn't buy a lovely item just because you were too cheap to "give" on the last US$5 of haggling. In the end, put your ego aside, give in, and buy what you really want. Only you and the merchant will know who really won this game, and once you return home the US$5 will seem to be such an insignificant amount. Chances are you still got a good bargain compared to what you would pay elsewhere if, indeed, you could even find a similar item!

4. **Play the role of an intelligent buyer in search of good quality and value**.

Shopping in Egypt involves playing the roles of buyer and seller with lots of expressive drama. It's one of the best shows in town. Egyptian merchants, especially those in the bazaars, are terrific role players. When you encounter an Egyptian merchant, you are often meeting a very refined and sophisticated role player. Therefore, it is to your advantage to play complementary roles by carefully structuring your personality and behavior to play the role of buyer. If you approach sellers by just "being yourself" – open, honest, somewhat naive, and with your own unique personality – you may be quickly walked over by a seasoned seller. Once you enter a shop, think of yourself as an actor walking on stage to play the lead role as a shrewd buyer, bargainer, and trader. Take, for example, this common scenario. Merchants will kindly invite you into their shop, ask you to sit down, pour you tea, and try to become your friend. Then they will abuse your wallet in very dramatic ways. Now that your guard is supposedly down because of their hospitality, they may quote you a high initial price for an item that interests you – not exactly what a friend should do to another! You may counter with a low price and they will respond by becoming very animated – as if you just insulted a good friend: *"Oh, my God! I'll lose money."* They will tell you what an absurd price you're offering, that they can't lose money, and that you'll have to pay a lot more to do business with them. At this point you may feel overwhelmed with the drama. Don't worry. It's all part of the role-playing game. Stick in there and continue with another absurd counter offer. Better still, become equally animated. Hit your forehead with the palm of your hand and counter by loudly saying *"Oh, my God; how can you expect me to pay such a high price!"* This role reversal will often catch the merchant off-guard as he tries to top your drama.

5. Establish good will and a personal relationship.

A shrewd buyer also is charming, polite, personable, and friendly. You should have a sense of humor, smile, and be light-hearted during the bargaining process. But be careful about eye contact which can be threatening. Keep it to a minimum. Sellers prefer to establish a personal relationship so that the bargaining process can take place on a friendly, face-saving basis. In the end, both the buyer and seller should come out as winners. This cannot be done if you approach the buyer in very serious and harsh terms. You should start by exchanging pleasantries concerning the weather, your trip, the city, or the nice items in the shop. After exchanging business cards or determining your status, the shopkeeper will know what roles should be played in the coming transaction.

6. **Let the seller make the first offer.**

If the merchant starts by asking you *"How much do you want to pay?,"* always avoid answering this rather dangerous set-up question. He who reveals his hand first is likely to lose in the end. Immediately turn the question around: *"How much are you asking?"* Remember, many merchants try to get you to pay as much as you are willing and able to pay – not what the value of the item is or what he or she is willing to take. You should never reveal your ability or willingness to pay a certain price. Keep the seller guessing, thinking that you may lose interest or not buy the item because it appears too expensive. Always get the merchant to initiate the bargaining process. In so doing, the merchant must take the defensive as you shift to the offensive.

7. **Take your time, being deliberately slow in order to get the merchant to invest his or her time in you.**

The more you indicate that you are impatient and in a hurry, the more you are likely to pay. When negotiating a price, **time** is usually in your favor. Many shopkeepers also see time as a positive force in the bargaining process. Some try to keep you in their shop by serving you tea while negotiating the price. Be careful; this nice little ritual may soften you somewhat on the bargaining process as you begin establishing a more personal relationship with the merchant. The longer you stay in control prolonging the negotiation, the better the price should be. Although some merchants may deserve it, **never** insult them. Merchants need to "keep face" as much as you do in the process of giving and getting the very best price.

8. **Use odd numbers in offering the merchant 40 percent to 60 percent less than what he or she initially offers.**

Avoid stating round numbers, such as 700, 1800, or 1,000. Instead, offer 62, 173, or 817. Such numbers impress upon others that you may be a seasoned haggler who knows value and expects to do well in this negotiation. Your offer will probably be 20 percent less than the value you determined for the item. For example, if the merchant asks E£100, offer E£40, knowing the final price should probably be E£60. The merchant will probably counter with only a 20 percent discount – E£80. At this point you will need to go back and forth with another two or three offers and counter-offers. In some cases you want to initially offer 75 percent less than the asking price, depending on the item and seller. Bus stop tourist shops often have extremely inflated prices; a 75 percent discount in these places would be a fair price!

9. **Appear a little disappointed and then take your time again.**

Never appear upset or angry with the seller. Keep your cool at all times by slowly sitting down and carefully examining the item. Shake your head a little and say, *"Gee, that's too bad. That's much more than I had planned to spend. I like it, but I really can't go that high."* Appear to be a sympathetic listener as the seller attempts to explain why he or she cannot budge more on the price. Make sure you do not accuse the merchant of being a thief! Use a little charm, if you can, for the way you conduct the bargaining process will affect the final price. This should be a civil negotiation in which you nicely bring the price down, the seller "saves face," and everyone goes away feeling good about the deal.

10. **Counter with a new offer at a 35 percent discount.**

Punch several keys on your calculator, which indicates you are doing some serious thinking. Then say something like *"This is really the best I can do. It's a lovely item, but E£162 is really all I can pay."* At this point the merchant will probably counter with a 20 percent discount – E£200.

11. **Be patient, persistent, and take your time again by carefully examining the item.**

Respond by saying *"That's a little better, but it's still too much. I want to look around a little more."* Then start to get up and look toward the door. At this point the merchant has invested some time in this exchange, and he or she is getting close to a possible sale. The merchant will either let you walk out the door or try to stop you with another counter-offer. If you walk out the door, you can always return to get the E£200 price. But most likely the merchant will try to stop you, especially if there is still some bargaining room. The merchant is likely to say: *"You don't want to waste your time looking elsewhere. I'll give you the best price anywhere – just for you. Okay, E£190. That's my final price."*

12. Be creative for the final negotiation.

You could try for E£180, but chances are E£190 will be the final price with this merchant. Yet, there may still be some room for negotiating "extras." At this point, get up and walk around the shop and examine other items; try to appear as if you are losing interest in the item you were bargaining for. While walking around, identify a E£10 item you like which might make a nice gift for a friend or relative, which you could possibly include in the final deal. Wander back to the E£10 item and look as if your interest is waning and perhaps you need to leave. Then start to probe the possibility of including extras while agreeing on the E£190: *"Okay, I might go E£190, but only if you include this with it."* The "this" is the E£10 item you eyed. You also might negotiate with your credit card. Chances are the merchant is expecting cash on the E£190 discounted price and will add a 2 to 6 percent "commission" if you want to use your credit card. In this case, you might respond to the E£190 by saying, *"Okay, I'll go with the E£190, but only if I can use my credit card."* You may get your way, your bank will float you a loan in the meantime, and your credit card company may help you resolve the problem in case you later learn your purchase was misrepresented. Finally, you may want to negotiate packing and delivery processes. If it is a fragile item, insist that it be packed well so you can take it with you on the airplane or have it shipped. If your purchase is large, insist that the shop deliver it to your hotel or to your shipper. If the shop is shipping it by air or sea, try to get them to agree to absorb some of the freight and insurance costs.

This very slow, civil, methodical, and sometimes charming approach to bargaining works well in most cases. However, Egyptian merchants do differ in how they respond to situations, and many of them are unpredictable, depending on whether or not they like you. In some cases, your timing may be right: the merchant is in need of cash flow that day and thus he or she is willing to give you the price you want, with little or no bargaining. Others will not give more than a 10 to 20 percent discount unless you are a friend of a friend who is then eligible for the special "family discount." And others are not good businessmen, are unpredictable, lack motivation, or are just moody;

they refuse to budge on their prices even though your offer is fair compared to the going prices in other shops. In these situations it is best to leave the shop and find one which is more receptive to the traditional haggling process.

This bargaining process often takes on additional drama in the bazaars and factories frequented by tourists. In some bazaars you may encounter merchants who play "bait and switch": they urge you to come into their shop where you can buy a particular item for the cheap price of E£10, but once you enter the shop, the price mysteriously goes to E£50. His objective is to get you to come into his shop where he believes he will be in control of the negotiation process. As noted earlier, he'll probably soften you up by offering you a cup of tea. We discovered four additional rules that work well in such situations – the "8 Foot Rule," "Oh, My God! Rule," "Never Ask Your Tour Guide to Negotiate for You Rule," and "The Best Deal is After Everyone Leaves the Place Rule." They go like this:

13. **Observe the "8 Foot Rule" for negotiating your best deal:** Egyptians like to maintain close personal space – at times they are literally in your face. Merchants maintain control by bringing customers into as well as keeping them in their shops. If you stand outside the shop to bargain (stay 8 feet from the merchant and his goods), you'll be in a much stronger bargaining position. However, if you're already in the shop, it may be time to make a "10 percent exit" – your exit could be worth another 10 percent discount! Do the following. Once you get near a final negotiated figure, walk 8 feet outside the shop. Yes, 8 feet and the price drops again. Tell the merchant his final price is too much and that you need to think about it as well as look elsewhere. Say goodbye, turn around, and literally walk 8 feet from the entrance of the shop and stop. Turn around and look at the shop and merchant and then look up and down the street. Look as if you are trying to decide where to go next. Chances are your new friend will still be talking to you, trying to persuade you that he offered you an excellent price and asking you to please come back into the shop and talk. Shake your head and say *"It's too expensive. I really need to look some more."* Whatever you do, do not go back into the shop at this point; you'll be at a disadvantage if you do. You should now be in control of the situation. Make the merchant come to you in the street – that's your turf. Take your time and don't move from

your position for at least three minutes. There's a high probability (70 percent or better) the merchant will come out and agree to give you the item at the final price you offered. For some unexplained reason, 8 feet seems to be the perfect distance for this final negotiation (we literally count our steps to make sure our final exit stops at 8 feet!); inside the shop the merchant may be within 6 inches of your face which may make you feel uncomfortable. By going into the street, you take final control of the negotiation. The merchant knows once you turn to leave, you'll probably be gone forever. The wise merchant knows it's better take less or lose out forever.

14. **Be just as expressive as the merchant by repeating the** *"Oh, my God!"* **phrase.** Many merchants in the bazaars have a flair for the dramatic. Indeed, the whole buying and selling transaction at times is high drama. Merchants often respond to your counter-offer by exclaiming *"Oh, my God"* as if you've just insulted them. This is part of their game. Don't be intimidated by·such an extreme expression. Dish it back to the merchant by saying *"Oh, my God"* (add a little more drama by hitting your forehead with the palm of your hand as you make this exclamation) when they quote you a price. This often puts you on an even playing field – they understand that you understand their psychology. You can now cut through the dramatics and get down to the real business of determining the final price.

15. **If you're with a tour group, bargain hard on your own.** Do not ask your tour guide or driver to help you negotiate a price. Since most of these service personnel are being paid commissions on everything you buy at their recommended shop, don't expect them to be an enthusiastic participant in helping you bargain for a good deal. Many will tell you the prices are fixed, which indeed they are . . . and you are the recipient of the "fix"!

16. **If you're visiting a bus stop shop or factory, don't buy where the crowds congregate, or be the last one out.** Remember, the herd never gets a good deal – it only gets taken to the slaughter. And he who buys early in the crowd tends to pay a high price. After all, the salesperson has no incentive to discount when he knows lots of naive tourists are willing to pay the full asking price. At this point, it's to your advantage to survey the competition

next door or across the street. There are often similar shops nearby that do not have a busload of tourists shopping inside. If you visit these places, you may discover similar items are one-half to one-third the prices being asked at the other shop. If there are no comparable shops around, it's best to wait until everyone leaves the shop to get back on the bus. Being the last one out, chances are you can negotiate a good deal. After all, once you're gone, there will probably be little or no business until another bus comes. The one exception is if you find an item, one of a kind, that you absolutely must have. In this case, bargain as much as you can and then buy. If you walk out, you may return to find that someone from the bus has already purchased "your" item.

Whatever you do, have lots of fun bargaining for your loot. If you follow our rules, you'll approach such situations with confidence, and you'll walk away with a good deal. Some locals may even compliment you on your ability to bargain so well. Indeed, you'll probably be a much better bargainer than most locals! But make sure you really want something before you go through this whole process.

BARGAIN FOR NEEDS, NOT GREED

One word of caution for those who are just starting to learn the fine art of Egyptian bargaining. **Be sure you really want an item before you initiate the bargaining process.** Many tourists quickly learn to bargain effectively, and then get carried away with their new-found skill. Rather than use this skill to get what they want, they enjoy the process of bargaining so much that they buy many unnecessary items. After all, they got such "a good deal" and thus could not resist buying the item. Be very careful in getting carried away with your new-found competency. You do not need to fill your suitcases with junk in demonstrating this ego-gratifying skill. If used properly, your new bargaining skills will lead to some excellent buys on items you really need and want.

EXAMINE YOUR GOODS CAREFULLY

Before you commence the bargaining process, carefully examine the item, being sure that you understand the quality of the item for which you are negotiating. Then, after you settle on a final price, make sure you are getting the goods you agreed upon. At this point, do two things:

1. Take a photo of your purchase, ideally with the merchant posing with the item.

2. Ask for an official receipt that states what you bought, for how much, and when. Make sure the shop includes its name, address, phone, and/or fax and email address.

You should carefully observe the handling of items, including the actual packing process. If you bought several items, make sure you count and recount exactly what you bought. It's often easy to get distracted at the end and forget to account for everything. Use your receipt as a final checklist before you leave the shop. If at all possible, take the items with you when you leave. If you later discover you were victimized by a switch or misrepresentation, contact the Egyptian Tourist Authority as well as your credit card company if you charged your purchase. You should be able to resolve the problem through these channels. However, the responsibility is on you, the buyer, to know what you are buying.

BEWARE OF SCAMS

Although one hopes this will never happen, you may encounter unscrupulous merchants who take advantage of you. The most frequent scams to watch out for include:

1. **Switching the goods.** You negotiate for a particular item, such as a piece of jewelry or a rug, but in the process of packing it, the merchant substitutes an inferior product.

2. **Misrepresenting quality goods.** Be especially cautious in jewelry and gem shops. Precious stones may not be as precious as they appear. Synthetic stones are sometimes substituted for real stones. Real ivory is beautiful, but many buyers unwittingly end up with bone at ivory prices. In fact, since it is now illegal to bring ivory into many countries, you are really better off with carved bone – but at bone prices! Some merchants may try to sell "new antiques" at "old antique" prices.

3. **Goods not included in the package(s) you carry with you.** You purchase several items in one shop. The seller wraps them and presents them to you, but "forgot" to include one of the items you paid for. You've become distracted in the process of paying for everything and talking with the shopkeeper to the point of forgetting to check your package(s) carefully.

4. **Goods not shipped.** The shop may agree to ship your goods home, but once you leave, they conveniently forget to do so. You wait and wait, write letters of inquiry, fax, make phone calls, and email the shop; no one can give you a satisfactory response. Unless you have shipping and insurance documents, which is unlikely, and proper receipts, you may not receive the goods you paid for.

Your best line of defense against these and other possible scams is to be very careful wherever you go and whatever you do in relation to handling money. A few simple precautions will help avoid some of these problems:

1. **Do not trust anyone with your money** unless you have proper assurance they are giving you exactly what you agreed upon. Trust is something that should be earned – not automatically given to friendly strangers you may like.

2. **Do your homework** so you can determine quality and value as well as anticipate certain types of scams.

3. **Examine the goods carefully**, assuming something may be or will go wrong.

4. **Watch very carefully how the merchant handles items** from the moment they leave your hands until they get wrapped and into a bag.

5. **Request receipts** that list specific items and the prices you paid. Although most shops are willing to "give you a receipt" specifying whatever price you want them to write for purposes of deceiving Customs, be careful in doing so. While you may or may not deceive Customs, your custom-designed receipt may become a double-edged sword, especially if you later need a receipt with the real price to claim your goods or a refund. If the shop

is to ship, be sure you have a shipping receipt which also includes insurance against both loss and damage.

6. **Take photos of your purchases.** We strongly recommend taking photos of your major purchases, especially anything that is being entrusted to someone else to be packed and shipped. Better still, take a photo of the seller holding the item, just in case you later need to identify the person with whom you dealt. This photo will give you a visual record of your purchase should you later have problems receiving your shipment, from being lost or damaged. You'll also have a photo to show Customs should they have any questions about the contents of your shipment.

7. **Protect yourself against scams by using credit cards** for payment, especially for big-ticket items which could present problems, even though using them may cost you a little more. Although your credit card company is not obligated to do so, most will ask the merchant for documentation, and if not satisfactorily received, will remove the charge from your bill.

If you are victimized, all is not necessarily lost. You should report the problem immediately to the Egyptian Tourist Authority, the police, your credit card company, or insurance company. While inconvenient and time consuming, nonetheless, in many cases you will eventually get satisfactory results.

Shipping With Ease

Shipping can be a problem in Egypt. What will you do if you discover a wonderful piece of furniture or a large earthenware pot? Some people have reported problems in receiving shipments from Egypt. Others ship trouble-free. And still others encounter problems which eventually get resolved, such as initially arranging for the shipment to be sent by sea but later being informed it must be sent by more expensive air freight rates.

You should not pass up buying lovely items because you feel reluctant to ship them home. Indeed, some travelers only buy items that will fit into their suitcase because they are not sure how to ship larger items home. But you can easily ship from Egypt and expect to receive your goods in good condition within a few weeks. We seldom let shipping considerations affect our buying decisions. For us, *shipping is one of those things that must be arranged*. You have numerous shipping alternatives, from hiring a professional shipping company to hand carrying your goods on board the plane. Shipping may or may not be costly, depending on how much you plan to ship and by which means.

Before leaving home, you should identify the best point of entry for goods returning home by air or sea. Once you are in Egypt, you generally have five shipping alternatives:

1. Take everything with you.

2. Do your own packing and shipping through the local post office (for small packages only).

3. Have each shop ship your purchases.

4. Arrange to have one shop consolidate all of your purchases into a single shipment.

5. Hire a local shipper to make all arrangements.

Taking everything with you is fine if you don't have much and if you don't mind absorbing excess baggage charges. If you are within your allowable baggage allowance, you can have large items packed to qualify as part of your luggage. Indeed, on our recent trip to Egypt, we purchased a large old pot which the shop crated so it could be checked through as part of our check-through luggage. If you have more items than what is allowable, ask about the difference between "Excess Baggage" and "Unaccompanied Baggage." Excess baggage is very expensive while unaccompanied baggage is less expensive, although by no means cheap.

If items are small enough and we don't mind waiting six to eight weeks, we may send them through the local post office by parcel post; depending on the weight, sometimes air mail is relatively inexpensive through local post offices.

Doing your own packing and shipping may be cheaper, but it is a pain and thus no savings in the long run. You waste valuable time waiting in lines and trying to figure out the local rules and regulations concerning permits, packing, materials, sizes, and weights.

On the other hand, most major shops are skilled at shipping goods for customers. They often pack the items free and only charge you for the actual postage or freight. Many of these shops use excellent shippers who are known for reasonable charges, good packing, and reliability. For example, if you decide to have jewelry custom-made, the jewelry shop will most likely arrange to have your purchase sent to you within three days by using the reliable international courier DHL. If you choose to have a shop ship for you, insist on a receipt specifying they will ship the item. Also, stress the importance of packing the item well to avoid possible damage. If they cannot insure the item against breakage or loss, do not ship through them. Invariably a version of Murphy's Law operates when shipping: *"If it is not insured and has the potential to break or get lost, it will surely break or get lost!"* At this point, seek some alternative means of shipping. If you are shipping only one or two items, it is best to let a reputable shop take care of your shipping.

If you have several large purchases – at least one cubic meter – consider using local shippers, since it is cheaper and safer to consolidate many separate purchases into one shipment which is well packed and insured. Sea freight charges are usually figured by volume or the container. There is a minimum charge – usually you will pay for at least one cubic meter whether you are shipping that much or less. Air freight is calculated using both weight and volume and usually there is no minimum. You pay only for the actual amount you ship. One normally does not air freight large, heavy items, but for a small light shipment, air freight could actually cost you less and you'll get your items much faster. However, many shops in Egypt prefer shipping everything by air freight rather than sea. Since this can be very expensive, make sure you understand the costs before deciding to purchase a large item. When using air freight, use an established and reliable airline. In the case of sea freight, choose a local company which has an excellent reputation among expatriates for shipping goods. Ask your hotel concierge or front desk personnel about reliable shippers. For small shipments, try to have charges computed both ways – for sea and for air freight. Sea shipments incur port charges that can further add to your charges. If you have figures for both means of shipping, you can make an informed choice.

We have tried all five shipping alternatives with various results. Indeed, we tend to use these alternatives in combination. For example, we take everything we can with us until we reach the point where the inconvenience and cost of excess baggage requires some other shipping arrangements. We consolidate our shipments with one key shop early in our trip and have shipments from other cities sent to that shop for consolidation. The ideal consolidation point for sea shipments is Cairo.

When you use a shipper, be sure to examine alternative

shipping arrangements and prices. The type of delivery you specify at your end can make a significant difference in the overall shipping price. If you don't specify the type of delivery you want, you may be charged the all-inclusive first-class rate. For example, if you choose door-to-door delivery with unpacking services, you will pay a premium to have your shipment clear Customs, moved through the port, transported to your door, and unpacked by local movers. On the other hand, it is cheaper for you to designate port to port. When the shipment arrives, you arrange for a broker to clear the shipment through Customs and arrange for transport to your home. You do your own unpacking and dispose of the trash. It will take a little more of your time to make the arrangements and unpack. If you live near a port of entry, you may clear the shipment at Customs and pick up the shipment yourself.

We simply cannot over-stress the importance of finding and establishing a personal relationship with a good local shipper who will provide you with services which may go beyond your immediate shipping needs. A good local shipping contact will enable you to continue shopping in Egypt even after returning home.

Great Destinations

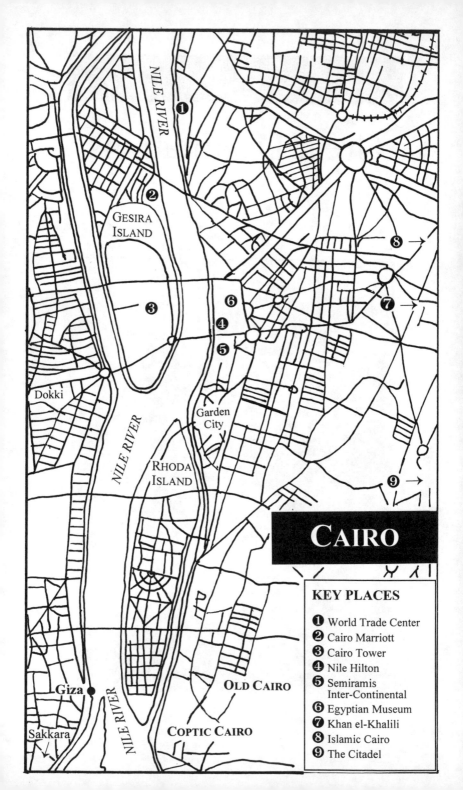

CAIRO

KEY PLACES

1. World Trade Center
2. Cairo Marriott
3. Cairo Tower
4. Nile Hilton
5. Semiramis Inter-Continental
6. Egyptian Museum
7. Khan el-Khalili
8. Islamic Cairo
9. The Citadel

NILE RIVER

GESIRA ISLAND

Dokki

Garden City

RHODA ISLAND

Giza

Sakkara

OLD CAIRO

COPTIC CAIRO

Cairo

I
T'S BIG AND SPRAWLING. A CITY OF NEARLY 18 million people, Cairo is the largest urban center in all of Africa. A fascinating amalgam of Egyptians, Africans, Arabs, and international residents and visitors from all over the world, Cairo is an extremely interesting Third World city with a very diverse population. With nearly 4 million people commuting into the city each day, Cairo is very congested with people, buses, and cars – a city you can easily learn to hate if it weren't for its many treasures and pleasures that attract millions of visitors each year. But stay a few days to explore this intriguing city and you may fall in love with Cairo.

Cairo is a city of great museums, mosques, churches, markets, minarets, high-rise hotels, and commercial buildings. Unfortunately, many jet-lagged visitors on hectic cultural and historical tours (the monuments and tombs crowd) rush into Cairo for only a day or two. At most they may visit the Egyptian Antiquities Museum, the Pyramids of Giza, and the Khan el-Khalili Bazaar and they head for Luxor, the Nile Valley, and Aswan for their remaining days in Egypt. Some become instant drive-by experts on Cairo – they've determined it's crowded, chaotic, and time consuming to get from one point to another. Such short-term time travelers only scratch the surface of what could be an extremely rewarding city for anyone with a few days to spend exploring Cairo's many other unique treasures and pleasures.

Just when you think you understand this city, it unfolds with more surprises. For history buffs, Cairo is the center for visiting Egypt's two major attractions – the Pyramids of Giza and the Egyptian Antiquities Museum. Spend a few days here and you will come away with renewed appreciation for Egypt's great treasures and pleasures. You'll spend hours walking its monuments and tombs and exploring its many streets and markets. You'll discover nearly 5,000 years of Pharaonic, Muslim, and Christian history all packed into a relatively small area within 45 minutes of downtown Cairo. The memorable sights, sounds, and shopping of Cairo are certain to last a lifetime.

A NEW CITY

Known by historians as the "Mother of the World," Cairo is a relatively new city when placed within the context of more than 5,000 years of Egyptian history. While today's Cairo represents a patchwork of many diverse elements, its origins are related to three major nearby settlements: **Heliopolis**, the capital of a united Upper and Lower Egypt in 3100 BC; **Memphis**, the capital of the Old Kingdom (2686 - 2181 BC); and the **Fort of Babylon**, the site of the Roman garrison in Old Cairo (98 - 640 AD). With the Muslim capture of the Fort of Babylon in 640 AD, the evolution of today's Cairo began near this site (Fustat) in the south of the city. Today you can still see the ruins of the Fort of Babylon as well as nearby **Fustat**, the first Arab settlement in Egypt from which Islam was established and subsequently spread throughout Egypt.

GETTING TO KNOW YOU

Colorful, crowded, congested, and always a fascinating sensual experience, today's Cairo throbs from early morning to late at night. It constantly unfolds with new, interesting, and diverse sights. Get into its traffic, walk its streets, explore its narrow market lanes, take a peaceful ride in a *felucca* along the Nile, or experience the varied nightlife, and you will discover a fascinating city that offers numerous opportunities to sightsee, shop, dine, and meet friendly people. Cairo is a great place to both begin and end an Egyptian travel adventure. While this city may occasionally frustrate you, its constant unfolding will most likely fascinate rather than disappoint you.

Flying into Cairo gives you a glimpse of what lies ahead. Rising like a huge oasis in the desert, Cairo embraces both the east and west banks of the Nile River. The desert sands seem to lap at this sometimes windy and dusty palm-fringed city that runs several kilometers from north to south. High-rise commercial buildings and residential blocks rise like a phoenix from the banks of this fertile river delta that serves as the lifeblood of Egypt's economy. Viewed from the sky, there's something about Cairo that looks unreal – as if it really doesn't belong in the middle of a desert. Once on the ground, however, it all seems to make good sense. Where else would one expect to find a city in the desert? As you later venture to the outskirts of Cairo to visit its many monuments and ruins, the abrupt transition from city greenery to desert sands reminds you that this is indeed a fragile oasis that for centuries has been dependent on the waters of the Nile River for its survival.

A CITY OF MANY HISTORIES

For history buffs, Cairo is all about the ancient Egyptians, pharaohs, pyramids, Romans, Christians, Muslims, and 20th century revolution and its attendant political, social, and economic transformations. It is definitely a history not to be missed. While its ancient history is well represented in the Egyptian Antiquities Museum and amongst the many pyramids that dot the southwestern outskirts of the city, make sure you don't overlook Cairo's other important histories: Islamic, Coptic, and modern. Spend a day or two exploring Cairo's pharaonic past, but be sure to leave enough time to discover its other more contemporary history. Explore its many churches, mosques, museums, and galleries to discover a fascinating city that pulsates with living history. Visit the more than 1,000 shops and vendors that comprise the huge bazaar, Khan el-Khalili, and you'll see business being done as usual in what is essentially a Muslim city and country. In the end, you'll find Cairo to be much more than just another big Third World city. Its people and places enthrall even the most jaded travelers, who find this city to be a truly unique experience.

THE STREETS OF CAIRO

Cairo is a big, sprawling, and at times disorienting and frustrating city. The best way to orient yourself to this city is to get a good map and then start by viewing the city from both east/west and north/south orientations. The Nile River splits the city into east and west sections, with most major commercial and historical areas located on the east bank. Two major islands, Gezira and Rhoda, stand between as well as link the two banks to one another.

The city encompasses several diverse geographic, historical, and cultural areas that often defy clear demarcation but encompass distinct historical and cultural areas: Central Cairo, Islamic Cairo, Old Cairo, Island Cairo, Giza and the Pyramids, and the suburbs of Maadi and Heliopolis. Taken together, these areas constitute an extremely interesting city for those who have the time to explore its many unique treasures and pleasures.

CENTRAL CAIRO

It's sometimes difficult to define Central Cairo because of the city's sprawling nature and its many neighborhood enclaves. An area of approximately five square kilometers, Central Cairo is located directly east of Gezira Island. It generally runs from the east bank of the Nile River, at the 6th of October Bridge, extends north to the World Trade Center, goes northeast to Ramses Square (train station), stretches east to Port Said Street, and runs south to Garden City. Within this area you will find many of the city's major hotels, restaurants, shops, historical sites, embassies, and commercial and government buildings. Highly congested, it includes wide streets, broad squares, grand 19th century architecture, and many worn structures that have seen better days. It's not a particularly attractive area from the standpoint of architecture when compared to other older sections of the city. Nonetheless, you'll find many interesting places to visit in Central Cairo. Many visitors prefer staying at a hotel in this area, especially one located along or near the Nile River.

❏ Nearly 4 million people commute into the city each day and contribute to its overall congestion.

❏ The abrupt transition from city greenery to desert sands reminds you that Cairo is indeed a fragile oasis.

❏ The Nile River splits the city into east and west sections, with most major commercial and historical areas located on the east bank.

❏ Cairo is a great place to both begin and end your Egyptian adventure. It never disappoints even the most jaded traveler.

Within Central Cairo, the major downtown section encompasses the **Corniche** which lies along the banks of the Nile River and is where the city's major hotels can be found – Conrad International, Semiramis, Nile Hilton, Nile Ramses, Sherpherd, Le Meridien, and Gezireh Sheraton – and extends to a triangle of squares – Midan Tahrir, Midan Ramses, and Midan Attaba. This is a beehive of commercial activity. Just off the Corniche and southeast of the Nile Hilton Hotel is **Midan Tahrir** (Liberation Square) which used to serve as the parade grounds for British and Egyptian troops but is now a major public transportation terminus with a fume-choked local bus and mini bus station located just behind the Nile Hilton Hotel and northwest of the square. Today this area is best known as the downtown section of Central. Here you'll find the famous Egyptian Antiquities Museum, Arab League Headquarters, Mogamma, American University of Cairo, Nile Hilton Hotel, and Semiramis Intercontinental Hotel. You can easily walk from this area to many of Cairo's famous sites as well as get public transportation to take you to other parts of Cairo. Most visitors to Cairo either start here or eventually end up here because of the museum, hotels, and Corniche. The highlights of this area are the museum and the air-conditioned hotel shopping arcades; the low points are the chaotic and polluted public transportation center and the Mogamma, a kind of passionately pathetic public mafia without a purpose. Hopefully you won't have to go here for a visa extension (first floor). The dreaded government bureaucracy is crammed into the infamous and imposing Mogamma, the 14-story building that houses 14 ministries, numerous departments, and 18,000 bureaucrats who abuse nearly 50,000 local residents and visitors each day with long lines and seeming bureaucratic nonsense!

The **World Trade Center**, located to the north and along the river, is Cairo's premier shopping center. Attached to the relatively new five-star Conrad International Hotel, this is one of Cairo's most desirable oases for luxury and comfort. It's a great place to stay given the shopping action as well as close proximity to fine restaurants.

Less than two kilometers northeast is **Midan Ramses** (Ramses Square) which is adjacent to two of Cairo's major transportation hubs – Cairo Railways Station and Gizeh Railways Station – and the Railways Museum. The Armenian Orthodox Cathedral is immediately to the west of Ramses Square.

Port Said Street lies nearly one kilometer east of Ramses Square. Running north and south, this main transportation artery divides the older parts of Cairo which lie to the east and southeast from Central Cairo and east of this street. The section between downtown Cairo and Port Said Street encompasses many interesting sites, including the Abdinc Presidential Palace, Islamic Museum, Post Office Museum, and Supreme Court.

The southern boundary of Central Cairo includes **Garden**

City with its noted British Embassy and remaining gardens. The U.S., Canadian, Japanese, Belgium, and Italian embassies also are found here. Once an upscale suburb for Cairo's English expatriates and known for its English garden ambience and elegant villas, Garden City still maintains an air of British civility despite the invasion of traffic and new residential and commercial development. The northern section of Garden City also encompasses the People's Assembly (Parliament).

ISLAMIC CAIRO

Make no mistake about it. This is a Muslim city and country with a heavy dose of intriguing medieval architecture that has survived nearly 1,000 years of urban settlement. And much of this history, both monumental and living, is found in the section of the city called Islamic Cairo. Despite Cairo's close association with pharaonic history – because of its close proximity to the Pyramids of Giza, Sakkara, and Memphis – this city was largely founded and developed by Muslim rulers during the past millennium. Located east of Central Cairo (beginning at Midan Ataba) and extending from the gates of Al-Qihira in the north to Fustat in the south, this is the medieval section of Cairo consisting of many fortresses, minarets, domed mosques, winding alleys, and chaotic streets complete with donkeys and carts that compete with noisy cars and buses. The unique sights, sounds, and smells and strong character of Islamic Cairo transport you into another time and place. The skyline with its many minarets and domes at times appears to be part of an exotic movie set and the stuff from which came the tales of *The Thousand and One Nights*. Shaped by powerful and infamous Muslim rulers, this whole area encompasses more than 800 Islamic monuments that can easily keep you busy sightseeing for weeks. However, most visitors focus on this area's major highlights which include the great Khan el-Khalili Bazaar, Mosque of Al-Azhar, the Citadel, Mosque of Mohammed Ali, Mosque-Madrasa of Sultan Hassan, Mosque of Ibu Tulun, Gayer-Anderson Museum, Museum of Islamic Art, Northern Cemetery, and Southern Cemetery. The Khan el-Khalili is the big drawing card here for visitors who have an opportunity to experience the Middle

❑ Despite Cairo's close association with pharaonic history, this city was largely founded and developed by Muslim rulers during the past millennium.

❑ Cairo's skyline with its many minarets and domes at times appears to be part of an exotic movie set.

❑ One of the best kept secrets in all of Cairo is the fascinating, but often overlooked, Museum of Islamic Art.

East's largest bazaar; many return again and again to browse its many interesting shops, stop at the famous Fishawi coffee-house, or dine in a local restaurant or café. The mosques, walled Citadel, and cemeteries add architectural drama to this fascinating area. For many visitors, one of the best kept secrets in all of Cairo is the fascinating, but often overlooked, Museum of Islamic Art.

OLD (COPTIC) CAIRO

While you may think Islamic Cairo is Old Cairo, this designation is reserved for the area south of Garden City and south-west of Islamic Cairo. Also known as Coptic (Christian) Cairo, this is actually the oldest section of the city, predating Islamic Cairo by several centuries. Originally known as the Fort of Babylon, it was first settled by both Jews and Christians in the early centuries AD and became the center for the Roman garrison from 98 AD until its fall to the Arabs in 640 AD. Today this is a charming walled area that includes Egypt's oldest synagogue, a few noted mosques, and more than 20 Christian churches. In many respects, this area has the look and feel of the more tranquil parts of Israel's Old Jerusalem. A very laid back area, it lacks much of the chaos associated with other parts of Cairo, especially Islamic Cairo. Highlights of this area include the Ben Ezra Synagogue, Coptic Museum, The Hanging Church, Church of St. Sergius and St. Bacchus, Church of St. Mercurius, and the Church of St. George. Visit this area and you will acquire a quick education on the Egyptian Christian tradition, which is different from the Greek and Roman Christian traditions. Intriguing old churches with beautiful icons make this a very special area of the city to visit, a high-light for many visitors to Egypt.

ISLAND CAIRO

Cairo has two islands in the middle of the Nile River, one old and one relatively new. The two islands connect the east and west banks of Cairo. The first island, Gezira, is the newer and more vibrant of the two. It's located directly west of Central Cairo and includes the upscale commercial and residential district of Zamalek in the north. Intersected by 26 July Street and directly across from the World Trade Center, Zamalek includes the huge salmon-pink Cairo Marriott Hotel and shopping complex as well as several art galleries and antique shops lining the streets behind the Marriott, especially near the intersection of Hassan Sabry and Brazil. You'll also find several good restaurants in this area. The southern section of the island is intersected by the east-west 6th of October Bridge, which connects in the east to Midan Tahrir, and El Tahrir Street. Highlights of this area include the Gezireh Sporting Club, the imposing Cairo Tower, Zohria Gardens, Cairo Opera House, Museum of Modern Art, and the Gezireh Sheraton Hotel.

The oldest island, which is often included as part of Old Cairo, is Rhoda Island. Located south of Gezira Island and connected by bridges to Garden City in the north and Coptic Cairo in the east, Rhoda Island has a long history dating from pharaonic and Roman times. Today, it is a somewhat run-down residential area mainly noted for the Manial Palace Museum and Le Meridien Cairo Hotel in the north and the Nilometer and Munasterli Palace in the south. Most visitors skip this island altogether, although the Nilometer, which was built in the 9th century to measure the rise and fall of the Nile, draws some visitors.

GIZA AND THE PYRAMIDS

Cairo's most popular drawing card for visitors are the Pyramids of Giza. Located in the southwest outskirts of Cairo, approximately 45 minutes form Central Cairo, this is one of four key sites that define what is popularly known as pharaonic Cairo in contrast to Muslim and Coptic Cairo. The other three elements include the nearby pyramids of Sakkara, the ancient city of Memphis, and the Egyptian Antiquities Museum.

Crowded Giza is where everyone heads to visit one of the great wonders of the world and the only survivor of the "Seven Wonders of the Ancient World". Standing majestically in the desert sands are the three great adjacent pyramids: The Great Pyramid (Cheops), The Second Pyramid (Chephren), and the Third Pyramid (Mycerinus). Nearby is the famous Sphinx and the Solar Boat Museum. Because of the heavy tourist traffic that plies this area, Giza also offers lots of tourist shopping as well as the famous Mena House Hotel with its fabulous location facing the pyramids (see the section on Accommodations). Visitors usually stop at the pyramids, the ancient city of Memphis, and the tombs of Sakkara as well as shop at the textile schools and carpet shops along the road to Sakkara. Keep in mind that this whole area is organized for the wall-to-wall tourist traffic that passes through the major streets, roads, villages, and towns. Not surprisingly, this is the area where you will encounter numerous touts and shops that are used to working with tour guides who steer traffic to their shops in exchange for commissions. If you're here to visit for the day, a great place for lunch is the Le Meridien Giza Hotel. If you plan to stay overnight, consider staying at the fabulous Mena House Hotel – and request a room with a view of the pyramids. From early morning camel traffic to sunsets at night, the view from a choice Mena House room is simply unforgettable.

The drive from Cairo to this area on the outskirts of the city is especially interesting as you begin to see much of Egyptian village life. The scenes are at times biblical: women dressed in black; adobe houses; irrigation canals; cornstalk fences; colorful young women; burrows with riders; children climbing trees for dates; and carpet weavers practicing their trade. Yes, the Pyramids of Giza are an important part of pharaonic Cairo, but this whole area comes alive with many more treasures and pleasures of Egypt.

SUBURBS

Cairo has several suburbs, but the most interesting ones for visitors are Maadi and Heliopolis. **Maadi** is a relatively upscale suburb in South Cairo that is home to many of Cairo's expatriates. It's also a popular district for Cairo's middle to upper middle class. Here you'll find numerous shopping centers and fast food outlets that especially appeal to local residents. **Heliopolis** is located north of the city on the way to the international airport. This is a relatively upscale suburb boasting many quality shops, especially designer boutiques. While important lifestyle centers for expatriates and Egyptian middle and upper classes, these suburbs have little to offer most visitors who have many more interesting things to see and do in Cairo.

SHOPPING CAIRO

Shopping in Cairo can be both fun and frustrating. It's fun for those who know where to go and bargain hard in an in-your-face retail shopping culture. It's frustrating for those who have difficulty finding places and handling the local shopping culture. If you follow the rules we outlined in Chapter 4 on shopping and bargaining in Egypt, your forays into the shops and bazaars of Cairo should be fun and rewarding. You'll leave Cairo with some very special treasures as well as meet many interesting people in the process of shopping.

If you are planning to do a lot of sightseeing in and around Cairo – especially the pyramids and tombs at Giza and Sakkara, the ruins at Memphis, and the museums, mosques, and churches in Central Cairo, Islamic Cairo, and Coptic Cairo – be prepared to unexpectedly shop along the way for arts, crafts, and textiles. The general shopping rule is this: wherever tourists congregate, expect to find numerous street touts and sidewalk vendors hawking tourist kitsch as well as shops and factories organized to handle tour groups. Many of these sellers can be very persistent and annoying. If you're not interested, just say "no," don't make eye contact, and keep on walking as if you know where you are going. Since many of these people and places inflate prices, you are well advised to bargain according to the rules we outlined in Chapter 4. Don't be surprised if you finally get a 40, 50, 60, or even 70 percent discount if you bargain hard! However, some places are reluctant to bargain and may only extend a 10 to 25 percent discount. It really depends on the shop. Top quality shops are less likely to bargain; some may tell you they have "fixed prices" and indeed they do.

If you plan what to buy and where to shop, you may need to set aside at least two but preferably three full days for shopping in Cairo's major hotel shopping arcades, shopping centers, department stores, street shops, factories, and bazaars. It's best to take taxis or rent a car with driver for the day to take you around to the various shopping areas. As you'll quickly discover, this is a very big city which is best covered via convenient transportation. A car with driver will cost anywhere from US$30 to US$50 a day, depending on where you plan to go and how hard you bargain for a daily rate. It's well worth the price given the convenience of finding addresses and being able to leave your purchases in the car as you go from one shopping destination to another.

Chances are you will spend a disproportionate amount of your shopping time in one of the world's greatest bazaars, the irresistible Khan el-Khalili. While this place may initially appear touristy, you'll quickly discover this is also a favorite shopping destination for many local residents, who claim to get both good quality and good prices at their favorite shops; they know exactly where to go and with whom to deal on everything from jewelry to pots and pans. Be prepared to do a lot of walking and expect to spend more time in this market maze than you initially planned. Indeed, you can easily spend most of a day visiting many of the more than 1,000 shops that make up this bazaar. Go early and plan on lunch in one of the major restaurants in the heart of the bazaar. Chances are you may want to return to Khan el-Khalili more than once during your stay in Cairo.

When you shop in Cairo's hotel shopping arcades, shopping centers, and department stores, expect to find fixed prices and sales. While some shops in these retail outlets will bargain, especially jewelry stores, most prices are labeled on goods and you are expected to pay the fixed price.

Many shops in Cairo accept major credit cards and can arrange international shipping. However, don't assume they will ship according to your expectations or the cheapest ways. As with shipping elsewhere in Egypt, most shops prefer using international courier services or air freight, which are the most expensive ways to ship. Make sure you understand your shipping options *before* making a major purchase. You may discover the cost of shipping may be two to three times higher than the cost of the goods.

WHAT TO BUY

You'll find just about everything in Cairo. Most products we outlined in Chapter 3 are more or less available in Cairo.

❑ **Fine art:** Egypt's best art tends to gravitate to Cairo's many art galleries and shops. Look for traditional and contemporary paintings, batik, tapestries, sculptures, and photography. Many of the best art galleries are found along the streets in the Zamalek area which is located behind the Marriott Hotel. One of the city's best contemporary art galleries is the **Mashrabia Gallery** at 8 Shar'a Champollion, Tahrir Square (Tel. 578-4494). For outstanding tapestries and batiks, be sure to visit the **Ramses Wissa Wassef Art Center** at Harrania Village, Sakkara Road (Tel. 384-3104). For original lithographs, stop at **L'Orientaliste** at 15 Qasr al-Nil (Tel. 575-3418) which also is a great place for rare, used, and new books. One of the best resources for identifying galleries and exhibitions in Cairo is the monthly edition of *Egypt Today*, which is available in most hotel news shops and bookstores.

❑ **Gems and jewelry:** Just step into the Khan el-Khalili Bazaar and you'll get a quick education on your gem and jewelry alternatives in Cairo: gold, silver, and precious stones. Excellent selections within the bazaar can be found at **Mihran and Garbis Yazejian** (Tel. 591-2321), **Nassar**, and **Jewellery Egypt Inc.** (8 Saket El Badestan, Tel. 592-5083). Also look for tribal arts and crafts shops offering a good selection of exotic tribal jewelry. Prices range from inexpensive beaded jewelry to very expensive designer gold jewelry. For fabulous designer gold jewelry, make a special effort to visit **Nakhla** at 10, Rue El-Nil-Guizeh, (Tel. 571-3457). Excellent quality jewelry also is available at **Al Ain Gallery** at 73 El Hussein Street, Dokki (Tel. 349-3940).

❏ **Leather goods:** Cairo is flooded with numerous leather goods that are primarily produced in leather factories near Alexandria. Look for attractively designed shoes, handbags, coats, jackets, belts, wallets, and other accessory items. Many items are knock-offs of popular European designer labels, such as Fendi, Chanel, and Yves Saint Laurent and are produced in unusual colors. Some shops, such as **MM**, also have genuine imported shoes and handbags from Italy mixed in with the local products. Expect to encounter numerous shoe stores throughout Cairo. Indeed, the local media often jokes that Egypt may be a country of 62 million centipedes rather than 62 million people – a country that may have a foot fetish! Look for tons of shoes throughout Cairo – the true "Mother of the World"!

❏ **Arts, crafts, and souvenirs:** You'll discover a profusion of Egyptian and tribal handicrafts in the shops and bazaars of Cairo. The problem is sorting out the tourist kitsch from the truly good quality arts and crafts. The tourist kitsch tends to be found near the major tourist sites where street touts, roadside vendors, and bus stop shops complete for the tourist dollar. There's no shortage of brassware, copperware, inlaid boxes, perfume bottles, baskets, woven bags, stuffed toys, and kitschy papyras paintings and related products. The best quality crafts will be found in a few shops and galleries that specialize in quality arts and crafts, such as **Bashayer** at 58 Mosadek Street, Dokki (Tel. 336-1006). For tribal arts and crafts, be sure to visit the main gallery of **Nomad** at 14 Saraya Al Gezira, 1st Floor, Zamalek (Tel. 341-1917) and its shop in the Cairo Marriott Hotel (Tel. 341-2132). For top quality reproduction papyrus paintings, visit **Dr. Ragab's Papyrus Institute** which is located on a houseboat docked by Corniche El-Nile which is near the Cairo Sheraton Hotel in Giza (Tel. 348-8177).

❏ **Carpets and tapestries:** If you tour the Pyramids of Giza and Sakkara, there's a good chance you will stop at one of the several carpet and tapestry factories along Sakkara Tourist Road. There you can view demonstrations of young girls being trained on looms as well as master tapestry weavers who are men. One of the best shops is **Akhnaton Carpets and Tapestry School** (16, KM. Sakkara Tourist

Road, Giza, Tel. 201-488). The second floor is jam-packed with a wide range of carpets and tapestries. Expect to bargain here – maybe get a 25 percent discount. This place will take credit cards, pack, and ship.

❑ **Antiques and collectibles:** While Alexandria is Egypt's most important center for antiques and collectibles, don't overlook Cairo, which holds its own in this department. Local antiques tend to be very European. Large items include everything from furniture to chandeliers. Look for old glass, icons, sculptures, paintings, tables, chairs, chests, jewelry, and knick knacks. For old art, collectibles, prints, textiles, and village artefacts, be sure to visit **Senouhi** (54 Sh. Abdel Khalek Sarwat, Apt. 51, Tel. 391-0955).

❑ **Home decor and furnishings:** Cairo also is the country's design center and importer for home decor and furnishings. For a good overview of such items, check out several shops on the second and third floors of the World Trade Center as well as in the Semiramis Hotel shopping arcade.

❑ **Appliqué work:** Like many of Cairo's arts, crafts, and souvenirs, the colorful appliqué work is an acquired taste. Look for many brightly colored items such as tents, cushion covers, toaster covers, wall hangings, and bedspreads. Most of these items are concentrated along one street in the Khan el-Khalili – Street of the Tentmakers behind Bab Zuwela.

❑ **Clothes:** Numerous shops throughout Cairo carry beautiful traditional Egyptian garments, such as the long *galabiyyas*, Bedouin costumes, beautiful wool scarves, leather coats, and T-shirts. You'll also find several upscale shops, such as **MM** and **BTM** in the World Trade Center, shopping centers, and hotel shopping arcades, carrying stylish lines of men's and women's clothes.

❑ **Linens and fabrics:** Cairo is a great place to shop for good quality linens and fabrics made from the legendary Egyptian cotton as well as silk. Look for cotton sheets and fabrics designed with Egyptian motifs. Several shops at the World Trade Center, such as **Tanis**, and at the Nile Hilton Mall, such as **Fame**, offer good quality fabrics and linens.

❑ **Ceramics and pottery:** Several shops in and around Cairo offer interesting ceramics and pottery. Some shops, such as **Bashayer**, occasionally carry old village water pots which make attractive home decorative pieces. Other shops, such as **Samir El Guindi** (261 El Sudan Street, Muhandiseen, Dokki, Tel. 347-3445), are actually pottery factories. Some of the best quality artistic ceramics are available at the artist studio of **Nabil Darwish** along Sakkara Road (3 km.) and at **Assila** at 98 Mohi el-Din Abou el-Eiz Street, Dokki (Tel. 337-9826).

❑ **Metal work:** Numerous shops in the Khan al-Khalili Bazaar and elsewhere offer a wide selection of brass, copper, and silver and other metal work. Copper cookware and engraved brass trays and plates are ubiquitous. For excellent quality metal work (lanterns, chandeliers, mirrors, ornamental chests, tables, candle holders, incense burners, and other decorative pieces) that is literally fit for the homes of celebrities and the palaces of royalty, be sure to visit Azza Fahmy's **Al Ain Gallery** at 73 El Hussein Street, Dokki (Tel. 349-3940).

❑ **Glassware:** You can't miss the Muski glass in the Khan al-Khalili Bazaar. Look for green, blue, red, and translucent white handblown vases, pitchers, and drinking glasses as well as small perfume bottles. The **Mosque Glass House** (8 Wikalat al-Makwa) and **Sayed Abd El-Raouf** (8 Khan el-Khalili, Tel. 933-463, red glass) are well worth visiting.

WHERE TO SHOP

You'll find shopping everywhere in Cairo. However, much of it is concentrated in shopping centers, hotel shopping arcades, and department stores as well as along major commercial streets and, of course, in the Khan el-Khalili Bazaar. While many top quality shops will be found in the World Trade Center, Ramses Hilton Hotel, Cairo Marriott Hotel, and the Semiramis Inter-Continental Hotel, others are found throughout the city and will require some sleuthing on your part – hopefully with a good map, car, and driver – to find them.

KHAN EL-KHALILI BAZAAR

You can't say you've shopped, or even been sightseeing in Egypt, unless you've been to the grand Khan el-Khalili Bazaar, the Middle East's oldest and most noted bazaar. A major trading and craft center for centuries, it's jam-packed with everything from gold, silver, copper, and brassware to handicrafts, antiques, clothes, leather goods, glassware, perfumes, and spices. It's as much a souvenir, gift, and craft center as a serious shopping center for local residents, who have been coming here for centuries to do their shopping. But most important of all, the Khan is about people, lots of people involved in buying, selling, taking pictures, and dining. This is the Egypt many people envision before coming to Egypt – thoroughly chaotic, crowded, colorful, noisy, intriguing, and in-your-face. This is not a tent bazaar. It's a labyrinth of shops and workshops in a centuries-old setting that both meets and dispels many stereotypes of Arab and Middle Eastern bazaars and shopping.

Stroll down its narrow, crowded, winding, and chaotic lanes, step into its specialty *souks* (markets), or people-watch as you sip a glass of mint tea or a cup of coffee at one of its smoky coffee houses or cafes, and you may feel transported into a different era. The Khan is many things to many different people. On the positive side, it's seen by many visitors as a unique cultural experience, an area rich in monuments and architecture, one of the most interesting sightseeing attractions, the best place to people-watch, the highlight of Cairo, a fun place to snap up bargains and buy gifts, a great place to see artisans at work, or the best place to get lost and found in Egypt. Free-spirited, adventuresome, and inquisitive types tend to have a good time here. On a negative side, some visitors find the Khan to be very intimidating, a highly overrated market, a tourist trap, or a waste of time. If you don't like shopping, chaos, and just wandering around in what at times may seem to be a maze, than the Khan may not be for you. Whatever your travel likes or dislikes, chances are you will not be neutral about this place. But hopefully it will be a very positive experience for you.

The Khan tends to elicit strong emotions. It's much more than just shopping or another tourist attraction. It's a chance to relatively painlessly experience a bit of medieval Cairo which remains an important working market for locals. Above all, the Khan draws huge crowds each day, rivaling the Pyramids of Giza as Egypt's main tourist attraction! Even for local residents, who regularly shop here for their daily needs, the Khan is a very special place to visit. While it definitely attracts tourists, it's much more than a tourist market. It's a living market of shops, merchants, and craftsmen who have served the needs of local residents for centuries. In many shops you can observe artisans in small workshops that are often found up narrow staircases on the upper floors of shops. After being served a glass of tea or cup of coffee, you may be invited to see the upstairs area where you will meet and observe the craftsmen at work and admire their unique treasures.

The Khan also is an important historical site with lots of interesting architecture, from shops to mosques and gates. The word *"khan"* itself indicates an interesting commercial and residential phenomenon that continues to dot the bazaar: a combination hotel, trading center, and warehouse which includes a gate, courtyard, shop area, and rooms for traveling merchants. One of the best examples of a *khan* today is the Wakalet El Ghuri near El Azhar which is now used as a studio for craftsmen.

You may have visited markets and bazaars in other countries and cities, but except for the exotic markets in Istanbul, Old Jerusalem, and Bangkok and the *souks* in Fez and Marrakech, most markets pale in comparison to the huge Khan el-Khalili. Located in the heart of Islamic Cairo, this medieval bazaar is nearly 600 years old and is home to over 1,000 shops. Many visitors to Egypt put this bazaar at the top of their "must see" and "must return to" list of things to do. Some primarily come here to sightsee and experience the café culture, especially the famous Fishawy's café, while others come here for a day of bargain shopping as they wander through a maze of winding lanes. It's a very noisy and colorful in-your-face market where touts, vendors, and merchants constantly pester you to enter their shops. While still exotic and traditional, it's also a thoroughly modern market complete with window displays, air conditioned shops, and credit card processing.

The Khan is a totally different shopping culture from what you will encounter elsewhere in Cairo. Here you are expected to bargain with very aggressive vendors. Whatever initial price you are quoted, counter with an offer that is 50 to 80 percent less. You'll know you've reached the correct price when the merchant becomes very adamant about your low offer! Don't worry. He's still making money – he has just reached his expected profit margin. The general rule here is to bargain in most shops (expect 20-70 percent discounts), although some of the older top quality shops bargain very little since they have an established reputation for fair pricing. Jewelry shops may only discount by 20 percent, and some shops display a "fixed prices" sign. At the same time, don't expect your new-found bargaining skills to be effective in other shops in Cairo. The Khan has its own bargaining culture that may or may not transfer well to many other shops. Indeed, some merchants elsewhere in Cairo may remind you that you're not shopping in the Khan any longer!

The best way to approach this market is to get a good map of the area or a guide who really knows the in's and out's of the

Khan. However, a guide may expect commissions from shops where you make purchases, an added shop cost that is usually included in your price. Not that you will get lost, for getting lost and then discovering your way out is half the fun of exploring the bazaar. Rather, there's a lot to this market you may miss if you don't have a good map or guide. It also can be a very disorienting bazaar consisting of many different markets and confusing streets, lanes, and landmarks. Ola Seif's *Khan al-Khalili: A Comprehensive Mapped Guide to Cairo's Historic Bazaar* (American University in Cairo Press, 1993) is still the "bible" of the area. Somewhat hard to find these days, nonetheless, this combination book and map may be found in some bookstores and museum shops. It provides a historical overview, offers shopping tips, and plots every shop in the Khan on a fold-out map.

But don't expect a guide or a guidebook, including this one, to point you to all the great places to shop. Remember, this is an area of more than 1,000 shops which are constantly changing their product mixes, names, ownership, and sales personnel. What was true last week, month, or year may not be true today or tomorrow. Constantly changing, the Khan is one of those delightfully serendipitous places where your best guide will probably be your eyes, ears, and intuition. The Khan is meant to be experienced by wandering, often aimlessly, down lanes, up staircases, and into back rooms of shops where you are likely to discover many interesting products and people. You'll encounter everything from truly hospitable, friendly, and honest merchants to pestering touts, aggressive in-your-face merchants, and the clever con-man who sees lots of suckers coming down his street or lane each day.

Getting lost, and doing so several times in a single day, is probably the best way to experience the Khan. Plan to block out two to three hours for the area, start at its main entrance at Hussein Square, note a few places you want to visit on your map, walk straight into the bazaar and usually keep to your left, and then just get lost for the next one to two hours. It's especially fun to get lost with a friend. In the end, you'll probably emerge with some very interesting stories of places you discovered, people you met, and great buys you found along the way. Just getting through the bazaar in a haphazard unplanned manner is half the fun. If you're with a group, plan to meet them at a set time either at the Badestan Gate (Khan El Khalili Restaurant) or at Hussein Square where you can all see the landmark minaret from the depths of the Khan.

In planning your daily itinerary, keep in mind that most shops in the Khan are open from 10am to 9pm, Monday through Saturday. Most shops close on Sunday and for one hour on Friday for prayers (around noon). However, the famous Fishawy's café remains open 24 hours a day.

If you are traveling on your own, the best way to get here is to take a taxi. Ask to be taken to al-Azhar, Khan el-Khalili, al-Muski, or al-Husayn. The taxi will normally stop at **El Azhar Mosque**, at the eastern end of the bazaar, where you will see a blue footbridge. This also is a good place to later get a taxi since taxis found within the main streets of the bazaar tend to be expensive. From here you cross the busy El Azhar Street, cross the parking lot, and enter **Hussein Square** which may be crowded with tour buses and cars. You can't miss Hussein Square and its landmark minaret at the large Mosque of El Hussein on your right. In fact, one of the best kept secrets in navigating the Khan is the **minaret** – always keep it in view for directions rather than follow the alleys within the bazaar. If you get lost, always head for the minaret rather than try to find specific alleys. Around this square you'll find coffeehouses that are good for roasted pigeon and smoking the ubiquitous *shisha* pipes. You also can walk from central Cairo to the bazaar. It takes about 20 minutes to walk from Ataba Square to Muski or Azhar Streets which are at the western end of the bazaar.

The bazaar includes numerous streets and a maze of lanes along which merchants noisily hawk a dizzying array of colorful and exotic goods, from spices and perfumes to jewelry and prayer beads. Don't be turned off by the many shops that offer tacky tourist trash, especially as you initially enter the Khan from Hussein Square You'll also discover many top quality shops throughout the Khan. In fact, much of the "good stuff" is often found in back rooms or up narrow staircases where shops keep their best treasures.

One of the defining aspects of the Khan are the many *souks* or markets that feed into the Khan. Most of these *souks* specialize in a particular product, such as spices, perfume, copper, brass, and gold, and have a very loyal following of local shoppers.

The major streets from which many small lanes feed include Shari' al-Mashhad al-Husayni (separates the Khan from the Mosque of El Hussein), Sikkit al-Badestan (Khan el-Khalili Street), Sagha/Shari al-Mu'izz li-Din Allah, al-Muski, and Shari' al-Azhar.

You can enter the Khan from several different directions. But the most interesting passage into the Khan is the craft lane to the right of the coffee houses and at the left corner of the Mosque of El Hussein – **Khan el-Khalili Street** (also goes by the name Sikkit al-Badestan). Here you'll find hundreds of densely packed shops offering a wide variety of varying quality goods: water pots, inlaid boxes, papyrus paintings, jewelry, silver, glasswork, leather goods, clothes, carpets, and antiques (mainly porcelain and furniture). Jewelry shops are especially prevalent in this area. Along this pathway, about mid-way into the bazaar, you'll also discover one of the best combination restaurant and coffee houses in the Khan on your right, the Oberoi-managed **Khan El Khalili Restaurant and Naguib Mahfouz Coffee Shop** (5 al-Badestan Lane, Tel. 590-3788). Located next to the 16ᵗʰ -century Badestan Gate, this is a great oasis in the middle of the bazaar! Stop here for lunch as well as use it as a central point from which to explore the bazaar to the south and west. Everything on the menu is good, but the popular dessert *Om Ali* is simply outstanding – the best we found in all of Egypt. In fact, the *Om Ali* here is so good that it gave us a terrific excuse to come back and visit the Khan several times during our stay in Cairo!

Most visitors spend 50 percent of their time shopping along the densely packed Khan el-Khalili Street (al-Badestan). It's a shopper's paradise for arts, crafts, jewelry, gold, silver, brass, copper, leather, antiques, clothes, and rugs. If you venture into the lanes to the left (south) of this street – especially between the huge El-Kahhal carpet shop (on left) and the Khan El Khalili Restaurant (on right) – you'll find many other shops offering similar items. Unfortunately, many shops do not have signs or numbers to identify their locations. You may have to ask for directions to various shops that are known by name only. Some of the better shops in this area include:

❑ **El Aguz Carpet Shop:** Located at the entrance to Khan el-Khalili Street – across from Mosque of Hussein. Good selections and prices on *kilims* (rugs), camel bags, and scenic Egyptian rugs.

❑ **El-Kahhal:** Huge carpet shop on left side of street.

❑ **Saad of Egypt:** Tel. 589-3992. *www.saadofegypt.com.* Offers some of the best quality silver items (trays, letter openers, boxes, candle holders, small decorative pots) at reasonable prices in Cairo. Also has shops at the Ramses Hilton Hotel and in Heliopolis.

❑ **Galal's:** Well known gold shop that produces excellent cartouches.

❑ **Hazem Moustafa Nonn and Brothers:** Large collection of antique furniture, chandeliers, lamps, icons, and glass. Be sure to go upstairs where you will find many additional treasures.

❑ **Amir's:** Specializes in beads and Bedouin necklaces and bracelets.

❑ **Mihran and Garbis Yazejian:** One of the best places in Egypt to acquire custom-made gold cartouches.

❑ **Nassar:** Offers very good quality jewelry. Look for silver, gold, precious stones, and lapis lazuli. Also includes some Bedouin jewelry.

❑ **Jewellery Egypt Inc.:** Almost looks like it doesn't belong here in the bazaar. A very classy shop offering top quality jewelry. Owns one of the largest gold and diamond factories in Egypt. Be sure to see the jewelry selections on the upper floors. Operates a gold market on the third floor where many small shops in the bazaar buy before marking up prices.

❑ **Abbas Hegazi:** Produces excellent quality *galabiyyas* at good prices.

❑ **Saad Leather Shop:** Good quality leather purses, briefcases, belts, and suitcases.

❑ **Osama's Copper and Brass:** Reasonably priced old and new copper and brass pieces. Does good quality custom work.

❑ **Saad Copper:** Offers both old and new copper pieces.

❑ **Mohamed El Sisi:** Offers good quality Mashrabeyya screens and tables.

❑ **Mustafa's Copper Shop:** Friendly shop offering good quality old and new copper and brass items at reasonable prices.

❑ **Inlay Work:** Top quality inlaid boxes, game boards, tables, and jewelry boxes.

❑ **Khorshani:** Good place to shop for precious and semi-precious unset stones. Also includes fake stones but very honest about the differences.

❑ **Mohamed Ali Mustafa:** Includes a huge selection of handicrafts and silver at excellent prices.

❑ **Adly M. Haddad Jeweleries:** Deceptive-looking small shop that opens into a very large shop offering lots of jewelry as well as silver, glassware, pharaonic furniture, inlaid boxes, and chandeliers. Beautiful ceiling.

If you wander the length of Sikkit al-Badestan, you'll eventually come to a main thoroughfare which is called al-Sagha. If you turn right (north), you'll find lots of small shops selling pots and pans and other household goods; this is the area of the copper and brass market. If you turn left (south), you'll see numerous jewelry stores, which are mainly gold shops, on both sides of the street; this is the area of the gold market. Since many local residents shop here for their jewelry, most of the jewelry designs appeal to local tastes. At the intersection of Muski Street you'll find a couple of important mosques on your right and the spice and perfume markets on your left; you'll smell the markets as you go by. Be careful with the aggressive perfume merchants who are known to tell tall tales about themselves and their little over-priced concoctions. At this point the street, Sagha, changes its name to Muizz la-Din Allah Street.

If you continue south along Muizz la-Din Allah Street, your next big intersection will be with Azhar Street. If you turn right, this street will take you to Ataba Square and the downtown area. If you turn left here, this wide street will circle to the left and take you back to where you started – Hussein Square. If you walk straight ahead, you'll leave the bazaar area and enter the Tentmakers' Street, El Khaymiya.

Some visitors to the Khan dismiss this market as a tourist trap and thus quickly navigate through this maze of shops and people within 45 minutes. Others take the whole day leisurely shopping, dining, and sightseeing. And still others return in the evening or for another day. We tend to be return visitors – for both shopping and our favorite *Om Ali* dish at the Oberoi restaurant. As you'll quickly discover once you go into the depths of this place and overcome any sense of intimidation, the Khan has something for everyone. It can be a very rewarding experience in more ways than one. While it is ostensibly a shopping center where you can do some very serious shopping, at the same time, this is a fascinating craft, cultural, historical, architectural, dining, and people-watching center. It constantly unravels and captivates visitors. Each time seems to be a new experience. Take your money, camera, and sense of adventure and you'll surely have a great time exploring the many treasures and pleasures of this marketplace. Indeed, the Khan el-Khalili Bazaar may well become one of your most memorable experiences in Egypt! It may be the only place you really want to shop in Egypt because it also is a unique cultural experience.

SHOPPING CENTERS

Going from the Khan el-Khalili Bazaar to a major shopping center takes some cultural adjustment. Indeed, you'll be going from seeming street chaos, intimidation, uncertain pricing situations, questionable quality products, aging buildings, and street dirt to relatively clean and modern air-conditioned centers with nice window displays, fixed prices, and quality selections. While initially more appealing because of their familiarity, the shopping centers may be less fun because of the people: you may encounter disinterested salaried salespeople rather than shop owners who bathe you in hospitality and conversation and who often demonstrate their work. Nonetheless, some of Cairo's best quality shopping can be found in its attractive shopping centers.

Cairo has several modern shopping centers which primarily cater to local residents. The ones of most interest to visitors are located adjacent to major hotels. These include:

❏ **World Trade Center:** *1191 Corniche El Nil.* Facing the river directly across from Gezira Island and located adjacent to the Conrad International Hotel, this is Cairo's largest upscale shopping center with nearly 100 shops. It's an interesting, although by no means the most exciting, place for visitors to shop. One to two hours here should be plenty, depending on your shopping interests. This center also tends to be very quiet; some shops have closed recently. Consisting of three levels with an atrium and open restaurant at the center of the main entrance, this attractive center is filled with home decorative, clothing, and leather goods shops. However, you must really probe the three floors in the atrium area because many shops are found off to the sides and in back of the main atrium – a true modern labyrinth of shops! While the shops in the atrium area represent some of the best shops in the World Trade Center, be aware that the third floor (from the escalator) extends into another building where you will find many additional clothing and home decorative shops. The overall emphasis here is on home furnishings and decor as well as clothes and leather goods. As soon as you enter the World Trade Center, you'll see a Mercedes dealer on your left as well as several small vendors with carts. In the center of the atrium is an open restaurant. Cheers and Baskin Robbins are found on the left. The ground floor includes many nice fashionable clothing and accessory stores. For leather shoes and handbags, visit **T.A. Egypt**. For nice Egyptian-made men's sweaters, shirts, sport coats as well as women's blouses and blazers, stop at **MM** (Tel. 580-4034); one of 20 such shops in Cairo, MM also offers good quality leather handbags and shoes which are what they predominantly offer in their other shops. **Choices**, which also has shops in the Ramses Hilton Shopping Annex and elsewhere in Cairo and Alexandria, offers a very attractive selection of leather handbags, briefcases, and belts, as well as jewelry. For some of the best quality fashionable men's and women's clothing, be sure to stop at **BTM/Marie Louis** (Tel. 574-8516). BTM is the clothing line for men and includes nice quality cotton shirts, ties, jackets, and pajamas displayed on the ground floor. The women's clothes, under the Marie Louis label, are found on the first floor and include silk and cotton blouses, dresses, and coats. Other good quality shops in this area include **Club Executive** for men's clothes and **Signee** for ties and shirts.

The first floor, which is accessible by escalator just behind Baskin Robbins to the left of the entrance, includes several very nice home decorative shops along with a few leather goods and handicrafts shops. **Genuine** (Tel. 578-4244) has a good selection of shoes, handbags, and luggage in many unusual and interesting colors. You'll also find several knock-offs of Fendi and Yves St. Laurent handbags and luggage here. **Art Zone Gallery** (Tel. 580-4153) has a good selection of glassware, lamps, paintings, trays, and Plexiglas items. **Gallery Asfour** includes paintings, crystal figures, carpets and furniture as well as the famous Asfour crystal. **Le Prince** (Tel. 576-9489), one of the center's most attractive home decorative shop with additional shops in Cairo (largest is in Heliopolis), Amman, and Crete, has a good collection of lamps, dishes, candles, knick-knacks, picture frames, and soap dishes as well as specialty clocks that make nice collectibles. **Tanis** (Tel. 580-4160) is one of the best textile and home decorative shops in Egypt with a very attractive selection of cotton, silk, and linen upholstery and drapery weight fabrics in beautiful Egyptian designs; the shop also offers attractive chandeliers and towels. Next door is **Sucre** (Tel. 577-6140) which has a very tasteful collection of home decorative items – paintings, glassware, picture frames, silver, tapestries, tribal jewelry (from Tunisia), and furniture. **Mona E. Siag** (Tel. 576-6955), at the other end of this floor, offers an unusual selection of large silver and brass pots. The second floor leads into a whole new section of shops called the New Annex. Look for **Pandora's Box**, a small but nice boutique, and **Invention** (Tel. 580-4237), a home decorative shop offering an interesting collection of paintings, lamps, and stained glass screens.

❑ **First Mall:** *The First Residence, 35 Giza Street, Giza.* Located next to the new Four Seasons Hotel, this is Cairo's newest and most upscale shopping center. It's actually part of the multi-mix complex known as The First Residence. It includes the Four Seasons Hotel, an apartment complex, and a casino. First Mall consists of 64 exclusive and elegant boutiques and galleries that offer everything from imported goods to Egyptian arts and crafts. Since opening in early 2000, First Mall has become very popular with locals as well as visitors to Cairo.

❑ **Ramses Hilton Shopping Annex:** This 8-story shopping mall is located directly across the street from the Ramses Hilton Hotel. A pleasant air-conditioned oasis from the teeming traffic outside, it's especially popular with locals, who shop here for fashionable and inexpensive leather handbags, some of which are good knock-offs of European brand name leather goods. Indeed, you may be overwhelmed with the many shops offering so many handbags as well as shoes. You'll immediately see why Cairo has a reputation for having a foot fetish! But look for many other types of shops here: clothing, textile, sportswear, book, art, electronics, jewelry, tailor, linen, cotton, handicraft, toy, and luggage. Most shops are found on the ground to third floor, but don't forget to go to all floors, especially fourth and fifth. The top floor, however, is a food and entertainment center with McDonald's, the Hilton Billiard Hall, and a movie theater. The ground floor has three shops of particular note: **Ed-Dukhan** (Tel. 575-2752) for fashionable Egyptian clothes using gorgeous Egyptian cottons and silks; **New Cardinal Jewellery** for all types of jewelry; and **Ani** for handicrafts. The first floor includes several shoe and handbag shops that include many knock-offs. The second floor is a shoe and handbag fetish's delight – lots of shops offering many unique designs and colors including many knock-offs of brand names such as Chanel and Fendi. The third floor is primarily devoted to both men's and women's shoes. The fourth floor is a mix of furniture, home decorative, clothing, carpet, shoe, toy, and silver shops. The standout shop here, as well as for the shopping center as a whole, is **H.H.** (Tel. 579-6582) with its gorgeous Egyptian clothes, jewelry, and dolls. The fifth floor is again heavy with shoe, handbag, clothing, toy, and luggage shops. One of the best shops here is **Choice** (Tel. 348-0760) which carries very unique handbags and luggage that are produced in its factory in Alexandria; it also has shops in the World Trade Center, Mohandessin, Heliopolis, Alexandria, and Taba. You also may want to visit the Ramses Hilton Hotel which has a few excellent quality shops, such as **Saad of Egypt** (Tel. 577-7444, Ext. 3109) for silver trays and figures.

You'll find other popular shopping centers and strip mall sections in suburban **Heliopolis, Maadi, Mohendiseen**, and **Dokki**. However, these places are of most interest to expatriates and middle to middle class Egyptians.

HOTEL SHOPPING ARCADES

Several four- and five-star hotels have shopping arcades attached to their main properties. Although the World Trade Center and the First Mall could also be included in this section, they appear in the previous section as "Shopping Centers" because they are not attached to the main property. Hotels with the largest such shopping arcades include:

❑ **Nile Hilton Mall:** *Corniche El Nil Street at Tahrir Square.* Located next to the Egyptian Antiquities Museum, this shopping arcade is attached to the rear of the Nile Hilton Hotel. It includes several jewelry and clothing stores as well as a nice carpet shop (**El Kahhal Oriental Carpets**), bed linen and cover shop (**Fame**), and a glass shop (**Scarabe**). Includes a food court at the lower level. The Nile Hilton Hotel next door has a few nice shops.

❑ **Cairo Marriott Shopping Arcade:** *Shar'a Saray al-Gezira, Zamalek.* This two-level shopping arcade includes several good quality clothing, letter, and jewelry shops. **Nomad** (Tel. 341-2132) especially stands out with its attractive collection of Bedouin textiles and collectibles. The jewelry store next to the elevators offers a beautiful collection of fine jewelry.

❏ **Hotel Semiramis Inter-Continental Shopping Arcade:** *Corniche El Nil at Tahrir Square.* This pleasant two-level shopping arcade includes numerous clothing, leather, jewelry, toy, and handicraft shops as well as a convenient 24-hour bank. The ground floor only has a few shops, such as **Leather Home** (Tel. 357-1820, ext. 1914) which offers a good selection of nicely designed shoes, handbags, belts, and coats. The first floor (mezzanine) includes several shops worth visiting: **MM** (Tel. 355-7493) for nice leather handbags, shoes, and briefcases; **Heba** (Tel. 354-0573) for a fine collection of Egyptian cotton bed linens, towels, and bathrobes (also has shops at the World Trade Center and the First Mall); and **Genny** (two shops across from each other), a home decorative shop offering an eclectic collection of antiques, furniture, paintings, silver, brass, carpets, and glassware which you may or may not consider tasteful.

SHOPPING AREAS AND SPECIALTY SHOPS

Except for shoe stores and souvenir shops that seem to locate near each other, some of the best shops are scattered throughout Cairo. Most are difficult to find unless you have transportation and a good map or guide to get around into the various suburbs and neighborhoods.

❏ **Central Cairo:** There's little here of interest to visitors except the cultural experience of watching the locals shop for shoes and handbags. This section of the city is overrun with shoe stores that all seem to congregate next to each other. However, you will find a few antique shops and art galleries worth visiting. For example, **Mashrabia** at 8 Shar'a Champollion, Tahrir Square (Tel. 578-4494) is one of Cairo's most noted contemporary art galleries. We especially like a small fine arts, crafts, and book shop called **Senouhi** at 54 Sh. Abdel Khalek Sarwat, Apt. 51 (Tel. 391-0955) which is piled high with all kinds of unique treasures. Along **Borsa Street** (hard to find but it's between Kasar El Nil Street and Sulaiman Pasha), look for six antique shops ("galleries") that offer furniture and collectibles.

❏ **Zamalek and Gezira Island:** Some of Cairo's most upscale shops are found in the Zamalek area on Gezira Island. Located behind the Cairo Marriott Hotel, this area is filled with boutiques, jewelry stores, and art, antique, and home decorative shops. You can easily spend a couple of hours exploring the main shopping street, **26 July Street**, and adjacent streets. For antique reproduction furniture and accessories, one of the best shops in Cairo is **Les Galeries Odeon** at 110 26 July Street (Tel. 341-2172); be sure to visit the lower level which is a huge warehouse of model reproduction furniture. Les Galeries Odeon also has a branch shop in Heliopolis and a factory and shop in Alexandria. For an eclectic collection of top quality furniture, one of the very best shops is **Alef** at 14 Muhammand Anis (Tel. 342-0848). Zamalek also has two tribal arts and crafts shops worth visiting. One of the best in all of Egypt is **Nomad** which is located in both the Cairo Marriott Hotel shopping arcade (Tel. 341-2132) and 14 Saraya Al Gezira, 1st floor (Tel. 341-1917). The Saraya Al Gezira shop, which is referred to as the **Nomad Gallery**, is the main shop with a large and colorful selection of good quality Bedouin textiles, jewelry, bags, silver, baskets, plates, cards, pots, and carpets from the Western Desert oases and the Sinai Peninsula. **Egypt Crafts Center** at 27 Yehia Ibrahim, Apt. 8 (Tel. 341-5123 and *www.egyptcrafts.com*), which is operated by the nonprofit Marketing Link Project that supports village women, offers a small but reasonably priced collection of village handicrafts such as rugs, food baskets, clothes, textiles, embroidery, and cards. One of Egypt's most outstanding jewelers is found along the river – **Nakhla** at 10 El Nil Street (Tel. 392-2000). Located close to the dock for The Pharaohs cruise ship, this small shop produces exclusive designer jewelry that represents various Egyptian civilizations.

❑ **Dokki:** Located on the west bank of the Nile River and fusing with the district of Mohandiseen to the north, Dokki is a lively suburban shopping area. Some of the best shops are located just south of the Shooting Club, where Mohandiseen and Dokki meet. This area includes several clothing, fabric, home decorative, antique, arts, crafts, and ceramics shops. This is not an easy area in which to find the best shops. You may frequently get lost and have to ask directions. Some of the best shops in this area include **Bashayer** at 58 Mosadek Street (Tel. 336-1006 – also has a shop in Sharm el-Sheikh) for a good collection of arts and crafts, especially ceramics, alabaster, textiles, fabrics, pillows, paintings, batiks, lamps, boxes, bags, and carpets; **Clarine** at 11 Soliman Abaza Street, a very small shop behind the Shooting Club (Tel. 360-8393), for antique furniture and silver; **Assila** at 98 Mohi el-Din Abou el-Eiz Street (Tel. 337-9826), a design studio offering a nice collection of quality lamps, ceramics, glass, boxes, paintings, and old pots; **Al Ain Gallery** at 73 El Hussein Street (Tel. 349-3940) for excellent jewelry, silver, arts, crafts, textiles, ceramics, furniture, and metal work; and **Samir El Guindi** at 261 El Sudan Street (Tel. 347-3445) to purchase ceramics and decorative clay pottery directly from the factory and workshop. **Dr. Ragab's Papyrus Institute**, which exhibits and sells some of the best quality papyrus products, is located on boats in front of the Cairo Sheraton at Midan Gala' (Tel. 989-476).

❑ **Maadi:** Located southeast of Old Cairo, this is a popular suburb for expatriates. Especially along Road 9, it's filled with numerous shops and restaurants of most interest to local residents. However, it has a few good quality shops of interests to visitors. If you are in this area, you may want to visit the **Bedouin Market** at 15 Road 231 Degla, beside Degla Market (Tel. 517-3800) which includes a large selection of Bedouin textiles, rugs, and silver jewelry; **Ethno** at 38 Road 7 (Tel. 350-6473) for ethnic designed clothes; **Morgana** at 59 Road 9 (Tel. 375-1089) for antiques; **La Scarpa** at 10 Road 218, Digla (Tel. 352-7159) for excellent quality shoes; **Graffiti** at 28 Nerco Building off Road 213 (Tel. 353-1426) for art; and **Azza Fahmy Gallery** at Street 15 Road 216 Deglas (Tel. 517-0935) for gold and silver jewelry as well as many fine arts and crafts (same operation as Al Ain Gallery in Dokki).

❑ **Heliopolis:** Located north of the city, this is perhaps Cairo's most upscale suburb. Within the past few years, Heliopolis also has been going crazy with new upscale boutiques and shopping centers. Most shopping is found along Sharia Harun al-Rashid and on Midan al-Gami. Some of the more interesting shops for visitors include **Hazem Hafez** at 35 Nizih Khalifa (Tel. 258-1376) for an excellent selection of Bedouin clothes and beautiful, and surprisingly stylish, woven wool scarves worn by Egyptian farmers; **Hassan Elaish** at 10 Harun al-Rashid (Tel. 258-1845) for gold jewelry; **Saad of Egypt** at Mirghani and Hoprreya Streets (Tel. 290-9466; *www.saadofegypt.com*) for silver; and **Arvest** at 21 Menouf Street (Tel. 419-5726) for top quality imported (Spain and Italy) home decorative items, from wonderful furniture to fabulous chandeliers, as well as Egyptian carpets.

❑ **Giza/Sakkara:** Both Giza and the road to Sakkara have numerous bazaars and shops offering lots of tourist kitsch. The problem here is sorting the trash from the treasures. If you visit the Pyramids of Giza, Memphis, and Sakkara, the shopping will come to you in the form of touts who want to sell you souvenirs at inflated prices. Within the city of Giza, you'll find the streets, especially Pyramids Road – Shara el-Haram, lined with numerous arts, crafts, jewelry, and souvenir shops selling similar items to tourists. Some of the best shopping is found along Sakkara Road. You may want to stop at these three places: **Ramses Wissa Wassef Art Center** at Harrania Village, Sakkara Road (Tel. 384-3104) for beautiful woven wall hangings and ceramics housed in attractive domed Nubian buildings; **Akhnaton Carpets and Tapestry School** at 16 Km. Sakkara Road (Tel. 201-488) for his huge collection of woven tapestries and rugs; and **Nabil Darwish** at 3 Km. Sakkara Road (Tel. 385-5894) for very attractive ceramic pots and plates produced by one of Egypt's leading ceramic artists (which may or may not be for sale, depending on the quirky artist's mood; if not for sale, check out Assila in Dokki (see page 125) which may have a few of his pieces).

❑ **Museums, churches, and universities:** Most museums, churches, and universities have small shops offering books, maps, postcards, videos, and some handicrafts. The bookstore at The American University in Cairo has an excellent bookstore which includes many books on Egypt published by the university.

BEST OF THE BEST

If you have limited time for shopping in Cairo, you may want to concentrate on the following shops which we found to be some of the best in Cairo. It's best to get a car and driver to take you to several of these places since parking and finding taxis are sometimes difficult:

ART

❑ **Mashrabia:** *8 Shar'a Champollion, Tahrir Square, Tel. 578-4494. Open 11am to 8pm; closed Fridays.* Don't expect to find much Western contemporary art in Islamic Egypt. After all, depiction of human figures in art forms is frowned upon in Islam. Nonetheless, you'll find a few contemporary art galleries in Cairo. Most are listed in the monthly *Egypt's Insight Magazine* and *Egypt Today*. Mashrabia represents one of the very best such galleries. It exhibits the works of artists from both Egypt and abroad.

JEWELRY

❑ **Nakhla:** *10 El Nil Street, Tel. 392-2000.* Somewhat difficult to find, this small shop is located near the dock for *The Pharaohs* cruise ship. If you only have time to visit a few jewelry shops in Egypt, make sure you start with this exclusive and extremely talented jewelry designer. Produces exquisite gold jewelry in a variety of unique collections representing various Egyptian civilizations. Many international celebrities and noted diplomatic personnel regularly shop here. You can easily spend an hour examining the many unique pieces produced by the engaging owner-operator.

❑ **Mihran and Garbis Yazejian:** *Khan el-Khalili.* This long established and highly reliable jeweler arguably produces the best custom-made gold cartouches in all of Egypt. Don't expect to bargain here – prices are fair to begin with, given the quality of workmanship. Includes an interesting workshop on the upper floors.

❑ **Nassar:** *Khan el-Khalili.* Offers excellent quality jewelry using silver, gold, precious stones, and lapis lazuli. Includes an attractive collection of Bedouin jewelry.

❑ **Jewellery Egypt Int. Co.:** *8 Saket El Badestan, Khan el-Khalili, Tel. 592-5083; and 10 Haron El Rasheed, El Gamaa Square, Tel. 258-0227.* One of the largest jewelers in Egypt. Specializes in gold and diamond jewelry.

❑ **Azza Fahmy Gallery:** *Street 15 Road 216 Deglas, Maadi, Tel. 517-0935.* This noted international jewelry designer specializes in producing unique gold and silver jewelry that incorporates many traditional Egyptian motifs. Also operates the Al Ain Gallery (arts and crafts) in Dokki.

SILVER

❑ **Saad of Egypt:** *Khan el-Khalili, Tel. 589-3992. Website: www.saadofegypt.com.* Also has shops at the Ramses Hilton Hotel and in Heliopolis. Offers some of the best quality silver items (trays, letter openers, boxes, candle holders, small decorative pots) at reasonable prices in Cairo.

CLOTHES

❑ **BTM/Marie Louis:** *World Trade Center, 1191 Corniche El Nil, Tel. 574-8516.* Offers fashionable men's and women's clothes under a local designer label. Silk blouses on the second floor are an especially good buy.

❑ **Ed-Dukhan:** *Ramses Hilton Shopping Annex, Ground Floor, Tel. 575-2752.* If you are looking for well designed and stylish traditional Egyptian garments for women using beautiful cottons and silks, be sure to check out the selections at this excellent shop near the entrance of the shopping center.

❑ **H.H.:** *Ramses Hilton Shopping Annex, Third Floor, Tel. 579-6582.* Offers a combination of beautiful Egyptian style garments, jewelry, and dolls in one of this shopping center's most interesting shops.

LEATHER GOODS

❑ **MM:** *World Trade Center plus 19 other locations in Cairo, Tel. 580-4034.* This chain of leather and garment shops offers good quality and fashionable handbags and shoes at reasonable prices.

❑ **Choices:** *Ramses Hilton Shopping Annex, Tel. 348-0760; World Trade Center, Tel. 575-5087; Mohandessin, Tel. 348-0760; Maadi, Tel. 375-6455; and Heliopolis, Tel. 263-5148.* Offers good quality leather handbags, luggage, briefcases, and belts in fashionable designs and colors.

❑ **Leather Home:** *Hotel Semiramis Inter-Continental Shopping Arcade, Tel. 357-1820, Ext. 1914.* Includes a full range of quality leather goods, from handbags and shoes to coats, in several interesting colors and designs.

ANTIQUES AND FURNITURE

❑ **Les Galeries Odeon:** *110 26 July Street, Zamalek, Tel. 341-2172.* This expansive furniture and home decorative shop includes good quality reproduction antique French-style furniture produced in its factory in Alexandria. Be sure to visit the lower level of this shop which includes a large inventory of model furniture and accessory pieces. Experienced in shipping abroad.

❏ **Alef:** *14 Muhammand Anis, Zamalek, Tel. 342-0848.* Excellent quality furniture shop especially popular with expatriates. Eclectic.

❏ **Clarine:** *11 Soliman Abaza Street (behind the Shooting Club), Tel. 360-8393.* This small antique furniture and silver shop is especially popular with expatriates and collectors. Offers limited but excellent quality selections.

❏ **Meubles Bamboo Anto:** *195 Ramses Street, Tel. 490-0738.* Produces attractive rattan and cane furniture for export. Take your designs with you or choose from existing models.

HOME DECOR AND FURNISHINGS

❏ **Tanis:** *World Trade Center, 1191 Corniche El Nil, Tel. 580-4160.* If you're looking for good quality upholstery and drapery-weight fabrics using silks and cottons, this is the place to shop. Includes many nice contemporary designs and colors. All fabrics sold by the meter.

❏ **Arvest:** *21 Menouf Street, Heliopolis, Tel. 419-5726.* This exclusive designer and home decorative shop includes gorgeous furniture, chandeliers, and accessory pieces from Spain and Italy. Also includes an excellent selection of Egyptian carpets.

❏ **Le Prince:** *World Trade Center, 1191 Corniche El Nil, Tel. 576-9489.* If you're looking for small home decorative pieces, from lamps to soap dishes, this shop includes a nice and eclectic collection of such items. Also has two other shops in Egypt (largest in Heliopolis) as well as in Amman, Jordan and on the island of Crete.

BED LINENS

❏ **Heba:** *Hotel Semiramis Inter-Continental Shopping Arcade, Tel. 354-0573; World Trade Center; and First Mall.* Offers an attractive collection of bed linens, towels, and robes made with fine Egyptian cottons.

ARTS AND CRAFTS

❑ **Nomad Gallery and Nomad:** *14 Saraya Al Gezira, 1st Floor, Zamalek, Tel. 341-1917; and Marriott Hotel Shopping Arcade, Tel. 341-2132.* These two shops represent some of the best Bedouin arts and crafts in Egypt. The larger of the two shops, Nomad Gallery or the Saraya Al Gezira shop, is jam-packed with excellent quality textiles, baskets, pots, carpets, jewelry, silver, plates, cards, and bags from various Bedouin groups of the Western Desert, oases, and the Sinai Peninsula. The smaller Marriott Hotel shop includes a nice collection of colorful textiles. You're bound to find something unique in these two shops, especially in the well stocked Saraya Al Gezira shop.

❑ **Senouhi:** *54 Sh. Abdel Khalek Sarwat, Apt. 51, Tel. 391-0955.* At first you might think you're in the wrong location as you walk through the dark hall to take a dingy elevator to Apartment 51. Once you arrive, this small shop is jam-packed with arts, crafts, antiques, textiles, and books. Watch where you walk since you are likely to stumble over a treasure or two. Take your time since you'll need to pick through piles to discover what's in this unusual shop. The back room (to the right of the entrance) may also have excess inventory which has not been put on display since space is so limited (the owners may also forget what they have in stock). Again, take your time to paw through all the stuff. You may be surprised at what you discover. Indeed, we acquired some beautiful antique grain measuring containers by accident – found under a pile of textiles. The aging owners of this shop are as interesting as the inventory!

❑ **Al Ain Gallery:** *73 El Hussein Street, Dokki, Tel. 349-3940.* This attractive shop offers a very nice collection of quality jewelry, silver, arts, crafts, textiles, ceramics, furniture, and metal work. Offers an interesting collection of metal lamps that make nice home decorative items. Well worth a special trip to the Dokki area. Operated by the same owner of Azza Fahmy Gallery in Maadi, the noted jewelry designer Azza Fahmy.

❑ **Azza Fahmy Gallery:** *Street 15 Road 216 Deglas, Maadi, Tel. 517-0935.* Specializes in producing unique gold and silver jewelry along with fine arts and crafts. Jewelry designs incorporate many traditional Egyptian motifs. Also operates the Al Ain Gallery in Dokki.

❑ **Bashayer:** *58 Mosaddak Street, Dokki, Tel. 336-1006.* This crowded three-level shop offers a wide selection of quality arts and crafts, from attractive ceramic plates, lamps, and textiles to boxes, carpets, and alabaster. A good source for purchasing attractive gift items. Also has a smaller shop in Sharm el-Sheikh.

❑ **Egypt Crafts Center:** *27 Yehia Ibrahim, Apt. 8, Zamalek, Tel. 341-5123. Website: www.egyptcrafts.com.* Operated by the environmentally-friendly Marketing Link Project, a non-profit organization supporting village women through the production and marketing of village handicrafts, this shop offers inexpensive rugs, baskets, clothes, textiles, embroidered items, and cards. Not the greatest quality or selections, but shopping here goes to a very worthwhile cause.

❑ **Dr. Ragab's Papyrus Institute:** *On boats in front of the Cairo Sheraton at Midan Gala', Tel. 949-476.* While you'll find tons of papyrus or so-called papyrus products (banana leaves) in Egypt, some of the best quality papyrus can be found here, where the art of papyrus making has been revived in recent years. The Institute includes an exhibit as well as a shop. If you're interested in this art form, you'll want to visit these boats to learn more about papyrus and perhaps make a purchase at the same time.

CERAMICS

❑ **Nabil Darwish:** *3 Km. Sakkara Road, Tel. 385-5894.* This is a quirky gallery run by a quirky artist who is not sure if he wants to sell his ceramic pots, but broadcasts to visitors that he is the world's greatest ceramicist! Nabil Darwish is indeed a highly acclaimed ceramic artist, and his pots and plates are quite attractive – very similar to Japanese raku ceramics. However, his ego may turn you off as he makes fantastic claims about his talents. Humor him. If you catch him when he's not in the mood to sell his creations (he sometimes claims his shop is a national museum), visit Assila in Dokki which sells a few of his creations. Don't be surprised if you become confused as to whether you are in a shop or a museum. It looks like a shop . . . but it may be a museum, depending on what the artist wants to call it during your visit. He finally sold us one pot after we convinced him that maybe one of his museum pieces might be for sale! He steadfastly refused to sell others.

❏ **Assila:** *98 Mohi el-Din Abou el-Eiz Street, Tel. 337-9826.* This design studio offers a wide range of varying quality lamps, ceramics, glass, boxes, paintings, and old pots, including a few works by Nabil Darwish. An eclectic shop that yields a few unique treasures. The large old pots, which are found in the hallway just outside the entrance, are an especially good buy. Does excellent packing.

❏ **Samir El Guindi:** *261 El Sudan Street, Zamalek, Tel. 347-3445.* In many cities this street shop would be classified as a nuisance since it also operates as a noisy factory/sweat shop. This long and narrow factory shop produces a wide range of varying quality ceramic and decorative clay pottery items, many of which incorporate Islamic designs. You may or may not find the designs appealing to your decorative tastes. Most of the items here are relatively inexpensive. Crowded, chaotic, and dusty, this is the type of shop in which you need to spend some time digging through the inventory. Craftsman on second floor can be observed producing various ceramic items. Plan to do your own packing and shipping, since this is a bare bones factory shop primarily focused on creating products.

WALL HANGINGS AND RUGS

❏ **Ramses Wissa Wasef Art Center:** *Harrania Village, Sakkara Road, Tel. 384-3104.* Offers a lovely setting (domed Nubian buildings which unfortunately are doomed to decay because of the rising water table in the surrounding area) for displaying some of the most beautiful woven wall hangings in Egypt. Many items on display are part of the Center's museum. If you want to see first-rate quality wall hangings, this is the place to visit. The small shop offers wall hangings for sale (very expensive) as well as a limited selection of ceramic pots, plates, and decorative items.

❏ **Akhnaton Carpets and Tapestry School:** *15 Km. Sakkara Road, Tel. 201-488.* This popular bus stop shop on the road to the pyramids offers a huge collection of woven tapestries and rugs. The quality is generally good. If you want to see a large selection of such items in a well organized tourist setting, this is the place to visit. Very experienced with packing and shipping. If you arrive here on your own, be sure to bargain hard for any purchases, since prices tend to be inflated for tour groups whose guides tend to be richly rewarded for making this obligatory stop.

❑ **El Kahhal Oriental Carpets:** *Nile Hilton Mall.* Offers a nice selection of Egyptian carpets in a relatively quiet setting.

BOOKS

❑ **The American University in Cairo Bookstore:** *Hill House, 113 Shar'a Qasr al-Aini, American University of Cairo, Tel. 357-5377. Sunday - Thursday, 8:30am to 4pm, and Saturday, 10am to 4pm.* Offers one of the largest collections of English language books on Egypt. Many are published by the American University of Cairo Press.

❑ **The Egyptian Antiquities Museum Bookstore:** *Egyptian Antiquities Museum, Midan Tahrir (north end).* This bookstore is located immediately to the left of the main entrance to the museum. It consists of two adjacent small and often crowded shops – "kiosks" might be a better term – jam-packed with postcards, books, and videos relevant to ancient Egypt and the museum exhibits.

❑ **L'Orientaliste:** *15 Kasr El Nile Street, Tel. 575-3418 or Fax 579-4188. 10am daily except Sunday. Website: www.orientaliste. com.eg.* This antiquarian bookshop is a good source of rare books, original lithographs, old maps, postcards from the turn of the century, and much more.

ACCOMMODATIONS

Cairo offers a good range of hotels for all styles and classes of travelers. Most of its international four- and five-star hotels offer excellent accommodations and restaurants. Several hotels also boast some of Cairo's top shopping arcades as well as popular bars and casinos. New five-star hotels, such as the Conrad International and the Four Seasons, are upgrading the overall quality of accommodations and service in Cairo which has often been drab, uninspired, and disappointing to visitors.

Depending on how long you plan to visit Cairo, you may want to stay in two different locations – Giza and Central Cairo. If you plan to spend some time visiting the pyramids, hotels such as the Mena House Oberoi, Four Seasons, and Le Meridien Pyramids in Giza, would make excellent choices. Most other hotels are centrally located in Cairo either on or near the Nile River and within walking distance or a short taxi ride of the major shops, restaurants, and sites.

GIZA, THE PYRAMIDS

❑ **Mena House Oberoi:** *Pyramids Road, Giza, Cairo, Egypt, Tel. (202) 383-3222, Fax (202) 383-7777, or toll-free from U.S. & Canada (800) 223-6800.* This is one of Egypt's truly grand and classy old hotels which exudes the ambience of a bygone era. Although it primarily caters to tour groups and independent travelers, given its close proximity to the pyramids (just look out your window!), as an Oberoi Hotel it manages to offer uncompromising facilities, excellent service, and attention to detail. Situated at the base of the great Pyramids of Giza, Mena House started life as a Khedive's hunting lodge. For Empress Eugenie's visit to Egypt upon the opening of the Suez Canal, the Khedive built a road so the empress could visit the pyramids in comfort, and the lodge was redecorated in regal splendor for her stop there. It is to the credit of the Oberoi Group that they spared no expense in restoring Mena House and retained the original ambience that dates back to the style of the Ottoman Empire. If you stay in the Palace section with a view of the pyramids, you will almost feel you can reach out and touch them. A member of the *Leading Hotels of the World* and frequent winner of traveler surveys, The Mena House Oberoi was selected among the Ten Best Hotels in the World by *Travel and Leisure* magazine for the second consecutive year. The proximity to the pyramids is wonderful, but the drive to Cairo city center takes at least 45 minutes. The 498 rooms offer all the expected amenities. The Palace section has atmosphere and a sense of history. The newer Garden Wing is modern, a bit farther from the pyramids and with not nearly as much atmosphere, although slightly less expensive. If you feel like splurging on a suite with a view, this is the place to do it. A suite in the Palace section with a pyramid view is an experience you will not forget. The large bedroom and sitting rooms with period furniture, spacious bath, and view of the pyramids from your bed, make the Palace suites a special experience. If you do have a room in the Palace section with a view of the pyramids, look out your window a little before 9am and you may see the camels being taken up to the pyramids for the day.

Five restaurants offer a variety of dining choices. Al Rubayyat, set with arabesque arches and lit by beautiful Ottoman lamps serves Continental cuisine. Dinner is accompanied by folk entertainment and music. The accolade-winning Moghul Room serves Indian cuisine in a classy Indian atmosphere. The Khan El Khalili Brasserie serves Egyptian and Continental dishes in an Ottoman decor with views of the pyramids. The Greenery, located in the Garden Wing, offers a buffet for all meals as well as an a la carte selection. The Oasis is a poolside coffee shop. A nightclub and discotheque offer entertainment. Fitness Center; Business Center; Conference and Banquet Facilities.

❑ **Four Seasons:** *The First Residence, 35 Giza Street, P.O. Box 663-12612, Al Orman, Giza 12311, Cairo, Egypt, Tel. (202) 573-1212 or Fax (202) 568-1616, or toll-free from US & Canada (800) 819-5053. Website: www.fourseasons.com/loca tions/Cairo.* Newly opened at The First Residence, a prestigious new development in Cairo which also includes a new upscale shopping center, the Four Seasons is now Cairo's premier five-star hotel. It offers 273 luxurious rooms and suites, the most spacious in Cairo. It's the city's only hotel with a dramatic view of three great attractions: Ancient Botanical Gardens, Nile River, and the Great Pyramids of Giza. Each room is beautifully appointed with a full marble bathroom, deep soaking tub, and separate shower and toilet stalls. Best of all, it comes with the legendary Four Seasons service! Breakfast, lunch, and dinner are served in the Seasons Restaurant which overlooks Cairo and the Nile and offers Mediterranean cuisine with North African flavors and influences from Lebanon, Morocco, and Italy. The Library Bar overlooks the Nile River. The elegant Tea Lounge and Lobby Coffee Bar serves light meals, afternoon tea, and refreshments. The Pool Bar and Grill offer relaxed, casual outdoor dining. Includes an extensive health club and spa. Business Center; Conference and Banquet Facilities.

❑ **Le Meridien Pyramids:** *El Remaya Square, Pyramids, Giza, Egypt, Tel. (202) 383-0383, Fax (202) 383-1730, or toll-free from US & Canada (800) 225-5843.* Le Meridien Pyramids is situated 10 km southwest of Cairo and within walking distance of the pyramids, and approximately 45 minutes from Cairo city center. Many of the guest rooms have views of the pyramids. The 523 guest rooms offer all the amenities expected in a five-star hotel. The numerous restaurants provide a variety of cuisines. The elegant La Farnesina serves Italian selections; La Pergola presents a poolside "all nations barbeque"; El Shams Coffee Shop has an extensive international buffet and a la carte menu 24 hours a day. Fitness Center; Business Center; Conference and Banquet Facilities.

CENTRAL CAIRO

❑ **Nile Hilton:** *Tahrir Square, Cairo, Egypt, Tel. (202) 578-0444, Fax (202) 578-0475, or toll-free from the US & Canada (800) 445-8667.* Located in the heart of Cairo, overlooking the Nile, adjacent to The Egyptian Antiquities Museum, and within walking distance of the main business and shopping district – though crossing the highway system makes walking hazardous – the Nile Hilton is ideally situated. Cairo's first international chain hotel has been well maintained by the Hilton chain, and the service is excellent. The 431 guest rooms and suites are spacious and the separate mirrored closet-filled dressing alcove makes it convenient as well. Most rooms have either a view of the Nile or the city. Balconies provide a place from which to view the traffic on the Nile or on the streets below. Executive Club floors offer additional amenities and services including complimentary breakfast, evening cocktails and hors d'oeuvres and snacks. Some of the many restaurant options include the Ibis Café, open 24 hours a day. Abu-Ali is an open-air, Oriental style terrace serving snacks, hot and cold drinks and water pipe. Café Ole, a Viennese-style café serves breakfast and light snacks and coffee throughout the day. DaMario offers authentic Italian specialties. Rotisserie Belvedere is an elegant rooftop restaurant offering breathtaking views of the Nile. There are many shops both within the hotel and within a shopping arcade attached to the hotel. Fitness Club; Business Center, Conference and Banquet Facilities.

❑ **Ramses Hilton:** *1115 Corniche El Nil, Cairo, Egypt, Tel. (202) 574-4400, Fax (202) 575-7152, or toll-free from US & Canada (800) 445-8667.* Located in the heart of Cairo on the east bank of the Nile within walking distance of the shopping district, The Egyptian Antiquities Museum, and the Nile Hilton. Walking is made difficult by the many large and congested highways around the hotel. Newer than the Nile Hilton and more of a high-rise tower, the Ramses Hilton has just undergone a major renovation (2000) and both the 836 guest rooms and the public areas have been redesigned and refurbished. All rooms have balconies with view of the Nile or city. Executive Club floors offer additional amenities and services. Several restaurants include the Terrace Café for 24-hour dining; Citadel Grill offers steaks and seafood in an elegant setting; The Regent serves Chinese selections; and Falafel, an ethnic restaurant serving Oriental cuisines in an Egyptian atmosphere with folk dancing and belly dancing as entertainment. Shops are located within the hotel as well as across the street at the Ramses Hilton Shopping Center. Fitness Center; Business Center; Conference and Banquet Facilities.

❑ **Cairo Hilton World Trade Center Residence:** *World Trade Center, Corniche El Nil, Cairo, Egypt, Tel. (202) 580-2000, Fax 579-0577, or toll-free from US & Canada (800) 445-8667.* Hilton World Trade Center Residence is the third property for Hilton in Cairo. Overlooking the Nile, the 26-story residential tower within the World Trade Center consists of 104 luxury furnished apartments, ranging from two to four bedrooms and available for rental from a week to a year. Nightly rates are provided, so ask if bookings permit a shorter stay if your plans are for less than a full week. Eat in – preparing meals in your own kitchen – or dine out at any of the many eateries in the World Trade Center. During the summer months, El Takeiba restaurant offers residence guests Oriental cuisine in an authentic atmosphere overlooking the Nile. Residence accommodations are ideal for traveling families – the larger units even have separate nanny quarters. Direct access to World Trade Center shopping and entertainment; 24-hour security; 24-hour room service; housekeeping services; free parking; full-service Business Center within the World Trade Center mall.

❑ **Conrad International Cairo:** *1191 Corniche El Nil, Cairo, Egypt, Tel. (202)580-8000, Fax (202)580-8080.* If you are looking for a newly built five-star luxury hotel with all the amenities – including a separate shower and tub in the bath – and with a balcony that overlooks the Nile and within a few steps of a major shopping venue, you need look no further. The Conrad International fits the bill. The guest rooms are spacious and comfortable, the bath is roomy with a separate tub and shower enclosure, and the balcony with a view of the Nile is nicely configured. Executive Floor guests enjoy several extra services, including private express check-in/check-out; complimentary buffet breakfast in the Executive Lounge; and complimentary cocktails and hors d'oeuvres in the evening. The Felucca Café presents all-day dining with choices of international cuisines in a setting overlooking the Nile. Villa D'Este serves outstanding Italian cuisine in an elegant setting. Sea Market serves fresh fish as well as a choice of meats. The Atrium is a lovely lobby lounge set amidst palm trees and a soothing but modernistic appearing fountain. The Conrad is attached to the World Trade Center and provides easy access to the many shops there. Fitness Facilities; Business Center; Conference and Banquet Facilities.

❑ **Semiramis Inter-Continental Cairo:** *Corniche El Nil, Cairo, Egypt, Tel. (202) 355-7171, Fax (202) 356-3020, or toll-free from US & Canada (800) 327-0200. Website: www.interconti. com.* Located in the heart of the city along side the Nile and a short walk from the Egyptian Museum, the Semiramis was the first hotel built along the Nile River. The present building was constructed in 1987. All 840 guest rooms have balconies affording views of the Nile or the city. On Club Floors – a concept developed by Inter-Continental – guests enjoy the speed of a special check-in/check-out counter, the use of a private lounge, meeting rooms, and complimentary breakfast. Ten restaurants provide choices of Middle Eastern, specialty and international restaurants. Try Spaghetteria for Italian fare; the Bird Cage for Far Eastern cuisine or the Felucca Brasserie for international choices. For a special evening, Cairo's premiere French restaurant, The Grill, offers delicious entrees in an elegant setting overlooking the Nile. The Casino is open through the night and Haroun Al Rashid nightclub features top artists. Shopping Arcade; Fitness Center; Business Center; Convention and Banquet Facilities.

❑ **Cairo Marriott:** *Shar'a Saray al-Gezira, Zamalek, Cairo, Egypt, Tel. (202) 340-8888, Fax (202) 340-6667, or toll-free from U.S. & Canada (800) 228-9290.* Drive up to the Cairo Marriott Hotel and you will think you have arrived at a royal palace. The public areas of the Cairo Marriott are some of the most spectacular you will encounter as befits its royal origins. The Gezira Palace was built to accommodate the Empress Eugenie of France and her entourage for her visit to Cairo on the opening of the Suez Canal. The Gezira Palace has been described as the most beautiful building of modern Arabic style in its category. It is this palace that forms the heart of the public spaces in the Cairo Marriott, which was awarded the honor of "Best 5 Star Hotel in Egypt" in 1999. Enter one of the Marriott's 1,250 guest rooms and you could be in a Marriott anywhere in the world. The trappings of the palace – carved ceilings, marble staircase, columns, and beautiful filigree lamps – are left behind as you enter one of the two modern towers that house the guest rooms. Executive Floor guests enjoy additional services and amenities. There are 185 guest rooms designated as "Rooms that Work." These are specifically designed for the business traveler. Seven restaurants include Omar's Café which offers international selections; Tuscany serves Italian cuisine; JW's Steakhouse serves American choices; and Roy's Country Kitchen offers Southwestern dishes. The Marriott has a sizeable area of shops on the main floor as well as shops on the lower level surrounding a courtyard. The jewelry shop near the tower elevators on the first floor will make you wish you were Empress Eugenie! Fitness Facilities; Business Center; Conference and Banquet Facilities.

RESTAURANTS

Many of Cairo's best restaurants are found in the major international hotels and offer a variety of international cuisines. New five-star hotels, such as the Four Seasons and Conrad International, have added to the city's growing number of fine dining restaurants staffed with talented international chefs and well trained servers. You'll notice a big difference in the quality of food and service in these restaurants compared to many other restaurants in the city where service tends to be slow and the food uninspired.

Cairo residents tend to dine late for both lunch and dinner. Hours will change by seasons. Lunch often takes place between 2 and 4pm. Dinner can start at 7pm in many restaurants but doesn't really get going until 9 or 10pm. If you are an early diner, you'll often find yourself nearly alone in many restaurants.

Most major restaurants will serve alcohol. However, you may want to avoid the local wine, which is both cheap and dreadful (except at Villa D'Este). The local beer tends to be good.

It's a good idea to make reservations at most restaurants since their clientele is often unpredictable – some evenings the city's most popular restaurants are nearly empty and other evenings they are full.

ITALIAN

❑ **Villa D'Este:** *Conrad International Hotel, 1191 Corniche El Nil, Tel. 579-9399. Open 7:30pm to 12:30am.* If you only have time to dine at one fine restaurant in Cairo and you enjoy Italian cuisine, make sure it's Villa D'Este. It doesn't get any better than this in North Africa. This is simply one of Egypt's very finest restaurants. Serves outstanding Northern Italian cuisine and accompanied by the best service we encountered in Egypt. Excellent selection of wines, including a surprisingly good Egyptian wine! Everything is good, including the exceptional spaghetti and the Pavarotti music to complement your meal. Hopefully the current Italian chef plans to stay here for awhile.

❑ **Cortigiano:** *4 Michel Bakhum Street, Dokki, Tel. 337-4838. Open 1pm to 1am.* This moderately priced restaurant offers a good range of Italian specialties, from pizzas and pastas to meat and fish dishes.

FRENCH

❑ **The Grill:** *Semiramas Inter-Continental Hotel, Corniche El Nil, Garden City, Tel. 355-7171. Open 7pm to midnight.* This well appointed restaurant serves excellent French cuisine in an elegant setting accompanied by a pianist. Try the braised fillet of grouper and tiramisu. Excellent service. Nice ambiance with several tables overlooking the Nile River.

❑ **Justine:** *Four Corners, 4 Hassan Sabri Street, Tel. 341-2961. Open 1 to 3pm and 8 to 11pm.* This has been one of Cairo's finest French restaurants for over 15 years. Everything is good here, from starters to desserts. An elegant restaurant with excellent service.

❑ **Les Trèfles:** *Corniche El Nil, Boulaq, Tel. 579-6511. Open noon to midnight.* Located along the river and across the street from the Conrad International Hotel. While it has a reputation for being one of the best French restaurants in Cairo, it's most exceptional for its romantic indoor and outdoor settings. Continues with its legendary slow service – from placing an order to getting the check. Patience is not rewarded here.

MIDDLE EASTERN

❑ **Khan El Khalili Restaurant:** *5, El Badestan Lane, Khan El Khalili, Tel. 590-3788 or 593-2262. Open 10am to 2am.* Located in the heart of the world's oldest bazaar, the Khan El Khalili, this is a terrific oasis from the crowds of the market. Offers a varied menu of Egyptian and Lebanese specialties. Be sure to try their house specialties as well as

Om Ali for dessert – one of the best in Cairo. Includes a very popular attached coffee shop, Dr. Naguib Mahfouz Coffee Shop. Operated by the Oberoi Hotel chain.

❑ **Papillon:** *Opposite Tersana Shopping Centre, 26ᵗʰ of July Street, Mohandiseen, Tel. 347-1672. Open 11am to 1am.* Serves excellent Lebanese cuisine, especially lamb kebabs.

MEDITERRANEAN

❑ **Seasons Restaurant:** *Four Seasons Hotel, The First Residence, 35 Giza Street, Al Orman, Giza.* The signature restaurant of the Four Seasons Hotel, which serves excellent Mediterranean cuisine.

INDIAN

❑ **The Moghul Room:** *Mena House Oberoi Hotel, El-Haram Street, Tel. 383-3222.* This small but elegant restaurant serves excellent Indian cuisine. You can choose from a set menu or order a la carte. Includes excellent tandoori specialties. The kitchen will spice your dishes according to your specifications. Includes live music.

STEAKHOUSE

❑ **JW's Steakhouse:** *Cairo Marriott Hotel, Saray El-Gezirah Street, Tel. 339-4661. Open 1 to 4pm and 6:30pm to midnight.* If you're hungry for a big juicy American steak, JW's should be on your "must dine" list. Serves large T-bone steaks, surf-n-turf, and crab cakes. An American-style dining experience. Excellent service.

JAPANESE

❑ **Sushiyama:** *World Trade Center, Ground Floor, 1191 Corniche El Nil, Tel. 578-5161. Open noon to 3pm and 6pm to midnight.* Popular with Japanese (always a good sign), this elegant restaurant serves excellent *sushi* and *teppanyaki* (yes, the cooks put on the knife show at the grill tables).

SEEING THE SITES

Cairo is all about more than 5,000 years of history. Its many historical monuments and sites draw millions of visitors to

Egypt each year. For many first-time visitors, Cairo is primarily of interest because of its gateway location for seeing the many famous pyramids of ancient Egypt as well as for being home to the world-famous Egyptian Antiquities Museum with its exhibition of the fabulous treasures of Tutankhamun. But Cairo also has many other interesting sites that represent three additional historical periods: Islamic, Christian, and Contemporary.

PHARAONIC CAIRO

The major sites representing pharaonic Egypt lie along the desert fringes of the southwest section of the city. Most are within a pleasant yet chaotic 45-minute drive from downtown Cairo which takes you past colorful adobe villages, irrigated fields, and carpet centers. During high season, expect to encounter numerous bus loads of tourists and taxis crowding these sites. You'll also be greeted by many friendly and persistent hawkers and vendors selling postcards, head dresses, souvenirs, tourist kitsch (do you want a replica of the pyramids or a statue of Ramses II?), and drinks as well as offering photogenic camel and donkey rides (don't be surprised if a cell phone rings under the garments of the what initially may appears to be a poor camel or donkey vendor!).

If you primarily head for the three popular pyramids of Giza, you'll miss out on some of ancient Egypt's most important monuments, or what are known as the Monuments of the Old Kingdom. Indeed, you'll skip some important evolutionary elements in the history of the pyramids, starting with Memphis, proceeding to the pyramids and tombs of Sakkara, and then ending with the three pyramids of Giza. In fact, you should visit these sites in this sequence, starting with the farthest site (Memphis) and working your way to the nearest site (Giza):

❑ **Memphis:** Located 29 kilometers southwest of Cairo. Known as the old capital, the first unified capital of Egypt, which was founded in 3100 BC. Not much left here (most structures have been removed over time) except for a few interesting stone sculptures – the huge reclining Ramses II statue in the museum area being the most impressive – and vendors selling tourist kitsch.

❑ **Sakkara:** Located 25 kilometers southwest of Cairo. This is the burial site for the ancient city of Memphis. These are mastaba-type (trapezoid-shaped) tombs which approximate a pyramid form. The most famous is the Step Pyramid of

Djoser. Not quite pyramids but very important in the evolution of the perfect pyramid.

❑ **Pyramids of Giza:** Located 12 kilometers southwest of Cairo. Giza's three pyramids of Khufu (Cheops or the Great Pyramid), Khafre (Chephren), and Menkaure (Mycerinus), along with the nearby Great Sphinx, are what draw millions of visitors to Egypt each year. This is a busy site with buses, taxis, vans, cars, camels, horses, and donkeys competing for space amidst the pyramids. Be sure to also visit the impressive nearby Solar Boat Museum which is the highlight of many visits to this area.

If time permits, you also may want to visit several other pyramids found at these three nearby sites: Zawiyat al-Aryan, Abu Sir (Sahure, Nyuserre, and Neferirkare Pyramids), and Dahshur (North, Bent, and Black Pyramids).

Any visit to Egypt and Cairo would be incomplete without visiting the **Egyptian Antiquities Museum**. This is one of the world's great museums, and if the crowds tell you anything, it is one of the world's most fascinating repositories of history. You can easily spend days here getting caught up in the history of ancient Egypt. Room after room is jam-packed with marble statues, granite sarcophagi, mummies, jewelry, tools, inscriptions, furniture, weapons, models, carvings, and numerous fascinating objects discovered in the tombs of pharaohs, royalty, and workers. The museum's most popular attraction is found on the second floor – the treasures of King Tutankhamun. The level and quality of sophisticated artistry are truly impressive. Much of the treasure is in gold and wood. Indeed, the wood furniture and statuary alone testify to the quality and preservation of this collection. On a busy day, you may have trouble navigating through this exhibit. It can be wall-to-wall people, many of these with organized tour groups, pushing and shoving to get from one fascinating exhibition to another. The largest crowds tend to appear in the morning, especially at opening time, 9am. The best time to visit is in the afternoon, around 1:30pm. The museum closes at 4:30pm. Our recommendation: visit the pyramids first and then visit this museum. The museum will have more meaning once you've had a chance to see many of the tombs and pyramids.

ISLAMIC CAIRO

In addition to the more than 1,000 minarets that accent Cairo's skyline, you'll find numerous monuments and museums that catalog Cairo's Islamic history. Some of the major sites to visit include:

❑ **Mosque of Ibn Tulun:** Completed in 879, this large complex is especially noted for its unique architecture – unlike any other in Egypt. Be sure to climb the crumbling staircase of the tower from which you can get a panoramic view of both the mosque and city. Great photo opportunity.

❑ **Gayer Anderson Museum (Bayt El-Kretlea):** Located near the Mosque of Ibn Tulun, this restored Ottoman house of Major Gayer-Anderson, an Englishman who served in the Egyptian civil service during the 1930s and 1940s, is well worth a visit for its fascinating architecture and furnishings.

❑ **Mosque and Madrasa of Sultan Hassan and Mosque of Al-Rifai:** These two adjacent mosques are rich with history. The Mosque and Madrasa of Sultan Hassan was built in the 14th century and remains one of the largest mosques in the world. The Mosque of Al-Rifai was built in the late 19th century and is noted as the burial site for members of the last royal family, the last Shah of Iran, and various religious leaders.

❑ **The Citadel:** Once the site of Cairo's great fortress which ruled over the city for over 700 years (from 1168), today this impressive hill houses the Museum of Military History, Mohammand Ali's Alabastor mosque and palace, and several other structures of historical note.

❑ **Museum of Islamic Art:** One of Cairo's best museums which is often overlooked by visitors. Includes a terrific range of items from more than 1,000 years of Islamic history in Egypt. You can easily spend an hour or more leisurely enjoying the many wonderful displays in the absence of crowds.

COPTIC CAIRO

Egypt has played a very important role in the evolution of Christianity. Its Coptic, or Christian, tradition dates from the time of Christ. Indeed, the Holy Family spent some time in Egypt evading persecution by Herod in what is today Israel. Many of Cairo's ancient churches have been preserved and are open to visitors interested in Egypt's Christian tradition.

One of the first things you need to know about Christianity

in Egypt is its Coptic origins. An orthodox religious sect, the Christians in Egypt are known as the Coptics. They have evolved their own doctrines and traditions separate from Christians elsewhere in the world. They even have their own pope which is neither recognized by, nor deferential to, the Catholic pope in Rome. The second thing you need to know is that the remains of the early churches in Cairo are very old – no grand architecture or huge edifices. Most of the churches are very small and in a continual state of repair or disrepair. Nonetheless, they are fascinating places to visit, with their many interesting sanctuaries and icons. The major Coptic sites worth visiting include:

❑ **Coptic Museum:** This rather eclectic and worn museum houses the largest collection of Coptic Christian artifacts. Displayed over two floors, it catalogs an important and continuing chapter in Egyptian history.

❑ **The Hanging (Al Moallaqa) Church:** Initially constructed in the 9th century and subsequently rebuilt several times, this is a most unusual church for most Christians. Includes an impressive marble pulpit dating from the 11th century, a sanctuary screen, and numerous icons.

❑ **St. Sergius Church:** The oldest church in Cairo originally constructed in the 5th century and rebuilt several times. Noted for its altar which was built over the area where the Holy Family is believed to have stayed while fleeing from King Herod.

❑ **Church of St. Mercurius:** Once the cathedral church of Cairo, today this aging structure houses many impressive icons, carved marble windows, and painted marble columns.

❑ **Convent of St. George:** Currently housing over 30 nuns, the convent is especially noted for its impressive reception hall with its huge wooden door.

Related to the Coptic tradition, as well as in the same general geographic area of Old Cairo, surrounded by 29 mosques and 20 churches, is Egypt's oldest Jewish synagogue, the **Ben Ezra Synagogue** (Hara al-Qadisa Burbara, Tel. 354-2695). This beautiful old structure is well preserved and well worth a visit while touring this section of Cairo. Today, only about 50 Jewish families remain in Cairo. Donations are welcomed.

CONTEMPORARY CAIRO

Cairo has a lot to offer visitors who want to understand contemporary Cairo and Egypt. Here are some of the favorite activities of many visitors to the city:

❑ **Cairo Tower:** Zoharia Gardens, Gezirah Island. 9am to midnight (closed during lunchtime). For a panoramic view of the city, go to the observation deck at the top of this 187-meter tower, the tallest concrete tower in the Middle East. Includes a café and revolving restaurant.

❑ **Dr. Ragab's Pharaonic Village:** Jacob's Island, Giza, Tel. 729-186. Visit this re-enactment of ancient Egyptian life and work. A guided tour takes visitors by a floating amphitheater.

❑ **Cairo Zoo:** Giza on Sharia Giza (near entrance to Cairo University). Open 8:30am to 4pm. Very popular with locals, this zoo offers a nice collection of tropical animals and birds.

❑ **Felucca ride:** Take a break from the hustle and bustle of street-level Cairo by hiring a *felucca* for a relaxing one- to two-hour sail along the Nile River in the downtown area along the Corniche. The boats take up to 10 passengers and are relatively inexpensive.

ENTERTAINMENT

You can always find something to do in this city which starts late and stays up late. Since dinner often begins around 10pm, you may find your evening fully occupied at a restaurant. Don't expect to find world-class entertainment here. The city is relatively sedate, although it does have its own brand of local entertainment. Many visitors focus on these forms of evening entertainment:

❑ **Dinner cruise on the Nile:** Several companies offer nightly dinner cruises on the Nile. This usually includes a buffet dinner accompanied by a belly dancer, whirling dervish dancers, musicians, and singers. A delightful way to spend the evening along the pleasant river with the city lights and restaurants lining the shore. Some of the best cruises are offered by The Pharaohs Cruising Restaurants which is operated by the Oberoi Hotels. Includes an excellent program of belly dancing and musicians.

❑ **Cultural events:** Check out the local English-language *Middle East Times, al-Ahram Weekly*, and *Egypt Today* for information on what's happening in the arts, especially art exhibitions, opera, and musical performances. If you are planning to be in Egypt during October, check to see if the famous Aida Opera will be presented at the Pyramids of Giza.

❑ **Sound and light show:** Don't miss the popular nightly sound and light show that takes place at the Great Sphinx in Giza. Check times for English language presentations.

❑ **Bars:** Most major hotels have bars which include some entertainment. Try **Harry's Pub** at the Cairo Marriott Hotel; **Oasis Bar** at the Cairo Sheraton Hotel; **Pyramids Bar** and **Traverne du Champs de Mars** at the Nile Hilton Hotel; **Windows on the World** at the Ramses Hilton Hotel; and **Cheers** and the **Piano Piano** at the World Trade Center.

❑ **Discos:** Most discos are found in hotels and operate from 9 or 10pm to 3 or 4am. Check out the action at **Jackie's Joint** in the Nile Hilton Hotel; **Le Disco** at the Gezirah Sheraton, Gezirah (11pm to 5am); **Barracuda** at the Le Meridien Heliopolis; **Papillon** at the Mövenpick Hotel in Heliopolis; and **Saddle** at the Mena House Oberoi Hotel.

❑ **Nightclubs:** Several nightclubs operate in Cairo. However, most of them are for locals and are in Arabic.

❑ **Casinos:** Designed for foreigners (Egyptians are prohibited from gambling due to Muslim strictures), several casinos operate in the major hotels: Cairo Sheraton, Helnan Shepheard, Mena House Oberoi, Sofitel Cairo, Semiramis Inter-Continental, Ramses Hilton, Sheraton Heliopolis, Nile Hilton, El-Gezira Sheraton, Mövenpick Heliopolis, and Cairo Marriott.

Alexandria

DON'T VISIT EGYPT WITHOUT AT LEAST spending a day or two in legendary Alexandria, once the second largest city in the Roman Empire. Known as "The Pearl of the Mediterranean" and hosting nearly 2 million visitors a year, who are mainly Egyptians, Alexandria is an ideal destination for independent travelers who wish to absorb the pleasant ambience of this city without the attendant pressure from tour guides, sightseeing schedules, and street touts that characterize visits to many other parts of Egypt. If you're tired of visiting another hot, crowded, and tout-laced tomb, pyramid, monument, and light show – and love ocean views and breezes and well as great seafood, outdoor cafes, and pleasant walks – consider heading for Alexandria as soon as possible. It's the Egypt many Cairo residents dream about.

WELCOME TO REAL CIVILIZATION

Welcome to a living civilization perched on top of a buried ancient civilization. Founded in 322 BC by Alexander the Great, Alexandria today is a relatively clean, green, uncongested, and tout-free city where nice beaches, restaurants, casi-

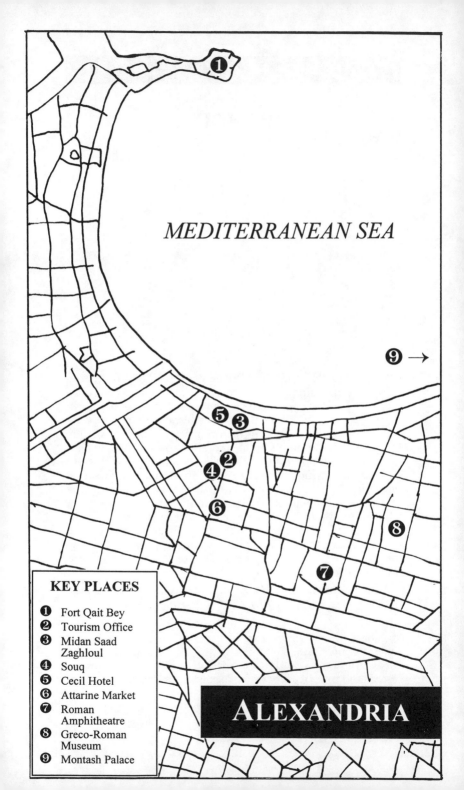

MEDITERRANEAN SEA

9 →

5 **3**

2

4

6

8

7

KEY PLACES

1 Fort Qait Bey
2 Tourism Office
3 Midan Saad
  Zaghloul
4 Souq
5 Cecil Hotel
6 Attarine Market
7 Roman
  Amphitheatre
8 Greco-Roman
  Museum
9 Montash Palace

ALEXANDRIA

nos, discos, nightclubs, shopping, and Internet cafes are the order of the day! Like a good wine, cosmopolitan Alexandria is best savored alone and on your own time. It's one of Egypt's, and the Middle East's, best kept travel secrets. Most important of all, Alexandria is a great escape from the hordes of tourists that occupy so many of Egypt's popular historical sites south of Alexandria.

If you're interested in a beach resort popular with locals, Alexandria has a lot to offer. However, it's not the same as the more Western-oriented beach resorts in the Sinai Peninsula, especially the world-class diving center at Sharm el-Sheikh or even Hurghada, which offer a good range of water sports, restaurants, and entertainment. Alexandria is essentially beach and seafood minus the many attractions that accompany major international resorts. For beach lovers, its main attraction is its convenience in relationship to Cairo: two hours up the highway and you're facing the blue waters of the Mediterranean Sea.

A SURPRISINGLY EUROPEAN CITY

Spread along the Mediterranean for nearly 20 kilometers, Alexandria is the second largest city in Egypt and the country's major port. It's also the principal beach resort destination for Cairo residents and the country's industrial powerhouse. Located nearly 230 kilometers northwest of Cairo and con- nected to it by two excellent highways (Delta Road and Desert Road) and a railroad line, it can easily be reached by car within two hours. It also can be reached by train which leaves hourly during the day between 5am and 10pm. Because of its close proximity to Cairo, many visitors make a day trip to Alexandria.

Alexandria often gets mixed reviews from culturally oriented travelers and travel guides that primarily focus on ancient history and culture. Some advise you to skip this city altogether since it appears unattractive and doesn't seem to have much noteworthy sightseeing compared to all the pharonic antiquities spread along the upper and lower Nile Valley. Not surprisingly, Alexandria often gets characterized like this: it's historically one of the world's greatest cities (the site of one of the Seven Wonders of the Ancient World, the Pharos Lighthouse, as well as famous for the Great Library, Cleopatra, Julius Caesar, Mark Antony, and Octavian), but it has little to show for all its great historical significance. In other words, lacking many excavated historical sites and monuments, it doesn't measure up well with the rest of ancient Egypt. True, but so what? There's a time and a place to be a "cultural" tourist – especially south of the Delta region – and there's a time and a place to be a relaxed and pampered traveler – which is what Alexandria is all about. Just don't come to Alexandria looking for things that don't exist. Instead, do with Egyptians do – enjoy the pleasures of this city.

Indeed, Egyptians love this place – great beaches, great seafood, great sidewalk cafes, great weather, great ambience – more so than many foreign visitors who seem to be in search of something else. Much of the "real Egypt" evacuates itself on weekends from Cairo and heads for relaxing Alexandria and its nearby beach resort areas west of the city. Transforming itself into a popular Middle East summer resort, with gorgeous beaches and attractive scenery running 40 kilometers along the Mediterranean – from Abu Kir in the east to Sidi Abdul Rahman in the west – the city also has very temperate winters that appeal to visitors. If it weren't for jobs being concentrated in Cairo, many Egyptians would move to Alexandria in a heartbeat; they dream of some day living in Alexandria where life can be wonderful!

❑ Alexandria is one of Egypt's, and the Middle East's, best kept travel secrets.

❑ Alexandria is the major beach resort destination for Cairo residents and the country's industrial powerhouse.

❑ Egyptians love this place, more so than many foreign visitors who seem to be in search of something else.

❑ Alexandria lacks the chaos, pollution, and stress of Cairo. It's a relatively clean and orderly city that works reasonably well.

❑ For Egyptians, this is a wonderful resort city boasting great restaurants, green parks, wide streets, pleasant walks, and friendly people.

Unless you are a diehard history buff who's obsessed with seeing more tombs and monuments, Alexandria more than holds its own when it comes to enjoying the treasures and pleasures of travel in Egypt. Just stop at one of its waterfront cafes or seafood restaurants overlooking the Mediterranean and you'll quickly understand why this is such a favorite destination for Egyptians. Alexandria is different from the rest of Egypt. In many respects, it has a lot more to offer than other more heavily trafficked tourist centers.

Alexandria is one of those surprising and seductive places you tend to discover once you get there. During its more than 2,300-year history, this fascinating city has undergone many transformations. Going from one of the world's greatest cities in the time of Alexander the Great to a relatively quiet backwater city for nearly 2,000 years, it re-emerged in the 19th century as a wild and decadent international city run by a combination of immigrant Greeks, Armenians, Jews, and Italians who controlled its fate well into the 20th century. Alexandria most recently became a relatively tame resort, port, and industrial city in the aftermath of the Egyptian revolution of the 1950s that saw many of its powerful nationalities flee the country due to a combination of wars with Israel and the nationalization of businesses. On top of lacking a monumental history, it no longer was much fun for the international jet set and expatriates who frequented its shores. The good news is that Alexandria is likely to soon transform itself again into a major tourist destination as it rises from its more than four decades of slumber.

Indeed, this city has many treasures and pleasures that require more time than a quick day trip from Cairo. In fact, many visitors lament the fact that they planned too few hours in Alexandria. Many wish they had allotted two to three days here, especially after discovering its antique market (Attarine) and many seafood restaurants. This unique city will give you a totally different perspective on this country – a Greco-Roman and Mediterranean rather than a pharaonic and desert view of Egypt. A sprawling oceanfront city of nearly 5 million people, Alexandria is very different from Cairo and other places in Egypt. Indeed, it's a different world for local residents and visitors alike. Above all, it's a city with an abundance of water lapping at its attractive shoreline.

If your image of Egypt has been largely shaped by the Nile, pyramids, tombs, temples, and desert of Cairo and Upper Egypt, Alexandria may come as a delightful surprise. Once a very colonial, cosmopolitan, and decadent European city, with a diverse mix of Greeks, Armenians, Turks, Jews, Christians, Arabs, French, Levantines, and other nationalities and religious groups – the place where many Europeans fled to during World War II – today's Alexandria is very much an Egyptian city that still retains a European and Mediterranean character, especially when it comes to restaurants and food. Except for the numerous Greeks and Armenians who remain and operate much of the city's commercial sector, gone are other national groups, who left as a consequence of the nationalist revolution, the national-ization of businesses, and the ruinous wars with Israel in the 1950s, 1960s, and 1970s.

Laid back, easygoing, and somewhat worn, with few foreign visitors, Alexandria is Egypt's main industrial and shipping city that also exudes a feel of an up-and-coming sleepy seaside resort. Best of all, Alexandria lacks the chaos, pollution, and stress of Cairo. Locals, with their bias toward things European, see themselves as more cultured, sophisticated, and worldly than their brethren to the south. It's a relatively clean and orderly city that works reasonably well. For Egyptians, this is a wonderful resort city boasting wonderful restaurants, green parks, wide streets, pleasant walks, and friendly people. It's a great escape from desert Egypt. It's also the gateway city to some of the Mediterranean's finest beaches, mostly located several kilometers west of the city, where Cairo residents increasingly escape to for long weekends and holidays.

Alexandria residents rightfully love their city. For them, there's no better place, even in Europe, than this Egyptian Riviera city. Its 25-kilometer long Corniche offers an attractive skyline with beaches, hotels, and restaurants – and Alexandria's two main attractions, Fort Qait Bey and the Montazah Palace grounds – facing the placid ocean. Excellent restaurants and cafes abound in this balmy city on the ocean.

Our advice: visit Alexandria soon before it becomes a major tourist attraction with all the attendant crowds, touts, and rising prices. In many respects, Alexandria is one of those undiscovered travel gems that surprises visitors, who often leave wishing they had scheduled more time for this city. Give it at least two, if not three, days of your travel time. Unless you are obsessed with discovering even more tombs, ruins, and outdoor monuments, you won't be disappointed with Alexandria. You just need to approach it differently from other places in Egypt – approach it like an Egyptian.

GETTING TO KNOW YOU

For history buffs, Alexandria may be a disappointment, especially after spending several days seeing Egypt's many pyramids, temples, tombs, mosques, and churches. From all physical appearances, Alexandria seems to lack a grand, monumental history. On the other hand, Alexandria may become one of the highlights of your trip to Egypt, especially if you have become "tombed out" from your tourist adventures in Cairo, Luxor, and Aswan. Pharonic, Islamic, and Christian Egypt lie south of Alexandria, along the Nile and in the desert. Greco-Roman history is centered in Alexandria, and it lies either under the ocean or beneath the city proper. Only a few historical monuments, such as the Roman Theater and Fort Qait Bey, remain visible in what was once the world's greatest city. The city also boasts over 200 churches in addition to its hundreds of mosques.

Alexandria is the city founded by Alexander the Great in the 4th century BC and subsequently became noted as a great Greek and Roman city, the place of Cleopatra, Julius Caesar, Mark Antony, the Great Library, and one of the Seven Wonders of the Ancient World – Pharos or the Lost Lighthouse of

Alexandria. All are gone. Many succumbed to the cataclysmic earthquakes that buried much of the city more than 12 meters below the ocean in the 6th and 7th centuries AD.

Since the present city is the culmination of several cities that have been built on top of each other, many ancient ruins lie only a few meters below the city. New construction projects often intrude into these ancient ruins. Indeed, modernizing Alexandria is a slow and often painful process because of all the delicate ruins that lie just below the surface. Constructing a building in Alexandria can become a construction-halting adventure in uncovering antiquities!

Unlike Cairo, Luxor, Aswan, and Abu Simbel, Alexandria has yet to fully uncover its rich historical past. Once it does, it will most likely become a major tourist attraction for those who enjoy seeing the physical remnants of history and culture. However, plans are underway to create a unique tourist experience to explore the ancient ruins – scuba diving and submarine tours of the old city that lies submerged off of the Corniche. Rather than recover the monuments from the ocean floor and resurrect them on land, the plan is to take tourists into the water to view the watery setting of the fabled city of Alexandria.

UNIQUE TREASURES AND PLEASURES

Alexandria offers numerous treasures and pleasures to keep you busy for at least three days. If you enjoyed shopping in Cairo, you'll find Alexandria to be added value and without the hassle of pushy merchants and pesky touts. While not numerous, its treasures are different, especially in the case of antiques, furniture, and leather. Indeed, Alexandria is the best place in Egypt to buy such items. Alexandria also is relatively hip, with its numerous fine restaurants, cafes, casinos, discos, nightclubs, and beaches. Unlike more conservative and Egyptian Cairo, Alexandria has a more international atmosphere and a greater tolerance for enjoying the good life.

Alexandria also has its share of historical ruins and monuments, although a great deal still lies under both the sea and city. Nonetheless, history buffs and sightseers will find enough interesting things to see and do for at least one full day.

In preparation for the treasures and pleasures of Alexandria, we recommend visiting these websites which provide relatively current information on all aspects of the city:

http://touregypt.net/alexandria/
www.alex-guide.com
http://ce.eng.usf.edu/pharos/alexandria
http://alexandriaegypt.com

The community BBS section on the *TourEgypt.net* site may put you in touch with recent travelers to Alexandria as well as local residents.

THE STREETS OF ALEXANDRIA

This is by no means a beautiful city. While its ocean-view setting is exquisite, its architecture leaves much to be desired. The streets may be wider, cleaner, quieter, and less polluted than in Cairo, but it still has a worn 50s look about it. Alexandria looks like it's somewhere between Havana and Tel Aviv. While it may be a popular seaside resort with many visitors from nearby Arab countries, it has a long way to go before it challenges other major beach-front cities of the world.

❑ This is by no means a beautiful city. It looks like it's somewhere between Havana and Tel Aviv.

❑ This is a sprawling east-west city that hugs the oceanfront for nearly 25 kilometers.

❑ Some of the best buys in Egyptian leather goods can be found in Alexandria.

❑ The most interesting shopping is found in the many antique and furniture shops that line the side streets of the Attarine Market district.

Alexandria is a city that promises to someday become an important tourist center. Compared to chaotic Cairo, Alexandria feels like a well planned city thrust along many kilometers of beautiful beaches. It's a kind of Islamic version of Miami, Rio, Cannes, and Monaco, minus the beautiful people and trendy shops, restaurants and entertainment spots; it even has its own summer palace with lovely gardens, scenic views of the ocean, and a boutique hotel (Salamlek) built to house Abbas II's mistress. It has the look and feel of a resort city that also is into the heavy lifting attendant to being a shipping and industrial center. Streets sometimes run parallel to each other and are relatively wide, orderly, and clean. With a good map of the city, you should be able to navigate Alexandria on your own. And with a car and driver, you'll be able to quickly navigate this city.

This is a sprawling east-west city that hugs the oceanfront for nearly 25 kilometers. The city has little north-south depth since it is set back only one to three kilometers from the attractive Corniche. As a result, the Corniche becomes the central reference point for navigating most parts of this city. It's a great place to walk and sightsee, although distances between major sites can be considerable. You'll find plenty of inexpensive public transportation, from trams to taxis, to take you around the city.

Most visitors focus on two sections of the city which are located approximately 18 kilometers from each other – the city center to the west, which includes Fort Qait Bey, and the Montazah Palace grounds to the east, which include beautiful gardens, luxury hotels (Palestine and Salamlek), and scenic views.

The center of the city extends from the city's main tram center at Midan Ramla to an adjacent large square, Midan Saad Zaghloul, that extends north to the ocean. It also includes the peninsula area that encompasses the city's major attraction, Fort Qait Bay. Within this two square-kilometer area you'll find numerous hotels, restaurants, shops, airline offices, and the tourist office.

You may want to initially start at the tourist office (Tel. 807-9885) where you can pick up brochures, ask questions, and arrange for a guide. This office is located at the center of the city at the southwest corner of Midan Saad Zaghloul. It's open from 8am to 6pm during most of the year (9am to 4pm during Ramadan).

SHOPPING ALEXANDRIA

Alexandria is by no means a shopper's paradise, especially after Cairo. While it has a few interesting *souks*, a unique antique market, and a few malls, it has nothing to compare to Cairo's massive Khan al-Khalili. Some of the best buys in Egyptian leather goods can be found in Alexandria simply because most of the leather factories are located near this city. However, this is not Gucci territory when it comes to quality leather goods.

Alexandria includes many small nondescript shops, *souks*, and old alleys in the center of the city (Sharia Nokrashi and Sharia Faransa Streets at Midan Tahrir or Midan Mansheiyya and the narrow streets south and west of Midan Saad Zaghloul) but nothing comparable to the shops and *souks* in Cairo or even Luxor. In fact, if you visit the tourist office at the southwest corner of Midan Saad Zaghloul, just walk a few meters and you will be in the heart of the downtown shopping district. You can easily shop this area within an hour or less. Here you'll find a large array of food, clothes, leather goods, cotton, silver, gold, and household items which primarily appeal to local residents. Leather goods, especially shoes, are a particularly good buy in

Alexandria since most Egyptian leather goods are produced at the factories in and around this city. Many of the best shoe stores, including ones that sell custom-made shoes, are found along Falaki Street. But don't expect to find many fashionable or quality shoes in Alexandria.

The most interesting shopping for visitors is found in the many antique and furniture shops that line the side streets of the **Attarine Market** district. This area alone is worth a visit to Alexandria. Variously spelled Attarine, Attereen, or Attarien, this market lies approximately 1,000 meters south of the historic Cecil Hotel and 500 meters directly west of the Masr Train Station.

Attarine Market is a working market with many shops also operating as workshops where you can observe artisans at work refurbishing antique furniture and other collectibles. It also represents the best antique and furniture market in Egypt. It includes dozens of shops offering rugs, furniture (both old and reproduction), inlaid boxes and tables, Syrian chairs, ceramics, French-style furniture, brass pots, coffee grinders, lights, clocks, pictures, and old house doors. Part of this market has the look and feel of an upscale flea market. But most of the market appeals to serious collectors of antiques and furniture. Many visitors and expatriates who prowl this market find the antique French reproduction and inlaid furniture and accessory pieces to be especially appealing.

If you've already shopped Cairo, you may recognize many similar items in the Attarine Market Indeed, much of the antiques and furniture found in Cairo, especially in the Zamalek area, come from these shops in Alexandria. Not surprising, prices on such items are much better in Alexandria than in Cairo, although it's always "buyer beware" when purchasing such items. While prices may initially seem high, be sure to bargain for everything in this market. Offering many treasures left behind by Alexandria's wealthy European residents who lived here prior to the Egyptian revolution of the 1950s, as well as excellent quality French reproduction furniture, these shops are fun to browse for unique items from Europe and the Middle East. If you only visit Alexandria for a day, you may discover you failed to leave enough time to shop this area of the city. The narrow streets are lined with many shops filled with treasures that can easily take a few hours of earnest shopping time. Plan to spend at least two hours going from shop to shop. You'll find numerous shops lining five narrow streets offering beautiful restored antique and reproduction furniture, chandeliers, and collectibles.

The Attarine Market area includes too many interesting

shops to list here. However, we especially like **Moutafa** for reproduction French antique furniture; **Mahmoed el Deray** (Tel. 495-1416, El Lethy Street) for beautiful old doors from Egyptian houses; **Hag Hassan Teima** (6 Rue El-Kefah, Tel. 490-9524) for inlaid furniture and brass items; **Abbas Hamza** (7, Youssef Moghaira Street, Tel. 493-0658) for French-style reproduction furniture; **El Shamy** (23 El-Shek Aly Ellice Street, Tel. 491-3104) for furniture, paintings, ceramics, and lights; and **Mohamed E. Habahy** (10, El-Shikh Aly Elp-Lesy Street, Tel. 492-0670) for two floors of antique and reproduction furniture.

While you may find some lovely furniture here, be sure to check on shipping before making a major purchase. While Alexandria is the country's major shipping center, many of these shops are primarily oriented to servicing the local Egyptian and expatriate market. They may or may not be experienced in international packing and shipping.

ACCOMMODATIONS

Alexandria offers a good range of three-, four-, and five-star properties as well as several budget hotels. Some of the best properties include:

❑ **Sofitel Alexandria Cecil:** *26 July Street, Saad Zaghloul Square, Alexandria, Egypt, Tel. (203) 483-7173 or Fax (203) 483-6401.* A grand old hotel, recently refurbished to suit the expectations of 21st century travelers. The classic revolving door at the main entrance and the elevators retain the elegance and period feel of the Cecil when it first opened in 1930. With a view of the harbor and its location in the heart of the business, shopping, and entertainment district, the Cecil's setting is ideal for these venues, although noise can be an issue for those unaccustomed to the bustle of a busy city center. The Cecil's 83 guest rooms and 3 suites offer the expected amenities. Though under French management, the staff is Egyptian, and a facility may be closed because the employee who has the key cannot be found. Restaurants include Le Plat d'Or for French cuisine, Le Rang Mahal for Indian food, and Le Jardin, a 24-hour café, serves buffets or a la carte. A full service hotel. Fitness Room; Business Services.

❑ **El-Salamlek Palace Hotel:** *Montazah Palace, (P.O. Box 258) Alexandria, Egypt, Tel. (203) 547-7999 or Fax (203) 547-*

3585. Built in 1892 by the Khedive for his mistress, this former palace has been converted to a boutique hotel. Sited on a hill overlooking the Mediterranean, many rooms have a water view. Each room is unique and guest rooms vary greatly in size and decor. Some guest rooms are spacious, whereas others seem cramped. So get particulars before booking. Al-Farida Café is open 24 hours serving a variety of snacks, sandwiches and fresh juices. Prince Café overlooks the Mediterranean and serves snacks, juices, ice cream and beverages. Many visitors stop by El- Salamlek Palace for lunch as part of a day's outing to the beaches in the area. Qatr El-Nada Garden overlooks the sea and gardens and serves lunch, dinner and snacks. Includes a casino.

❑ **Marriott Renaissance Alexandria Hotel:** *544 El Geish Avenue, Sidi Bishr, Alexandria, Egypt, Tel. (203) 548-3977 or Fax (203) 549-7690.* A modern high-rise hotel 20 minutes from downtown, the Marriott Renaissance overlooks the Mediterranean. Most rooms overlook the sea as well as the swimming pool. Guest rooms are modern and offer the expected amenities. Chinese cuisine is served in an authentic setting at Dynasty Restaurant; Northern Italian cuisine is served at Italian Restaurant; the El Bardy Coffee Shop serves a variety of dishes from Egypt as well as international fare. Full service hotel. Fitness Center; Business Center; Meeting Facilities.

❑ **Sheraton Montazah Hotel:** *Corniche Road, Montazah, Alexandria, Egypt, Tel. (203) 548-0550 or Fax (203) 540-1331.* One of the newer hotels in Alexandria–high-rise and modern. A beachfront location affords views of the Mediterranean, and 279 guest rooms and 17 mini-suites offer the expected amenities. Five restaurants serve a wide variety of cuisines. Fitness Facilities; Meeting Rooms.

❑ **Helnan Palestine Hotel:** *Montazah Palace Gardens, Postal Code #21919, Alexandria, Egypt, Tel. (203) 547-3500, Fax (203) 547-3378. Website: www.helnan.com.* The Helnan Palestine Hotel has a unique location overlooking the Montazah Royal Beach and Gardens surrounded by 350 acres of gardens inside the Montazah Park. The hotel was built to accommodate the Arab kings and heads of state participating in the Second Arab Summit in 1964. The hotel was most recently renovated in 1999. All 222 guest rooms and suites overlook the Mediterranean Sea and the Royal Gardens and offer all the expected services and amenities.

Pista Pasta features Italian cuisine; Sea Horse serves 24 hours a day and has a sea view; Sea Breeze is an open BBQ and is open during the summer months. The Zodiac Lobby Café and The Terrace serve light snacks and beverages. The Royal Garden features an Oriental Café. Water activities include diving, windsurfing, and fishing boats. Indoor activities include table tennis, billiards, computer games, a children's playground, and a pool. Business Services; Meeting Facilities.

❏ **Hilton Borg El Arab Resort:** *Matroub Road, Alexandria, Egypt, Tel. (203) 990 730, Fax (203) 990 760 or toll-free from the U.S. or Canada (800) 445-8667.* Located on the beautiful white sand of the North Coast with a view of the Mediterranean Sea, the Hilton's 247 guest rooms spanning four floors offer either sea or garden view rooms. Rooms are decorated in pastel turquoise, coral and beige that complement the colors of the beach and sea outside. Rooms have private balconies. Guest rooms have all expected amenities, and baths have separate tub and shower areas. Some restaurants include The Mermaid, which serves breakfast buffets and dinner theme nights. The Sun Set Café coffee shop serves snacks and light meals. Shells serves seafood and is open for lunch and dinner. Discotheque. Small Shopping Arcade. Fitness Club; Business Services; Conference and Banquet Facilities.

RESTAURANTS

Alexandria is well known for its wonderful seafood. Indeed, many residents of Cairo come to Alexandria just to sample its seafood restaurants which also tend to be relatively inexpensive. The city also is noted for its Greek dishes and pastries. You can't go wrong trying some of these restaurants which represent the best in dining when visiting Alexandria:

❏ **Fish Market:** *El-Mina El-Sharkeya, Bahari, Tel. 480-1119.* Located on the Corniche near Fort Qait Bey and overlooking the Eastern Harbour, this is one of three food outlets operated by the Americana Company (Grand Café and Tikka Grill are the other two). Serves excellent seafood in a delightful oceanfront setting. One of Alexandria's very best.

❏ **Tikka Grill:** *El-Mina El Sharkeya, Bahari, Tel. 480-5114.* One of our favorite restaurants with a wonderful waterfront setting overlooking the Eastern Harbour. Popular with locals, expats, and travelers, this restaurant serves a wide range of excellent dishes, including many spicy Indian dishes along with Egyptian, Italian, Greek, and seafood dishes. Offers an excellent salad bar.

❑ **Grand Café:** *El-Mina El Sharkeya, Bahari, Tel. 480-1119.* Open for dinner only. Located next door to the Tikka Grill, this romantic outdoor garden restaurant serves excellent Egyptian dishes, especially kebabs.

❑ **San Giovanni:** *San Giovanni Hotel, 205 Shari' el-Geish Stanley, Tel. 546-7774.* Excellent dining on the Corniche. Offers many fine European and Middle Eastern seafood dishes in a delightful setting.

❑ **Al-Saraya (also known as al-Fayrouz):** *El Geish Street, Stanley Bay, Tel. 546-7773.* Offers an ideal oceanfront setting for some of the best seafood in Alexandria. Excellent service.

❑ **Grand Trianon:** *Maydan Saad Zaghlul, Raml Station, Tel. 482-0986.* One of Alexandria's most elegant restaurants which exudes the style of a bygone era, especially the 1920s. More famous for its ambience and decor than for its many acceptable dishes. Still popular with Alexandria's French-speaking residents.

❑ **Zephrion:** *41 Khaled Ibn-el Walid Street, Abou Qir, Tel. 560-1319.* Located in a small village about 20 minutes east of Montazah, this popular seafood restaurant serves excellent fresh seafood along the beach. Worth the extra 40 minutes to get here from downtown Alexandria.

❑ **Alexanders:** *Ramada Renaissance Hotel, 544 Sharia el-Geish, Sidi Bishr, Tel. 549-0935.* Serves excellent seafood with a nice view of the sea.

❑ **Elite:** *43 Sharia Safeya Zaghloul, Tel. 482-3592.* Centrally located, this popular Greek restaurant serves everything from fresh seafood kebabs to a good range of tempting Egyptian dishes. Large portions.

❑ **Samakmak:** *42 Shara Ras al-Tin, Gomrouk, Tel. 481-1560.* Offers excellent seafood in a less than appealing neighborhood (down at the docks).

❑ **New China Restaurant:** *Corail Hotel, 802 Sharia el-Geish, Tel. 547-0996.* If you're looking for Chinese food with a nice view, this is the place for excellent seafood and beef dishes.

ENJOYING YOUR STAY

Despite what you may hear or read, there's actually a lot to see and do in Alexandria, from visiting archeological sites and museums to evening entertainment.

MUSEUMS

❑ **Greco-Roman Antiquities Museum:** *5 El Mathef Street, Tel. 483-6434.* This is one of Egypt's most impressive museums. Displays an interesting collection of Greco-Roman pieces from the 3rd to 5th centuries BC. Includes many intriguing sculptures, especially the Tanagra statues, and encaustic paintings (portraits painted on mummy cases). Altogether this impressive museum's 24 rooms house nearly 40,000 relics from the 5th century BC to the 7th century AD.

❑ **Bibliotheca Alexandria:** Located at the Eastern Harbour near the Silsileh Peninsula, and once famous in the ancient world for its Great Library (4th century BC) Alexandria's ambitious $185-million UNESCO-sponsored project to construct a new 13-story library has been recently completed. Exhibiting a stunning design by Norwegian architects, especially the roof of interlocking glass panels, this is now the largest and most modern library in the Arab world.

❑ **Royal Jewellery Museum:** *21 Ahmed Yehya Street, Glim, Tel. 586-8348.* Housed in the ornate palace of Princess Fatma el-Zahraa, a member of the former royal family, this museum includes an impressive display of jewelry and other items which became the property of the state after the abdication of King Farouk.

❑ **Hydrobiological Museum:** *Near Fort Qait Bey.* Houses a impressive collection of rare fish and other marine life.

❑ **Museum of Fine Arts:** *18 Manasha Street in Moharam Bey District.* Includes a large collection of paintings, sculptures, and architecture works. Holds exhibitions showcasing the works of contemporary Egyptian and foreign artists.

❏ **Cavafy Museum:** *4 Sharia Sharm el-Sheikh.* Representing the living quarters (third floor apartment over a former brothel) of Alexandria's greatest poet, the Greek Constantine Cavafy (1863-1933). Includes his furniture and books as well as numerous photos.

❏ **Dr. Ragab Papyrus Institute:** *40 Abdel Kader Ragab Street, Fort Qait Bey.* If you've missed papyrus museums elsewhere in Egypt, here's your chance to see the unique materials used in ancient times for paper and paintings.

ARCHEOLOGICAL SITES

❏ **Roman Amphitheatre (Kom al-Dikka):** *Raml Station Square, Tel. 490-2904.* Recently discovered (1964), this small but impressive site is the only Roman theatre found in Egypt. It dates from the 4th century AD. Includes 13 terraced rows of limestone seats arranged in a semicircle and facing a unique speaker's rock which resonates an echo (visitors usually try out this interesting design element with their own Senate speech). Used as the Senate in ancient Alexandria.

❏ **Qait Bey Citadel/Fort:** Built in the 15th century at the tip of the peninsula on the site of the famous Pharos of Alexandria (the legendary 400-foot tall Pharos lighthouse, one of the Seven Wonders of the Ancient World, which was built in 279 BC and collapsed with an earthquake in the 14th century) and incorporating huge red granite pillars from the ancient lighthouse into its outer walls, Fort Qait Bey almost looks out of place in Alexandria with its gingerbread architectural style. Its three floors include an interesting Naval Museum. A good place to get a beautiful view of the harbor and the city of Alexandria spread along the Corniche.

❏ **Pompey's Pillar and the Serapeum:** *Sharia Amud el-Sawari.* Constructed in 293 AD within the acropolis of Serapeum, this massive ancient pink granite column (88 feet high and 29 feet in circumference) carved from a single piece of stone is the only ancient monument still standing in Alexandria. Not much else here except for a couple of granite sphinxes and the remains of the Serapeum, which once was an important building in Alexandria.

❏ **Catacombs of Kom el-Shogafa:** *Near Sharia Amud el-Sawari.* These are the largest Roman catacombs found in

Egypt. Includes three burial levels of which only the two top tiers are accessible to the public. Originally built in the 2nd century AD as private tombs, they were later expanded and used as community tombs. The underground burial complex includes an impressive rotunda, a banquet hall (triclinium), and passageways to the tomb chambers.

❏ **Shatby Tombs and Mustafa Kamel:** *Port Said Street and Moaskar Romani Street, Roushdi.* These four subterranean tombs, first constructed in the 2nd century BC, are noted for their bright colors and relief inscriptions about daily life and religious beliefs of their occupants.

RELIGIOUS SITES

❏ **Mosque of Mursi Abul Abbas:** *In Al-Anfushi.* With its four domes and tall minaret, this is Alexandria's largest mosque. Built in Andalusian style.

❏ **Anglican Church of St. Mark:** While there are over 200 Christian churches in Alexandria, St. Mark's is one of the most interesting churches because of its blend of Western, Moorish, and Byzantine architecture and because of its history of the Anglican community dating from 1855.

PALACE AND GARDENS

❏ **Montazah Palace Gardens:** Consisting of palace buildings, two hotels (Helnan Palestine and El-Salamlek Palace), gardens, and nice ocean view, this compound is a popular destination for tourists. Built in 1893 for the khedive's Austrian mistress, the elegant building which is now the El-Salamlek Palace Hotel and Casino is Alexandria's most luxurious boutique (14 suites and 6 rooms and studios) hotel property. It includes a casino, fine restaurants, and a small shopping arcade. The imposing Italian-style Al-Haramlek building functioned as the summer residence of the former royal family, King Farouk, and is seasonally used by the current president of Egypt.

❏ **Alexandria International Garden:** Located at the entrance of the Desert Road, this is one of Alexandria's newest attractions. Includes numerous recreational and cultural activities along with water sports and exhibits.

❑ **Al Nozha Gardens:** Includes several gardens and a zoo – Flower Garden, Children's Park, and the Zoological Garden.

❑ **Antoniadis Gardens:** This attractive area of beautiful trees and flowers includes Greco-Roman marble statues and the Antoniadis Palace.

BEACHES

One of Alexandria's major attractions is its many beaches which stretch from east to west along the Corniche for more than 20 kilometers. The most popular beaches are Abu Kir, El-Maamoura, El-Montazah, El-Mandra, El-Asafra, Miami, Sidi Bishr, San Stefano, Glyme, Stanley, Rushdy, Sidi Gaber, Cleopatra Sporting, El-Ibrahimiya, and El-Shatby. Many of these beaches also boast good seafood restaurants.

❑ **Abu Kir:** Located in the suburb of Abu Kir, this is one of Alexandria's most popular beaches known for its calm waters, fishing, and excellent seafood restaurants.

EVENING ENTERTAINMENT

Except for a couple of casinos and discos and a few bars and nightclubs, Alexandria is a relatively tame and quiet city at night. Indeed, such action is centered in Cairo. Much of what passes for evening entertainment can be found in the city's major hotels, especially the El-Salamlek Hotel and Casino, Hilton Borg El Arab Resort, and San Giovanni Hotel:

❑ **Casinos:** Alexandria boasts two casinos that are only open to foreigners: El-Salamlek Palace Hotel and Casino on the ground of the Montazah Palace, and the downtown Cecil Hotel. Don't expect Las Vegas or Monte Carlo.

❑ **Bars, discos, and nightclubs:** All of the major hotels have bars serving alcohol and offering some level of entertainment. The **Al Fouad Bar** and **Khedive Salon** at the El-Salamlek Palace Hotel and the **San Giovanni King's Bar** and **San Giovanni Night Club** at the San Giovanni Hotel (205 El Gueish Avenue, Stanley) are especially popular with the evening crowds. The Al Fouad Bar is by far the most elegant place for a drink. Also try the **Aquarius** and **El-Phanar** at the Montazah Sheraton Hotel; **Dolphin Nightclub** at the Helnan Palestine Hotel; and the **Palace Suite** at the Plaza Hotel. Outside these hotels, look for some action at **Far & Away Extra** (14 Fouad Street, Downtown, Tel. 484-1881); **Café Royal Pub** (22 El Bakht Street, downtown, Tel. 483-34306); **Santa Lucia** (40 Safia Zaghloul Street, downtown, Tel. 482-420); **Cap d'Or** (4 Adib, downtown, Tel. 483-5177); **Portugal Club** (42 Abdel Kadri Ragab Street, Roushdi, Tel. 847-599); **Havana** (intersection of Sharia Orabi and Tariq al-Horreyya, Tel. 483-0661); and **Spitfire Bar** (Sharia Ancience Bourse, downtown, Tel. 480-6503). The most popular discos are **Black Gold** (Ramada Renaissance Hotel) and **Aquarius** (Sheraton Hotel).

❑ **Internet Cafes:** If you need to check your email or entertain yourself on the Internet, you're in luck in Alexandria. Several cybercafes now offer Internet access:

- **CyberAccessCafe:** Semouha Shopping Mall, Semouha. Tel. 425-5766.

- **Globalnet:** 29 Nabi Danial Street, Elghonemey Bldg., 6th Floor, Tel. 491-2289.

- **Passe Par Tout:** Sidi Gaber Towers, 2nd Tower, 10th Floor, Apt. 6, Tel. 425-5203.

- **Puregate:** 8 Samy Raouf Street, Tel. 555-4166.

- **Sat-Net:** 603 Horreya Avenue, Zizinia.

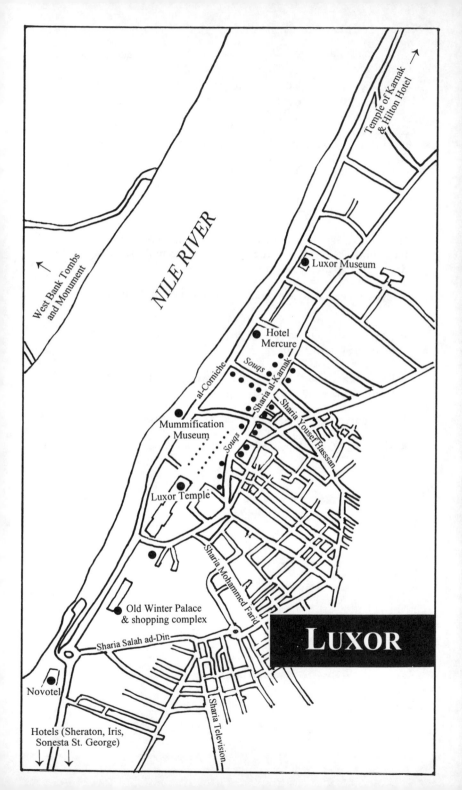

NILE RIVER

West Bank Tombs and Monument

Temple of Karnak & Hilton Hotel

Luxor Museum

Hotel Mercure

Souqs

al-Corniche

Sharia al-Karnak

Sharia Yousef Hassan

Mummification Museum

Souqs

Luxor Temple

Sharia Mohammed Farid

Old Winter Palace & shopping complex

Sharia Salah ad-Din

Novotel

Sharia Television

Hotels (Sheraton, Iris, Sonesta St. George)

LUXOR

Luxor and Beyond

K NOWN AS THE VALLEY OF THE KINGS, THE
Nile River at Luxor is where the myths and realities
of legendary and powerful ancient Egypt remain
enshrined in hundreds of inspiring temples, tombs,
and statuary. Referred to in antiquity as Thebes,
Luxor is Egypt's most impressive monumental city for discovering the great power and wealth of such ancient rulers as Ramses
II, Nefertari, and Tutankhamun. Given its wealth of history and
well preserved monuments, which date back more than 4,000
years, Luxor also is one of the world's top tourist destinations
and its largest outdoor museum.

REDISCOVERED TREASURES

Rediscovered by Europeans at the end of the 18th century,
when Napoleon's survey team visited what was then a small and
relatively unimportant provincial village, Luxor subsequently
became a major center for explorers, archeologists, and scholars
who flocked to this area to uncover Luxor's many buried
treasures. The graffiti etched on Luxor's major monuments by
French soldiers and adventuresome travelers testify to the
presence of many visitors to Luxor in the early to mid-19th

century. Indeed, Thomas Cook opened the area to tourists in the 19th century with the inauguration of tours to Upper Egypt. A steady stream of tourists, explorers, archeologists, and scholars have been coming here ever since to marvel at the wealth of Luxor's treasures. Today, Luxor is the most important tourist destination in Upper Egypt. It boasts an extensive tourist infrastructure – complete with cruise ships, tours, hotels, restaurants, nightclubs, bars, shops, and public transportation – that service more than 5,000 visitors who descend on this unique city each day.

TOURISTS, TOUTS, AND TREASURES

Luxor also is a tourist-clogged city where over 70 percent of the local population is dependent upon the tourist trade for their livelihoods. While this city of over 150,000 inhabitants is known for its colorful Nile-irrigated countryside planted in sugarcane, corn, and wheat, the city literally thrives, survives, or dies on tourism. For example, when terrorists killed over 65 European tourists in 1997, followed by another Gulf war in 1998, for two years tourism nearly died in Luxor. As tourists stopped coming to Egypt, the residents of Luxor disproportionately felt the effects of the severe drop in tourism. Idle tour boats and struggling travel agents, tour guides, shopkeepers, taxi drivers, horse buggy (*hantour*) drivers, and artisans suddenly found their livelihoods endangered. Some went out of business. Tourism slowly began to recover in 1999, surrounded by some of the most intense police and military security found anywhere in the world.

When tourism is fully functioning, Luxor is a lively and crowded city. Tour buses, vans, taxis, cars, and horse buggies jam the city's two-lane streets. In a good year, nearly 2 million visitors come to this city along with numerous scholars who continue to unearth and study Luxor's many monumental treasures. More than 300 cruise ships line the city's pleasant Corniche where you can enjoy a stroll along the river and watch the sunset. At times, especially early evening when the sun sets, Luxor may remind you of a bustling town along the French Riviera.

Luxor has a well deserved reputation for tourism, touts, and temple and tomb overload. Expect to find hundreds of tourists crowding the major sites, numerous aggressive and demanding merchants, pestering touts, and persistent taxi drivers and horse buggy drivers. There's never a dull moment here as you explore Luxor's many treasures and pleasures. The main problem is finding enough time to see all the sites and shop Luxor's many colorful bazaars.

In many respects, Luxor is both a history buff's and a shopper's paradise. There may be more treasures and pleasures per square meter in Luxor than anywhere else in all of Egypt. For both sightseeing and shopping tourists, Luxor is a challenging place to visit. Plan to spend a minimum of two days here. If you're joining a river boat tour that either originates or ends at Luxor, you may want to add an extra day to the tour's intensive one-day itinerary that most likely only highlights Luxor's major treasures and pleasures.

HAD ENOUGH TEMPLES AND TOMBS?

Let's talk truth about tourism in Luxor, and much of Egypt, rather than provide all the excruciating historical details on various temples and tombs. Luxor represents a fabulous outdoor museum which variously educates, entertains, and exhausts many visitors. The problem with Luxor is its over-abundance of antiquities, especially its many temples, tombs, and stone statuary. It is literally sensory overload, further complicated by hordes of tourists competing for visitation space. If there is one place in Egypt where you may tire of ancient history, as well as fellow tourists, while also being in awe of Egypt's many treasures, it's probably Luxor. After a while, and especially in the heat of the day, its hundreds of temples and tombs start looking the same. Indeed, many visitors quickly get "templed-out" or "tombed-out" and bored with the over-saturation of historical sites to visit. The old laments of the bored traveler – *"If you've seen one, you've seen them all," "Been there, done that,"* or *"Is there more to Egypt than just these temples and tombs"* – are frequently heard among visitors who are anxious to get off their tour bus to do something other than visit another recommended tomb or temple accompanied by another esoteric set of facts or stories. Luxor also demonstrates one of the major facts of life when visiting Egypt: its infrastructure is primarily geared to handle large groups of tourists rather than independent travelers.

If you love sightseeing and ancient Egyptian history, you'll be enthralled with the temples and tombs of Luxor. In fact, Luxor may become the highlight of your Egyptian adventure as you get up early in the morning (5am is recommended) to start what will most likely turn out to be a long and hot day of sightseeing. On a busy day, you may stand in long and hot lines to visit the major sites. You'll learn about the details of sculptures, sarcophagi, hieroglyphics, and paintings which can be both enlightening and extremely esoteric. You'll marvel at the tombs of Nefertari (if you're lucky to get one of the few tickets sold each day), Ramses II and VI, Amenophis II, Tutankhamun, noblemen, and workers, as well as stand in awe of the temples of Karnak, Luxor, and Hatshepsut and the wonderful displays at the Luxor Museum.

But if you're not a great history buff who enjoys a heavy dose of temple and tomb trekking nor acquiring esoteric knowledge about pharaohs and their followers, Luxor could become your trip from hell. After seeing a few major temples and tombs and perhaps visiting the local museum, you may want to know if there is more to Egypt than just temples and tombs. As you seek alternatives to Luxor's major attractions, you may want to spend some of your time focused on the city's bazaars and factories where you'll have a chance to interact with real people and acquire some local treasures. In so doing, you'll quickly discover this is a highly competitive tourist city where drivers and merchants primarily depend on the tourist trade to fuel their livelihoods. They're often aggressive, sometimes obnoxious, usually outrageously overpriced on their first quoted price, but always pesky as they attempt to get you to spend your money with them. Some try to improve their image by posting signs saying they are a "No Hassle" shop which means they have fixed prices – or they won't hassle you as badly as some other shops!

❑ Luxor is Egypt's most impressive monumental city for discovering the great power and wealth of its ancient rulers.

❑ Luxor is a tourist-clogged city where over 70 percent of the local population is dependent upon the tourist trade for their livelihoods.

❑ The major problem is finding enough time to see all the sites and shop Luxor's many colorful bazaars.

❑ Luxor's infrastructure is primarily geared to handle large groups of tourists rather than independent travelers.

Nonetheless, shopping in Luxor can be a fun adventure as you take a horse carriage through the narrow bazaars and occasionally stop at shops that appeal to your shopping tastes. Be it jewelry, clothes, alabaster bowls, papyrus paintings, carvings, T-shirts, replicas of antiquities, brassware, or the usual assortment of tasteless tourist kitsch, Luxor's colorful and noisy bazaars have lots of interesting things to offer visitors. In fact, the markets in Luxor are some of the largest outside Cairo. If you bargain hard here (50 to 75 percent discounts are not unreasonable in many tourist shops and factories), you should be able to walk away with some good buys. If approached right, shopping in Luxor may become one of your highlights in visiting this ancient city of the Upper Nile.

GETTING TO KNOW YOU

THE BASICS

Many visitors make Luxor their second stop in Egypt after briefly visiting Cairo. In fact, Cairo merely becomes a transit point for what is their primary destination, Luxor.

Luxor is an especially attractive destination for two reasons. First, it's the center for Egypt's most extensive collection of important ancient temples and tombs. Second, it's the jumping-off point for visiting several popular destinations along the Nile Valley by riverboat. More than 300 cruise ships (up from 30 in 1975) ply the waters between Luxor and Aswan, visiting several popular sites along the way, such as Esna, Edfu, and Kom Ombo, as well as continuing by road, plane, or ship to one of the great highlights of visiting Egypt – Abu Simbel on the shores of Lake Nasser.

WHEN TO GO AND GO OUT

Luxor can get miserably hot most of the year. The best times to visit are in the cooler months of October through February. However, even daytime temperatures during these months can get very hot. The sun starts blazing the area around 9am and continues until 5pm. It's usually a good idea to start touring temples and tombs very early in the morning – by 7am – or late in the afternoon. Shopping is best done after 5pm when the sun sets and a cool breeze graces the city. The city is most pleasant from 6pm to 9pm when the shops and streets really come alive.

WHAT TO TAKE

Given the heat and sun of Luxor, it's a good idea to pack well for your daily sightseeing forays. The essentials are a hat, sunglasses, bottle of water, good walking shoes, sun screen, hand fan, and maybe an umbrella. You won't find much shade in Luxor, except inside tombs or next to temple pillars. Also, take extra film with you since you'll probably want to shoot scenes of the beautiful countryside, villages, and monuments.

GETTING THERE

Luxor is located along the Nile River 420 miles south of Cairo and 130 north of Aswan. The quickest way to get to Luxor is by plane. The flight from Cairo takes a little more than one hour. The flight from Aswan takes just over 20 minutes.

You also can reach Luxor by road, train, and ship. Driving from Cairo to Luxor by private car, taxi, or bus takes four to five hours. The train leaves Cairo for Luxor four times a day and takes 10 to 12 hours. Numerous cruise ships link Aswan to Luxor and take from 3 to 5 days, depending on the ship's itinerary.

Tourist Offices

If you're traveling on your own, you may want to stop at the local tourist office for brochures and information. It is located, along with the tourist police, in the Tourist Bazaar which is adjacent to the Old Winter Palace Hotel and Corniche (Tel. 372-215). It's open daily from 8am to 8pm (Friday until 1pm). This office also more or less maintains a desk at the airport and train station.

Getting Around

You'll have no problem getting around Luxor – if you know the rules of the road. Given the long five-kilometer stretch of Luxor's Corniche, you'll find it more convenient to navigate the city by horse carriages (*hantour*) and taxis than by walking its hot streets. Numerous worn blue and white **taxis** line the main street. As might be expected, they usually overcharge tourists, if they can get away with it. Most rides from one end of the Corniche to the other should cost L£10. The taxis drivers usually quote a price of L£20. Tell them you'll pay L£10. Start walking away and they will quote L£15. As you walk further, they will say *"Okay, L£10."* You may be able to get some rides for L£5 to L£8, but L£10 is reasonable. Anything above L£10 is robbery.

The most pleasant way of navigating the streets and lanes of Luxor is by **horse carriage**. If you're walking along the street, these aggressive and pesky drivers will constantly approach you for a ride. Keep walking until the price gets right. Many will quote an initial price of L£20 or L£30. The correct price should be L£5 for an hour for two to four people per carriage. Make sure you repeat to the driver that you are paying L£5, not US$5, for an hour. He usually nods yes and then becomes a friendly and helpful driver for the first half hour and then a quiet and conniving driver the second half hour. The driver will most likely take you around town and through the bazaars where you can stop to shop. It's a very pleasant and entertaining ride where you can observe a great deal of market activity. However, expect your driver to take you to his favorite souvenir and carpet shops where he can get a commission on your purchases. His two favorite shops are likely to be **Fatah Market** and **Castle of Carpet**. Not bad shops, but you'll need to bargain hard in both places – go for 50 to 75 percent off the initial asking prices. Once you finish your horse cart trip, expect to encounter "price slippage" as you get hassled by what appeared to be a friendly and helpful driver – especially if you did not purchase in his recommended shops. He experiences a temporary loss of memory and integrity. The usual end-of-the-trip pitch goes like this: he whines that the journey was too long, or that he should be getting L£10 or L£15, or that his price was US$5 rather than L£5. Many of these drivers will attempt to intimidate you. It's all part of the street game designed especially for tourists. Don't argue with them. Give them the agreed upon L£5 and walk away without saying a word or making eye contact. The driver may continue to harass you for more money. Just ignore him and keep walking to your next destination. He'll finally go away after he figures out that you can't be intimidated. Unfortunately, many tourists give in to this form of extortion and thus reconfirm to these drivers that it is indeed possible to get more money out of their foreign passengers.

While you can navigate some of the city on foot, especially near major hotels such as the Old Winter Palace and the Hotel Isis, it's most pleasant to enjoy a tour of the city by horse cart. However, much of time you may want to quickly get around the city and adjacent Karnak by using taxis, which are readily available and cheap, if you bargain.

When traveling to the West Bank of the Nile, you need to join a tour or take a car and/or driver to get around from one site to another. Since this is a large, sprawling area, walking to different sites is not an option. Most travel agents can arrange a car and driver.

TOURS AND TRAVEL AGENTS

If you arrive in Luxor on your own, you can quickly join a tour or organize your own private tour by hiring a car, driver, and guide. You can also book one of the three- to seven-day Nile River cruises in Luxor which will probably be much cheaper than if you booked one prior to your arrival. Competition amongst the river cruisers is keen and prices drop accordingly once you are in Luxor.

Some of the best and most reliable travel agents are found in and around the Winter Palace Hotel along Corniche El-Nil: Thomas Cook (Tel. 372-196); American Express (Tel. 372-862); Travco (Tel. 376-445); Emeco (Tel. 370-332); and Misr Travel (Tel. 373-551). Not only can they arrange local tours and river cruises, they also can make tour, transportation, and hotel arrangements in other cities, such as Aswan, Cairo, Abu Simbel, Hurghada, and Sharm al-Sheikh.

ORIENTATION

Luxor actually consists of three different areas which result in three different travel experiences:

1. **City of Luxor:** east bank of the Nile River.

2. **Village of Karnak:** just north of the City of Luxor.

3. **Necropolis of ancient Thebes:** on the West Bank of the Nile River.

The **City of Luxor** is where most tourists stay and where the major tourist infrastructure is centered, from hotels and restaurants to shops, banks, tour operators, and museums. Especially lively after 5pm, when the city becomes cooler and after tourists have returned from a long day of touring Karnak and the west bank, the city finally comes alive as visitors head for restaurants and shop for souvenirs and jewelry in the city's many overpriced shops and markets. Although long and narrow, the city is relatively easy to navigate on foot or by taxi and horse carriage if you orient yourself to its three main streets: the Corniche, Sharia al-Karnak, and Sharia al-Mahatta. The **Corniche** (Al-Corniche) hugs the riverfront for over 5 kilometers. Here you'll find over 100 riverboats docked three to four deep and numerous hotels, shops, and restaurants facing the river. A very attractive area, especially viewed from the upper floors of a hotel facing the Corniche, this is a pleasant place to walk, although it can be a very long and tiring walk. Many visitors walk part of the area, especially near the boat docks, and then take a taxi or horse carriage the rest of the way. **Sharia al-Karnak** parallels the Corniche one block to the east and runs from Luxor Temple in the south to Temple of Karnak in the north. This street is lined with many restaurants, cafes, shops, and bazaars. **Sharia al-Mahatta** is an east-west street that runs from the Gardens of Luxor Temple in the west to the train station in the east.

The village of **Karnak** is located just north of the City of Luxor. Here you'll find the impressive Temples of Karnak, a huge complex of buildings, statues, sanctuaries, obelisks, pylons, colonnades, and reliefs. On a busy day, especially late in the afternoon, you'll encounter hundreds of tourists pushing and shoving their way through the many passageways.

The **West Bank**, also known as "The City of the Dead," is located directly across the river from Luxor. This area quickly transforms itself from green sugarcane, corn, and wheat fields fed by the Nile River to hilly and mountainous moon-scaped desert of heat, rocks, and sand. Representing the necropolis of ancient Thebes, this area includes a dazzling array of monuments, temples, and tombs, most of which are underground, that are largely responsible for attracting the nearly 2 million visitors a year to Luxor. Here you'll tour the Valley of the Kings and the Valley of the Queens, see the famous Temple of Hatshepsut, visit the popular tombs of Nefertari and Ramses, and shop in several alabaster and souvenir shops. You can easily spend two to three days just visiting the major sites; a week would probably cover nearly everything in this area.

SHOPPING ABOVE RETAIL

Next to temple and tomb trekking, shopping is Luxor's major attraction. Luxor is literally one big shopping center, the biggest south of Cairo. Within Luxor you'll find hundreds of shops lining the streets and bazaars as well as shops and shopping arcades in the major hotels. Indeed, most shops are found at the major hotels and shops fronting the main street or in the interior of the city with its colorful bazaars and markets. Except for the main bazaar that offers fruits, vegetables, meats, spices, and household goods for local residents, most of the shops and bazaars cater to the tourist trade. As a result, you'll find the usual mix of tourist items – jewelry, brassware, alabaster and limestone carvings, papyrus paintings, leather goods, T-shirts, clothes, and numerous tacky souvenirs.

High pricing of items in Luxor should come as no surprise given the fact that 70 percent of the local economy is dependent upon tourists. You'll also find lots of high prices aimed at gouging naive tourists who are not used to the fine art of bazaar bargaining. If you pay the first asking price in the bazaar, you are most likely paying three times what you should be paying. Don't be surprised to get up to 75 percent discounts on many items in the bazaar. When a merchant exclaims "*Oh, my God!*" to your low counter offer, you really haven't insulted him; chances are you're close to what you should be paying. A good rule of thumb in Luxor is to offer 25 percent of the asking price but never pay more than 60 percent. In other words, if someone in the bazaar or alabaster factory asks L£50 for an item, counter with L£10. He'll probably throw up his hands and exclaim "*Oh, my God!*" as he plays the "insulted merchant" game. Chances are you are within L£5 or L£10 of the final price – settle for L£15 but no more than L£20. If you go beyond that amount, chances are you've been taken by another enterprising merchant who is used to gouging tourists. If you are with a tour group, you may be surprised to see other members of your group actually paying the full asking price or only negotiating a 20 percent discount. Make a friend – help them bargain for the right price!

WHAT TO BUY

The shops of Luxor offer the usual assortment of tourist items – jewelry, T-shirts, alabaster carvings and vases, papyrus paintings, replicas of antiquities, carpets, clothes, scarves, leather goods, inlaid boxes, wall hangings, brassware, stone carvings, and spices – displayed in typical Third World emporium style. Most of what you encounter can be generally classified as tourist kitsch. Luxor does have a few good jewelry shops that offer nicely designed brooches, necklaces, and cartouches. Also look for shops that offer T-shirts with cartouches embroidered with your name (L£9 for children and L£12 for adults).

The problem with shopping in Luxor centers around the tourist nature of this area and the rush-to-buy mentality that often accompanies group buying behavior. Shopkeepers only have one type of repeat buyer – the tour guide who agrees to steer his group into particular shops in exchange for commissions – 20 to 60 percent – on everything his group members buy. This becomes the lucrative end of the tour guide business – take your group shopping in one of the "best" shops in Luxor. The "best" usually translates as the shops that give the guides the best commissions. As a result, if you go shopping with your tour guide, chances are you will be paying twice what you should be paying had you gone on your own and bargained vigorously. In fact, we've seen tourists in such shops pay US$300 for an alabaster bowl we had been offered for US$200 that should be fairly priced at US$100-150, and then gouged another US$200 in excess shipping charges. Shopping in Luxor often approximates our image of sheep being taken to the slaughter! Not only are prices far above retail, the quality of goods is often questionable since many shoppers tend to trust shops recommended by their tour guides. Our experience is that many products in such shops are at best mediocre quality.

WHERE TO SHOP

Luxor's shopping is confined to three major areas – shops in and around the major hotels, the tourist bazaar, and the regular bazaar. The best quality shops are attached to or located within a short distance from the major hotels. Dedicated shoppers should set their sights on five hotels: **Old Winter Palace**, **Sheraton**, **Isis**, **Hilton**, and **Mercure**. The Winter Palace Hotel includes a shopping arcade on the left side of the hotel which includes a few jewelry and handicraft shops. One of Luxor's best jewelry shops is located here: **Chez Georges Gaddis Jewellery**. This is a "no hassle" shop with fixed prices, but if you inquire nicely, you can probably get a small discount – we did. The Sheraton shop may be willing to give a larger discount than the Winter Palace shop. It includes lots of gold and silver jewelry with Egyptian motifs designed for upscale tourists. It's the only shop that makes copies of King Tut's jewelry. The Sheraton Luxor Resort also has a small shopping arcade (outside and to the left of the front entrance) that includes a branch of **Chez Georges Gaddis Jewellery** as well as a bookstore, souvenir shop, clothes store, and antiquities (replicas) shop. The clothing store offers T-shirts with personalized cartouches embroidered on the front (need to bargain for the going rate – L£9 for children and L£12 for adults). **Ancient Arts** offers a nice selection of overpriced replicas of antiquities, from temple and pharaonic figures to animals.

If you're in a hurry and don't want to hassle with shopping in all the aggressive bazaar shops, head for Luxor's one-stop shop for jewelry, handicrafts, and T-shirts – **Philippe** (across the street from the Isis Hotel, Tel. 375-677). This is as good as it gets in Luxor. This long-established shop is a favorite with tour groups. It includes a large selection of gold and silver jewelry as well as leather goods, alabaster, mother of pearl, watches, books, and all types of souvenirs. While the quality here is generally good for Luxor, don't expect to find international standards of workmanship and designs. Both the designs and craftsmanship tend to by very local and ethnic. If you're looking for something to remind yourself of Luxor, Philippe is a good place to shop. The shop maintains a factory downstairs. You can do some bargaining here but don't expect to get much of a discount, at least not like in the bazaar shops.

Luxor has two main bazaars that are popular with tourists. The **Tourist Bazaar** is located north of Luxor Temple near Sharia al-Karnak (Karnak Street) and next to the New Winter Palace Hotel. This densely packed bazaar is filled with dozens of small shops selling a wide range of typical tourist products and souvenirs, from jewelry and papyrus to brassware, water-pipes, and inlaid boxes. While you shouldn't expect great quality here, it can be a fun place to pick up some inexpensive gift items as well as practice your bargaining skills. Like bazaars elsewhere in Egypt, be sure to bargain hard for everything, expecting the first quoted price to be 50 to 75 percent more than you should eventually pay.

At the center of the city look for the **Regular Bazaar** which is very large and encompasses several adjacent streets. The heart of the bazaar is along El Souk Street (parallels Sharia al-Karnak). Here you'll find numerous shops offering a wide range of souvenir items. Be sure to stop at **El Hag Ahmad Shabib** (Tel. 373-742) which claims to be the biggest wholesaler in Luxor for brass items. Wedged between many other shops on a congested narrow street, this three-level shop is jam-packed with brassware, alabaster items, perfume bottles, drums, pipes, inlaid boxes, pots, ceramics, rugs, papyrus, lamps, musical instruments, walking sticks, and general tourist kitsch. If you tour this bazaar by horse carriage, which is one of the most interesting ways of seeing the city and its people and products, chances are your driver will take you to two of his favorite shops, Fatah Market and Castle of Carpet. Both are interesting to visit and you may find some things worth buying, although please heed our advice on bargaining and commissions. **Fatah Market** (Santa Maria Church Street, Tel. 370-140), which is somewhat off the beaten tourist path (one reason it needs the horse carriage drivers to "drop in" with guests), includes a wide selection of handicrafts, wall hangings, carpets, alabaster items, jewelry, silver, applique work, leather purses, papyrus, and inlaid tables. **Castle of Carpet** (El Souk Street, Tel. 373-412) includes two levels of handcrafted items. The carpets and wall hangings are found on the upper floor; brassware, stone pieces, leather jackets and purses, spices, scarves, T-shirts, and papyrus are found on the lower level.

Shopping on the West Bank is primarily confined to ala-baster, which is mined less than 100 kilometers northwest of the Valley of the Kings. You'll pass by numerous brightly painted village **alabaster factory shops** that are totally dependent on the tourist trade. In addition to having a showroom, these places have a demonstration area showing how the area's famous alabaster is cut and polished. Most of these shops are well organized to regularly receive taxis, vans, and bus loads of tourists. Indeed, these shops survive on their ability to persuade tour guides and drivers, through commissions rather than quality products, to stop at their places. Some guides and drivers are currently getting hefty commissions in the range of 50 to 60 percent! While much of the alabaster cutting and polishing process is interesting and some of the plates, bowls, and vases are beautiful, much of it also is of poor quality and somewhat tacky. In addition, you may find yourself both overwhelmed and captive in such shops, especially if your tour guide decides to spend 45 minutes at one of these places.

Well organized for tour groups, most of these alabaster factory-shops serve complimentary drinks and have many salespeople available to assist you. If you've heard or read that you should be able to get a 15 to 20 percent discount in these places, don't believe it. The general rule of thumb is that you will be quoted highly inflated prices that are 50 to 75 percent higher than fair market value. While a shop may only indicate a 15 to 20 percent discount, they have a lot more room to play with, even after giving your tour guide his or her commission on your sale. If you can't get at least a 50 percent discount on something you really like, we suggest doing the following: go next door or across the street where you will most likely find a similar shop but which has no tourists because their next bus load of tourists has not arrived; go into the shop and browse for comparable items. You will probably be amazed to discover that a US$50 vase where your group is currently shopping actually goes for US$15 in this tour-free shop. After all, this shop doesn't have to pay a 50 to 60 percent commission to your tour guide, they currently have no customers, except for you, and they know you know how to play this game. If you are shopping for price, ideally you want to identify a shop that has few if any people shopping in it at present.

One of the most popular alabaster shops on the West Bank with tour guides is **Obilisk Factory Albaster** (El Qurna, Tel. 310-745). They offer an interesting demonstration area just outside the entrance to the shop, which has some very nice alabaster bowls, plates, and vases on display. However, this place also charges 75 percent more for comparable items found in the shop. If you stop here, make sure you take the walk next door. If the competition has no buses, vans, or cars out front, you should be able to get some real good deals on alabaster items. Be sure to bargain very hard. These factory shops are very seasoned in dealing with foreign tourists.

Individuals interested in learning about papyrus and acquiring some quality items made from papyrus should visit the **Dr. Ragab's Papyrus Institute**. It's located on a boat docked along the Corniche just across the street from the Mercure Hotel. While somewhat expensive, the Institute does offer very good quality papyrus.

QUALITY SHOPPING

As you will quickly discover, Luxor is not a great place for doing quality shopping. Even the so-called best gold and jewelry shops, such as Gaddis and Philippe, have some nice items but the designs and handmade work are nothing to write home about. Much of the workmanship in Luxor looks amateurish. On the other hand, if you're not real picky about quality and just want to acquire some interesting local products, Luxor has a lot to offer. Best of all, shopping in the local shops and bazaars can be a great deal of fun as you practice your bargaining skills.

When shopping, always remember this is Luxor where nearly 2 million transient visitors pass through a city of 150,000 each year. As another tourist, you don't represent potential repeat business – only a one-time opportunity to make a sale. Given such a touristy shopping environment, expect to be quoted highly inflated prices on everything from alabaster vases to water pipes. Many of the bargaining skills you learned in Cairo may only be partially valid in Luxor. Except for the top jewelry and gold shops, think in terms of 50 to 75 percent discounts – when you are in a shop without a guide or driver.

ACCOMMODATIONS

Luxor has a good range of accommodations for all types of travelers. At the high end are such classic properties as the Sofitel Old Winter Palace which has seen its share of world leaders and celebrities over the past century. Since most visitors arrive as part of a tour group, the major hotels, such as the Sheraton, Hilton, Mövenpick, Isis, and Mercure, are well prepared to handle groups. Budget travelers have lots of alternatives to choose from, especially along Sharia Television. Many visitors bypass the hotels altogether by staying on the many ships that line the Corniche – a problem for hotels, which have been losing business to the ships since 1975.

If you arrive in Luxor without a hotel reservation, avoid being taken to a hotel by a local tout. Like everything else that has a price, hotel touts usually get 25 to 40 percent commissions from a hotel which, of course, will be reflected in your bill.

If you're not staying on one of the cruise ships (see pages 182-184 on these "floating hotels" which yield hundreds of additional rooms in Luxor), you may want to check out some of Luxor's best hotels which include the following:

❑ **Sofitel Coralia Winter Palace:** *Corniche El-Nil, Luxor, Egypt, Tel. (2095) 380-422, Fax (2095) 374-087, or toll-free from the US & Canada (800) 763-4835.* Wonderfully located a few minutes walk from the Temple of Luxor, it is frequently referred to as the "Old Winter Palace" to distinguish it from the New Winter Palace. Don't be put off by the word "old." The Old Winter Palace has history and charm and has been very well maintained. Originally built in 1886, the grand hotel's guest list reads like a "Who's Who" of world leaders and celebrities. The exterior has a regal look to it as you approach. Enter the vast lobby with its imposing staircase and it further conveys a regal ambience. The 102 rooms are spacious and each varies somewhat in configuration and decor. Many guest rooms have fireplaces. The high ceilings throughout further emphasize the sense of space – especially in the bathroom. Many of the rooms overlook the Corniche below and the Nile beyond. Looking out from the balconies on these front-facing rooms, one almost has the sense of being on the Riviera. Rooms in the New Winter Palace are smaller, with cookie-cutter similarity. Five restaurants offer diners a variety of menus. The 1886 Restaurant exudes ambience, with light reflected from crystal chandeliers, heavy silver and white linen. Tall windows open out onto a garden. Lots of shops in and around the lower level of the hotel. Fitness Facilities.

❑ **Sonesta St. George:** *Corniche El-Nil, Luxor, Egypt, Tel. (2095) 382-575, Fax (2095) 382-571, or toll-free from the US & Canada (800) 766-3782. Website: www.sonesta.com.* Located on the Corniche overlooking the Nile, the Sonesta St. George should satisfy those who want their surroundings to be a constant reminder they are in the land of the pharaohs. Some love it; others may consider the pharaonic profusion a bit much. The 224 guestrooms feature all the expected amenities and the service is excellent. Restaurants include Serapis, which features buffets offering Japanese and international selections; Beban, the coffee shop, features Italian fare, fresh pastries and premium ice cream; Miyako is gaining renown for its Japanese selections featuring sushi bar and teppanyaki tables. Located in the center of Luxor's shopping district, the hotel has luxury shops on the lobby level for jewelry and a variety of Egyptian handicrafts. Fitness Center; Conference and Banquet Facilities.

❑ **Hilton Luxor:** *New Karnak, Luxor, Egypt, Tel. (2095) 374-933, Fax (2095) 376-571, or toll-free from the US & Canada (800) 445-8667.* Located on the East Bank of the village of Karnak in Luxor, it is 2 minutes away from the Temple of Karnak. Set back from the road, the grounds include vast areas of greenery with gardens overlooking the Nile in a peaceful setting. Most of the 261 guest rooms provide views of the Nile and the expected amenities. Executive Club rooms offer additional services and amenities, including larger balcony space. The Palms Restaurant serves a daily buffet and a la carte selections. Bella Vista serves Italian fare in a riverside setting. If you're looking for a dramatic view of the Nile, you'll find it at Shadoof Restaurant and Bar located at the pool. Fitness Facilities; Conference and Banquet Facilities.

❑ **Mövenpick Jolie Ville:** *Crocodile Island, Luxor, Egypt, Tel. (2095) 374-855, Fax (2095) 374-936.* Crocodile Island, one of the lush islands in the upper reaches of the Nile, provides the setting for this tropical resort. Located 4km south of Luxor's downtown, a shuttle bus and boat carry guests between the hotel and downtown area. 332 bungalow rooms including suites and connecting rooms are simply decorated and immaculate. All rooms have a private terrace. Among the six food outlets, Mövenpick Restaurant serves a la carte meals; Jolie Ville serves buffet meals. Shehrazade is an open air restaurant overlooking the Nile; and Fellah's Tent offers charming oriental evenings. There are many activities for children, including a zoo. Fitness Facilities; Secretarial Services; Conference and Banquet Facilities.

RESTAURANTS

Like shopping for handcrafted items, the food in Luxor is nothing to write home about. You'll find many decent restaurants attached to the major hotels, but nothing stands out as exceptional. After all, this city does not attract top international chefs who cater to a discriminating international audience. Restaurants, whether found on ship or on shore, cater to the tourist crowd; many serve the ubiquitous tourist buffet of unenlightened cuisine. Most of Luxor's best restaurants also are found in the city's top hotels and include:

❑ **Miyako:** *Sonesta St. George, Corniche al-Nil, Tel. 382-575.* This relatively new Japanese restaurant, with a Japanese-trained Egyptian chef, continues to get good reviews for its excellent dishes and nice ambience. It serves several Asian dishes but it's especially noted for its *teppan-yaki.*

❑ **The 1886:** *Sofitel Old Winter Palace, Corniche al-Nil, Tel. 380-422. Dinner only.* This is Luxor's most elegant dining room, found in its most elegant hotel and served with old-world charm. The kitchen could use a good chef.

❑ **La Mamma:** *Sheraton Hotel, Corniche al-Nil South, Tel. 374-544.* Serves good pizza and tasty pasta in a charming and informal outdoor setting surrounded by shops. Excellent service. Watch out for the two active pelicans that may end up near your table.

❑ **Class Restaurant:** *Sharia Khaled Ibn el-Walid.* Serves good Continental and Oriental food. Excellent service.

❑ **Mövenpick Restaurant:** *Mövenpick Crocodile Jolie Ville, Crocodile Island, Tel. 374-855.* A European-style restaurant providing fine dining in a cozy setting and with good service.

❑ **Bella Vista:** *Luxor Hilton Hotel, New Karnak, Tel. 374-933.* Dine under a thatched umbrella and overlooking the Nile River. Serves excellent Italian dishes, from pastas and pizzas to fish and chicken.

❑ **Tutankhamun Restaurant:** *Located on the West Bank at the ferry landing, Tel. 310-918.* This long established eatery serves generous proportions of some of the best dishes in Luxor. Very good stews and chicken curry.

❑ **Le Flamboyant:** *Hotel Mercure, Corniche al-Nil, Tel. 380-944.* Serves excellent Continental dishes in a delightful candle-light setting overlooking the Corniche.

Seeing The Sites

One thing you won't lack in Luxor are places to sightsee. The choices, however redundant, are simply overwhelming. To do the basics takes at least two days, and then you only scratch the surface of this extremely rich archeological region. Luxor is all about temples, tombs, and tours. The touts will find you when you go shopping!

Be aware that most sites require entrance fees ranging from L£5 to L£100. If you plan to visit Queen Nefertari's tomb (the most expensive) on the West Bank, be sure you arrive very early in the morning (by 6am) to get tickets to this quickly sold-out site; it's first-come-first-serve at the ticket window. Only 150 lucky ticket holders are allowed to visit the tomb each day.

You are well advised to tour the temples and tombs with the assistance of a guide who knows the history and significance of each site. Each place has its own story that may be best told by a local guide. If you do hire a guide, you may want to brief him or her on your style of temple and tomb travel. You'll find many experienced guides, but really good guides that meet your needs may be hard to find. Many local guides spend hours explaining every little esoteric detail that you may not be interested in learning about. If you just want a good overview of each area and prefer moving along at a more rapid pace, have a nice talk with your guide after the first hour of touring. Let him or her know your style of cultural tourism. Unfortunately, many visitors to Luxor end up in a large group with a very knowledgeable but boring guide who knows lots of historical facts but who lacks the analytical ability to explain or relate those facts to processes that may be of greater interest to you. As a result, you may feel you are being dragged from one boring site to another, especially if you are out and about on a hot day. A day or two with this type of guide will really dampen your enthusiasm for the antiquities of Luxor. As a backup, you may want to take a good travel guidebook with you that provides details on each historical site (*Blue Guide* or *Lonely Planet Guide* to Egypt). At least you can read the book while the guide babbles on!

The following are the major sightseeing highlights of each area on the East and West Banks.

East Bank

❑ **Karnak Temples:** Located just north of Luxor, this huge sprawling temple complex is on a grand scale. You may not be prepared for such a massive display of buildings. Representing more than 13 centuries of history, the religious monuments include a regal avenue of ram-headed sphinxes, pylons, obelisks, courts, halls, and gateways. Since this is one of the most popular tourist destinations, you may want to arrive very early (between 6am and 8am) in order to avoid the massive crowds that grip this area from 9am to 6pm. Be sure to check out the impressive sound and light show which is conducted in seven different languages on alternative nights (English is done nightly).

❑ **Luxor Temple:** Located near the river and just north of the Winter Palace Hotel, this temple complex dates to the period 1390-323 B.C. and is dedicated to the Theban triad gods of Amun, Mut, and Khonsu. Includes impressive statues of Ramses II, an obelisk (a second obelisk was hijacked by the French – the centerpiece in the Place de la Concorde in Paris), colonnades, courts, and halls. An interesting architectural feature is the 13th century mosque (Mosque of Abu al-Haggag) built within this complex.

❑ **Luxor Museum:** Located between the Temples of Luxor and Karnak, this impressive three-level museum houses numerous bronzes, statues, reliefs, and other relics from the New Kingdom period.

❑ **Mummification Museum:** Located on the Corniche, just opposite the Mina Palace Hotel, this relatively new museum details the whole mummification process. Includes displays of mummified animals and an ancient official. If you're really interested in learning more about mummies and the mummification process, this is the place to visit.

WEST BANK

The West Bank is known as the City of the Dead or the Theban necropolis. Located approximately 4 kilometers from Luxor, this is where the pharaohs of the New Kingdom constructed their underground tombs in the rugged desert landscape. While they also constructed several above-ground structures – mainly mortuary temples – it's the secrets of the underground tombs that have intrigued the world for decades. This area, for example, is where the fabulous tomb of Tutankhamun was discovered in the Valley of the Kings. Most tombs have been robbed or, as in the case of Tutankhamun, the mummy and artifacts have been removed to museums. The only things that remain in the tombs are the inscriptions, reliefs, and paintings.

Many tombs, both large and small, are open to the public from 6am to 5pm daily. Because of the bright sun and heat, you are well advised to visit the major sites early in the morning or late in the afternoon when the sun is the least deadly. It can really get hot in this desert climate. The visitation experience is very similar wherever you go. You purchase tickets for each site which are only valid on the day of purchase. Tickets are sold at two locations between 6am and 4pm: at the ferry landing on the West Bank and at the Antiquities Inspectorate ticket office which is located 2 miles west of the ferry landing (near the Colossi of Memnon statues). Once you arrive at the parking lot of a site, you may have a long walk to the entrance of the site as well as to the various tombs. Be sure you're wearing comfortable walking shoes as well as carrying sufficient water with you to prevent dehydration. Since the sun is likely to be very bright and the weather very hot, make sure you apply sun screen and/or take a hat and umbrella to keep the hot sun off your head. Also consider carrying a small flashlight, which will come in handy in illuminating many dark sections of tombs (good lighting is hard to find underground), and lots of small change to get rid of self-appointed guides that attach themselves to you at various sites (unless you have your own guide).

Once you arrive at a tomb, you usually descend into a narrow passageway where you can view inscriptions and paintings on the walls as well as see the burial chamber. A good tour guide will explain the history of the tomb and attempt to interpret the inscriptions and stories behind the art work. On a hot day and with many visitors entering the tombs at the same time, the journey into the depths of these tombs can become both stifling and claustrophobic. Since a long day of touring the many sites on the West Bank can be very exhausting, pace yourself accordingly.

A journey into the West Bank can take days of visiting numerous sites and tombs that dot this inhospitable terrain. In planning your trip, consider visiting several of these popular sites:

❑ **Valley of the Kings:** Consisting of 62 tombs, this is one of the "must visit" areas on the West Bank. Each tomb is numbered and labeled. Each ticket you purchased before you arrived is good for visiting three tombs, although the Tomb of Tutankhamun requires a separate ticket which can be purchased at the site. Some of the most interesting tombs in this areas include:

- Amenhotep II (#35)
- Horemheb (#57)
- Merneptah (#8)
- Ramses II (#7)
- Ramses III (#11)
- Ramses IV (#2)
- Ramses IX (#6)
- Seti I (#17)
- Tutankhamun (#62)
- Tuthmosis III (No. 34)
- Tuthmosis IV (#43)

❏ **Valley of the Queens:** You won't need to spend much time in this area since few tombs are open to the public. This area includes 75 tombs, although most are relatively unadorned caves and only five are currently open to the public (#34, 44, 52, 55, and 66). The most impressive tomb, which is the showcase tomb of the West Bank, is that of Queen Nefertari (#66). However, daily access to this tomb is limited to 150 people (line up at the ticket office early, 6am or earlier). The entrance fee is L£100 for foreigners; L£50 for foreign students; and L£5 for Egyptians. The second most impressive tomb is that of Amunherkhepshep (#55), although nothing compares to Nefertari's tomb. Also look for the Tomb of Thyti (No. 52) and the Tomb of Khaemwaset (#44) which exhibit some of the fine workmanship found in the Valley of the Queens.

❏ **Tombs of the Nobles:** This is one of the least visited areas of the West Bank but it yields some of the most impressive tombs. Located near the old village of Gurna, this area consists of some 400 tombs of nobleman who worked in the service of the pharaohs. Only a few of these tombs are of special interest. Since this whole area is not well marked, you may want to hire a local guide to find the right tombs (take lots of small change with you as rewards for their services). The most interesting tombs in this area include:

- Khonsu, Userhet and Benia (#31, 51, 343)
- Menna and Nakht (#52, 69)
- Ramose, Userhet, Khaemhet (#55, 56, 57)
- Sennofer, Rekhmire (#96, 110)
- Nefer-Ronpet, Dhutmosi, Nefer-Sekheru (#178, 295, 296)

❏ **Mortuary Temples:** Not everything is underground on the West Bank. The pharaohs constructed several mortuary temples which were designed to glorify themselves by raising themselves to the level of gods amongst the population, both before and after their deaths. Many of the mortuary temples have been destroyed – in rubble or disappeared altogether. The two most impressive ones are the much-visited Deir al-Bahri (Mortuary Temple of Hatshepsut) and the underrated Medinet Habu (mortuary temple of Ramses III). Deir al-Bahri (Hatshepsut) unfortunately became the site of the terrorist massacre of more than 65 European tourists in 1997 which, in turn, was responsible for a dramatic decline in tourism to Egypt in the subsequent 18-month period. Medinet Habu is wonderful temple complex (the area's second largest after the Great Temple at Karnak) which has fewer visitors than most other sites. The major mortuary temples in various stages of preservation include the following:

- Deir al-Bahri (Hatshepsut) – complete
- Medinet Habu (Ramses III) – complete
- Ramesseum (Ramses II) – in ruins
- Seti I – partial ruins
- Colossi of Memnon – only two seated statues remain

❑ **Deir al-Medina (Monastery of the Town):** Named after a temple used by Christian monks, this is also known as the Village of the Workman. It includes a small temple, houses, and the tombs of the many artisans and workers who built the royal tombs and resided in this area. While small in scale, the three tombs (Sennedjem #1, Peshedu #3, and Aneuka #359) that are open to the public demonstrate the beautiful paintings and reliefs of the artists who lived here. Archaeologists also have unearthed over 70 houses in the areas. The villagers currently living in this area are very friendly and will try to sell you lots of tourist kitsch.

ENTERTAINMENT

After a long and hot day of temple and tomb touring, you may not think you have much energy left to go out on the town. However, there's lots to do in the evening, from strolling down the Corniche and shopping to taking in a sound-and-light show. Here are your major options:

❑ **Shopping**: Most shops and markets stay open until 10pm each evening, which makes good sense since during the day most people are outside the city touring.

❑ **Sound and light show:** One of the best sound and light shows in Egypt takes place nightly at the Temple of Karnak. Offered in seven different languages on alternative nights, English-language shows are held nightly at different times (shows start at 6:30, 7:45, and 9pm during most of the year except summer when they start an hour later). Check with your hotel or tour guide on appropriate dates and times for the different language presentations.

❑ **Cultural shows:** Several major hotels, such as the Isis, Winter Palace, Mercure Inn, and Mövenpick Jolie Ville, put on cultural shows which usually include an obligatory belly-dancer, local music, and maybe a snake charmer.

❑ **Bars, nightclubs, and discos:** Don't expect a lot from Luxor when it comes to bars, nightclubs, and discos. This is not Cairo, Sharm el-Sheikh, or Hurghada where there is a well defined Western-style nightlife. Most major hotels have bars and discos and maybe a nightclub. Check out what's going on at the Isis, Winter Palace, Mercure Inn (Mercure Nightclub), Sheraton, Mövenpick Jolie Ville, and Novotel Hotels.

❑ **Hantour (horse carriage ride):** A very pleasant way to enjoy the city is to hire a horse carriage for an hour ride up and down the Corniche and/or through the market areas. Be sure to heed our earlier advice on setting the price with the enterprising drivers who at times appear to be in the extortion business; you may end up in a shouting match when you try to settle the bill at the end of your journey – just thrust into his hand the money you agreed upon and walk away. Also, smell your horse before you rent the carriage. We've ended up with some horrendously smelling horses that nearly ruined our evening. Unfortunately, the poor stinking beasts of burden are seldom bathed by their owners who could also use a bath!

❑ **Felucca ride:** If you are in the city during the day and have time, one of the most pleasant things to do is take a one- or two-hour *felucca* ride on the Nile River. You'll find several of these boats for hire along the river. However, if you are planning to visit Aswan, you may want to postpone this ride until you get there. A *felucca* ride at Aswan is one of the highlights of visiting that city.

❑ **Golf:** Luxor has become a big center for golf. If you're interested in playing golf, check with the management at the Sheraton Hotel for details.

CRUISING SOUTH ALONG THE NILE

One of the highlights of any visit to Egypt is to take a river cruise from Luxor to Aswan or vice versa. As we noted earlier, over 300 cruise ships now ply the waters between Luxor and Aswan – up from 25 in 1975.

No trip to Egypt is complete without visiting Luxor with the nearby tombs of Thebes in the Valleys of the Kings and Queens and Temples of Karnak as well as the Aswan High Dam and other sights near the city of Aswan. Although it is possible to fly to both cities – Egypt Air provides several comfortable flights each day – the vessel of choice is a floating hotel – a Nile cruiser. The riverboats afford the opportunity to see the countryside and life along the river between Luxor and Aswan as well as make stops at the noted temples and archeological sites along the way. There are a staggering number of cruisers in service on the Nile. Travel along the Nile in Luxor in a small boat and you will see more than 200 large cruisers moored along the river banks. Not all are in service at present, but of those available the best include Abercrombie and Kent's Sunboats III and IV; Oberoi's MS Shehrazad and MS Philae; Pyramiza Hotel's MS Champollion; Travcotel's MS Regency and MS Royale; Sonesta's MS Nile Goddess and Sun Goddess; and Mövenpick's MS Radamis.

In keeping with our "best of the best" theme, we chose Abercrombie and Kent's (A&K) cruise which indeed confirmed that it was one of the best tour operators along the Nile. We were privileged to travel on its Sunboat IV between Luxor and Aswan. A&K operates several itineraries of Egypt. Our Nile cruise was part of A&K's 11-day Nile Explorer which begins with two days in Cairo visiting the Egyptian Museum of Antiquities, the ancient capital of Memphis, the nearby necropolis of Sakkara, the Pyramids at Giza, the Sphinx, and Solar Boat Museum. On the fifth day, travelers fly south to Luxor to board the Sunboat IV. Following the 5-day Nile cruise and a visit to Abu Simbel, the group returns to Cairo for a final day of sightseeing and shopping before boarding their return flight for home.

The Sunboat IV can carry 84 passengers, but each of the tour itineraries is limited to 24 travelers, and the sightseeing expeditions from the Sunboat with the Egyptologist are limited to that number as well, so everyone can always see and hear with no difficulty. When we approached the Sunboat IV for the first time, she was docked in Luxor. She looked regal compared to many other Nile cruisers we had passed along the way. Indeed, the docking facilities used by A&K at both Luxor and Aswan were in beautifully kept areas with gardens and greenery in abundance. We already felt privileged to be on this boat. Once we boarded, our expectations were again fulfilled. The interior was fitted with rich wood and gleaming brass in the spacious public areas. Our cabin was roomy for a boat, and space had been well utilized to make it feel gracious. The in-suite bath facilities were compact but provided everything we needed. The crew was superb. Whatever was needed was provided, yet the service was unobtrusive. The meals were beautifully served and the food presented allowed a wide choice catering to the palates of many different international passengers. For the final evening on board the Sunboat, there was a special program following dinner (as was the case most evenings) and when we returned to our cabin we found individual rose petals had been arranged on each bed to form a heart shape as part of the turn-down service. The rose petal hearts along with our evening candy made a memorable finish to our Nile cruise.

As indicated earlier, our Nile cruise was part of A&K's 11-day trip – The Nile Explorer. Our Nile cruise began in Luxor and then traveled south, or upstream, to Aswan. The tour is also operated with the reverse itinerary. We boarded the Sunboat and after lunch onboard, we left with our Egyptologist, Hoda, for a visit to Karnak. Our small number for the sightseeing excursions meant we could all see and hear and individual questions were welcomed. The Egyptologist was outstanding. Her knowledge was in great depth, but she didn't just spew facts. She was able to put information in context and make history come alive.

The next morning we visited the Colossi of Memnon, the Temple of Hatshepsut, and the underground tombs in the Valley of the Kings. The third day, in Esna, we visited the Temple of Khnum. The temple site is 36 feet below the level of the present town. While not much extra time was available for shopping, one really didn't need it. This is a small town of 30,000 which was once a major trading and weaving center. It's still a weaving center, and you'll find many locally produced handwoven materials and clothes in the market. The street leading to the temple goes straight through the bazaar which is filled with clothes and souvenirs which most people quickly pass through – a type of shopping gauntlet one knows will result in being hassled all the way to the main street! Indeed, the enterprising merchants here are good at enticing visitors into their shops with "bait and switch" tactics – quote one price on the street but raise it once you're in their shop. However, you may want to stop at a few shops to bargain for some unique locally produced materials and clothes. Many of the shawls, for example, are very beautiful and the prices can be relatively inexpensive, if you bargain hard. In fact, expect to get 50 to 65 discounts off the initial asking prices. These vendors are used to dealing with tourists who constitute nearly 100 percent of their market.

After a short cruise to Edfu, it was off the boat again to visit the Temple of Horus, the falcon god. The market area in front of this temple is lined with aggressive in-your-face vendors offering similar types of clothes, jewelry, alabaster, brassware, and souvenirs. Again, if you decide to buy anything, expect to get a 50 to 65 percent discount off an initial asking price.

On our final full day on the Sunboat, we visited the town of Kom Ombo and its famous Greco-Roman temple dedicated to two gods – Sobek, the crocodile god, and Haroeris, the sun god.

After docking at Aswan, we boarded feluccas – typical small boats with a sail – to sightsee in the local area. The following day we visited the Aswan High Dam and the Temple of Isis – moved stone by stone to a nearby island to save it from the rising waters the dam created and which submerged its original site on the island of Philae. Early that afternoon we bid farewell to our floating hotel and flew – still with our small group of travelers and Egyptologist – to Abu Simbel to visit the colossal temples of Ramses II and his queen Nefertari. We could not decide whether the greater feat was in the ancient building of the temples or in the modern engineering and moving of the temples some 60 feet to higher ground to save them from the rising waters of the lake created by the dam. From Abu Simbel we flew to Cairo where the A&K tour group had more time to explore the ancient and modern attractions of Cairo. Although most travelers book the entire tour with A&K, it may be possible to book just the Nile cruise portion of this and other tours separately. This option is available 30 days in advance of departure on a space-available basis.

To contact Abercrombie and Kent for brochures on this or other tours of the Nile and greater Egypt, call toll-free from North America at 800-757-5884; for other information, call 800-323-7308. From overseas, call 630-954-2922. Visit their website at *www.abercrombiekent.com* or write to them as follows: Abercrombie and Kent, 1520 Kensington Road, Oak Brook, Illinois 60523-2141 USA.

8

Aswan and Abu Simbel

L OCATED NEARLY 900 KILOMETERS (550 MILES) south of Cairo and 210 kilometers (133 miles) south of Luxor, Aswan is a Nubian city which also serves as the gateway to Africa, and especially to neighboring Sudan. Indeed, while the rest of lower Egypt appears to be very Middle Eastern, Aswan introduces visitors to the fact that Egypt is also an African country with a population and culture that are distinctively African. Aswan is Egypt's southernmost city, an attractive desert outpost for managing Egypt's major water and power resource, the Aswan Dam, and for welcoming thousands of tourists who visit the city by river cruise boat in search of more Egyptian antiquities. While they discover more temples and tombs in this southernmost outpost of ancient Egypt, they also get an interesting introduction to African Egypt.

Aswan is a popular destination because of the Aswan Dam and the resulting international effort to relocate major ancient monuments from the former Nile River valley which was inundated following the completion of the Aswan Dam. As a result, many visitors spend a day or two in Aswan visiting a few local monuments, learning a little about the Nubian culture, and then visiting the famous monuments of Abu Simbel, especially the temples of Ramses II and Nefertari, which are

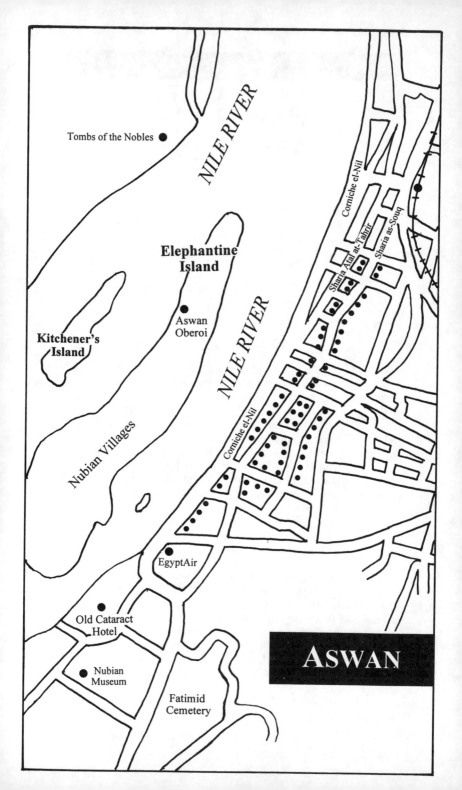

located 280 kilometers (175 miles) south of Aswan along the banks of Lake Nassar.

A CITY, A RIVER, A LAKE

For many visitors, a trip to Aswan and Abu Simbel is the highlight of their Egyptian adventure, a perfect ending to a fabulous journey into antiquity. After the noise and chaos of Cairo and the crowds, touts, and hassles of Luxor, laid back, sunny, and friendly Aswan comes as a pleasant surprise. The atmosphere here is more like a quiet resort surrounded with many interesting historical and cultural things to see and do, including shopping for unique items not found elsewhere in Egypt.

While Aswan is most noted as the gateway city to the famous Aswan Dam, Lake Nassar, and Abu Simbel, it's also Egypt's last major outpost to the African frontier that lies south of Lake Nassar. Strategically located, it has long served as Egypt's major link to Africa, the place where armies secured Egypt's frontier (and still do) and where caravan trade routes met to create a lucrative market for African and Egyptian goods. The Nubians, who are Egypt's unique black African population (also see pages 20-21) with their own language and culture, have long dominated this area and played an important role in the development of ancient Egypt. Largely displaced in recent years with the creation of the Aswan Dam which inundated their villages along the Nile River, today the Nubian influence is found everywhere in the Aswan area, from brightly colored villages and unique architectural styles to fascinating Nubian products found in the local bazaars. In fact, this is one of the added bonuses of visiting Aswan – discovering the Nubian culture and the many unique products created by this interesting population. If you wish to shop for Nubian items, as well as products from neighboring Sudan, especially woven baskets, knives, jewelry, pots, bowls, and walking sticks, the shops in Aswan will not disappoint you.

❏ Aswan is Egypt's southern most city, its gateway to Africa.

❏ The Nubians have long dominated this area and played an important role in Egypt.

❏ Except for the Nubian Museum, most major attractions are found outside the city.

❏ Aswan's most unique shopping reflects its close proximity to neighboring African countries.

❏ Merchants here tend to be less aggressive and more accommodating than those encountered in Luxor.

GETTING TO KNOW YOU

Aswan is a relatively easy city to get oriented to and navigate. Like Luxor, it has its East Bank and West Bank, an attractive Corniche, and numerous shops and hotels that define the center of the city. It also has a few interesting islands in the middle of the Nile River that are popular for sightseeing. As a major terminus point for cruise ships that ply the waters between Aswan and Luxor, you'll see dozens of river boats docked near the downtown area as well as many *feluccas* that sail up, down, and across the river – one of the major attractions for visitors who just want to relax on this charming section of the Nile.

The main part of the city stretches for over one kilometer along the east bank of the Nile River. For visitors, the city basically has two major north-south streets: **Corniche el-Nil** which runs along the river, and **Sharia as-Souq** which runs parallel to the Corniche and is Aswan's vibrant market street. Major hotels, banks, and airline offices are found along the southern stretch of the Corniche. The local tourist office and train station are located at the northern end of the market street, Sharia as-Souq.

Except for the fabulous Nubian Museum, most major historical attractions are found outside the city where visitors spend most of their day. Returning to their hotels and ships in late afternoon, visitors focus their evening activities on the city. Indeed, the city comes alive at night as visitors frequent restaurants along the Corniche or go shopping along the nearby streets for jewelry, clothes, and handicrafts.

SHOPPING ASWAN

Given Aswan's role as a center for Nubian culture and as a gateway city to Africa, and especially to neighboring Sudan, some of Aswan's most unique shopping reflects its close proximity to neighboring African countries. While you will find many of the same types of shops found elsewhere in Egypt, such as gold, jewelry, clothing, and handicrafts, also look for more and more shops reflecting local products. The market in particular has many vendors selling a wide selection of spices, musical instruments, papyrus, tribal jewelry, and antiques and artifacts from the Sudan. The merchants here tend to be less aggressive and more friendly and accommodating than those encountered in Luxor. The most frequent street conversation includes these friendly catch phrases thrown at tourists: *"No hassle," "Free to look," "Come into my shop,"* and *"Welcome to Alaska!"* Many of the merchants are delightful to engage in conversation and bargain over prices.

Not surprising, Aswan has two major shopping areas that correspond to its two major streets – Corniche el-Nil and Sharia as-Souq. In between these streets are a few other streets, such as Ahmed Maher Street, lined with interesting shops. While you will find a few shops in the major hotels offering the typical range of tourist jewelry, handicrafts, books, and postcards, most of Aswan's major and most interesting shopping is found in a few good quality shops along the Corniche as well as in the huge city bazaar that stretches the length of Sharia as-Souq.

The easiest and most productive way to approach shopping in Aswan is to start along the Corniche near the Egypt Air office. If you take a taxi to this office, you'll be at a good starting point. Just north of this office you'll come to a couple of distinctive looking shops that have been constructed to look like domed Nubian structures or cave buildings – **Hanafy-Bazar** (42 Corniche el-Nil Street, Tel. 314-083) and **Bazar Aboslah** (45 Corniche el-Nil Street, Tel. 304-657). These two adjacent shops are jam-packed with interesting antiques, artifacts, and handicrafts produced by the Nubians, Besharis, and Sudanese: woven baskets, knives, bowls, walking sticks, neckpieces, and pots. Many of the old pots are especially attractive. These two shops alone will give you a good overview of the types of local ethnic products available in Aswan.

As you leave these two shops, turn right and walk north along the Corniche until you come to a narrow corner shop variously called **Pacience & Faith Bazar** (sign outside) and **El-Sabr & El-Iman Bazar** (on business card). While you can easily miss this shop because of the poor signage, do make a special effort to find this shop. The unimpressive entrance, which has a few rugs on display, consists of a well carpeted staircase to the upper floor which opens up into a large room filled with rugs, wall hangings, appliqué goods, leather (camel) bags, clothes, and handicrafts. This place has real ethnic character.

After leaving this shop, turn right again and walk north until you come to several gold, silver, and brass shops which are located next to each other at 85 Corniche el-Nil. The three most interesting shops here are located adjacent to each other Hend Jewelry, St. George Bazar, and Tony Bazar. **Hend Jewellery** (Tel. 316-539) primarily specializes in gold and silver jewelry and is usually very busy at night. **St. George Bazar** offers a nice selection of loose stones, crystal, and handcrafted items. **Tony Bazar** (Tel. 303-176) offers a good selection of gold and silver jewelry as well as attractive necklaces made with semi-precious stones. Two blocks farther north is another good jewelry store, **Villa Bazar**.

The best place to turn into the main bazaar is at the corner where you'll find the big white **Government Store** (5 Corniche el-Nil Street), which also offers a large selection of jewelry and souvenirs. Turn right at the shop and go two blocks east (you'll pass by several gold shops) until you come to Sharia as-Souq. This is the main market street, with the majority of the market located to the left or north. Along the way, be sure to look for Ahmed Maher Street which has a few interesting arts and crafts shops such as Rafeal Store and African the Sudanese Bazaar. **Rafeal Store** includes a large selection of handicrafts (lots of tourist kitsch) as well as old silver jewelry (downstairs) and old Nubian and Beshari artifacts upstairs. Across the street and to the right is **African the Sudanese Bazaar** (Tel. 313-077), a Nubian shop filled with an interesting collection of baskets, boxes, knives, woven fruit and bread baskets, jewelry, brass-ware, loose stones, alabaster, leather bags, and musical instruments; this is one of the better shops in Aswan.

Sharia as-Souq is a fascinating street, a cultural experience in people-watching and bazaar shopping. The street scenes are a photographer's dream come true, although be careful whom you shoot without their permission. The sights and sounds are truly Third World, very ethnic, and nearly biblical at times. While you may find few things to buy along this street – since most items are for local consumption – you'll most likely have an interesting time just absorbing the colorful chaos, viewing the local activities, and occasionally conversing with the locals. Many of the market scenes are especially memorable: men smoking their *shishas* (pipes); women dressed in black; colorful and pungent spices piled high; butchers working their fresh kills; bakers producing breads in huge hot ovens; souvenir sellers engaged in aggressive "in-your-face" retailing; fresh-vegetable vendors; chickens turning on a fiery rotisserie; barros pulling carts; and cars honking in the midst of congested pedestrian traffic.

ACCOMMODATIONS

Similar to Luxor, Aswan has a good range of accommodations, from the classic Old Cataract Hotel (the equivalent to Luxor's Old Winter Palace Hotel) to the budget hotels. And like Luxor, many visitors use the cruise ships as their hotels. Some of the best properties in Aswan include the following:

❑ **Sofitel Old Cataract Hotel:** *Abtal El Tahrir St., Aswan, Egypt, Tel. (2097) 316-000, Fax (2097) 316-011.* Built in the Nubian Desert on the bank of the Nile opposite Elephantine Island, the legendary Old Cataract Hotel is majestically positioned on an outcrop of pink granite overlooking the Nile and the city of Aswan. Agatha Christie immortalized the hotel in her novel, *Death on the Nile*, and the film version was shot on location. Behind its Victorian earth-toned facade, the hotel retains its original beauty. The public areas are striking – the lobby with its polished marble floor and high classic ochre and cream colored Moorish arches transport the visitor back in time. Renovations have been made to add modern conveniences while retaining the hotel's character. The 131 guest rooms and suites vary in decor and configuration. The special touches, including Persian carpets, hand-carved furniture, and antique accents, are most likely to be found in the suites. Some rooms feature balconies with a Nile view. All eight theme suites (including Agatha Christie and Winston Churchill) offer a panoramic view from their terrace. The Terrace Restaurant commands a spectacular view of the Nile for drinks, snacks, and afternoon tea; Restaurant 1902 serves breakfast and an elegant a la carte dinner in majestic old fashioned surroundings. There is a small shopping area in The New Cataract Hotel located next door. Fitness Facilities; Conference and Banquet Facilities.

❑ **New Cataract Hotel:** *Abtal El Tahrir St., Aswan, Egypt, Tel. (2097) 316-000, Fax (2097) 316-011.* The New Cataract is a modern high rise, sharing the legendary Old Cataract Hotel location on the bank of the Nile opposite Elephantine Island, overlooking the Nile and the city of Aswan. The eight-story building lacks the old-world charm of the Old Cataract Hotel, but the views are superb and each of the 144 guestrooms is spacious and has a balcony from which to enjoy the view. The Nefertari Restaurant serves breakfast and a dinner theme buffet including Oriental and Nubian evenings during the winter season. Souno coffee shop is for snacks and light a la carte meals. Darna Restaurant offers a la carte authentic Nubian and Egyptian fares. Fitness Facilities. For Conference and Banquet Facilities, contact Old Cataract Hotel above.

❑ **Aswan Oberoi Hotel and Spa:** *Elephantine Island, Aswan, Egypt, Tel. (2097) 314-666, Fax (2097) 323-485.* The exterior has a rather block-like austere appearance, but once inside the first-class facilities, amenities and service for which the Oberoi chain is known make up for what the facade is lacking in character. The setting, an island in the middle of the Nile with lots of gardens, is attractive and the views of *feluccas* as they sail by provide a sense of place. The 244 guest rooms and suites provide all the expected amenities. Several Restaurants; Fitness Facilities.

RESTAURANTS

Most of the city's good restaurants are found in the major hotels or along the Corniche. While Aswan is not a major culinary center – food is acceptable – the best part of dining in Aswan is usually the view of the river and/or sunset. If you are with a cruise ship, chances are all your meals are available on board and thus you need not forage for food amongst the city's many questionable restaurants. Assuming you will dine sometime in Aswan, here are some of the best places to eat:

❑ **The 1902:** *Sofitel Old Cataract Hotel, Shar'a Abtal al-Tahrir, Tel. 316-000. Reservations and jacket required.* This is Aswan's most elegant restaurant in Aswan's most elegant old hotel. The large domed dining room, which resembles a 13th-century Mamluk mausoleum, has lots of old-world charm. Dine by candlelight and enjoy the restaurant's many unique specialties. Hotel guests have priority with reservations.

❑ **The Lotus:** *Shar'a Abtal al-Tahrir, Tel. 310-901.* This French-Continental restaurant offers both indoor and outdoor dining in a lovely setting. Great ambience.

❑ **The Darna:** *New Cataract Hotel, Shar'a Abtal al-Tahrir, Tel. 316-000.* This Nubian-style restaurant serves good Egyptian food, including a nice selection of *mezzes, tagines, rice khalta,* and *Om Ali.*

❑ **Al-Masry:** *Sharia al-Matar, Tel. 302-576.* Popular with locals, this relatively inexpensive restaurant is noted for its kebabs and *kofta.*

SEEING THE SITES

In addition to shopping and dining, there's lots to see and do in Aswan to occupy at least two full days. Here are some of the sightseeing highlights of visiting three areas in Aswan – East Bank, Islands, and West Bank.

ASWAN – EAST BANK

❑ **The Nubian Museum:** Opened in November 1997, this is one of Egypt's finest museums. Showcases the local Nubian history, art, and culture, from prehistoric times to the present day. Wonderful and informative displays that honor the Nubian people who sacrificed so much upon the construction of the Aswan Dam.

❑ **Unfinished Obelisk:** Located north of the Nubian Museum and east of the Fatamid Cemetery. If you want to see how the stone obelisks were made and transported, be sure to visit this old red granite quarry that used to supply materials for the ancient temples. The Unfinished Obelisk, which weighs 1,168 tons and is 41 meters in length, was abandoned because of a major flaw in the granite.

ASWAN – ISLANDS

❑ **Philae Temple and the Temple of Isis:** These are among the highlights of Aswan for many visitors. Constructed in the Ptolemaic period (332-30 BC), the temples were relocated from Agilkia Island by UNESCO in 1972-80 because of the construction of the Aswan Dam which eventually flooded the island. It's a magnificent reconstruction job. You must take a motorboat to reach the Philae Island which is itself a pleasant trip. You may want to attend one of the sound and light shows at night (three per night in different languages).

❑ **Elephantine Island:** This is reputed to be the original settlement in Aswan. Located opposite the Corniche, this two-kilometer long, 500-meter wide island includes the Aswan Museum, Temple of Satis, Temple of Khnum, Nilometer, and an interesting Nubian village at the northern end of the island. You can get to this island by taking a *felucca* along the Corniche or a public ferry at the southern end of the Corniche.

❑ **Kitchener's Island:** Located north of Elephantine Island, this is the site for Aswan's Botannical Garden, a 17-acre island with nearly 800 different tropical plans. The island can be reached by *felucca* or ferry (we prefer the much cheaper ferry – L£1 versus L£5). The docking area at the southern end of the island has a café and lots of vendors selling souvenirs. Using the toilet here can be a hassle, as the toilet touts try to rip off visitors for L£5 to use the public toilets – give them L£1 and walk away despite any protests.

ASWAN — WEST BANK

❑ **St. Simeon's Monastery:** Located on top of a hill on the West Bank, this 5th-century AD Coptic monastery is one of the most interesting places to visit in Aswan. You won't find many tourists around. Rent a camel and take the 15-minute camel ride from the monastery to the shores of Nile River. The ride itself is one of the highlights of this trip.

❑ **Tombs of the Nobles:** Located on top of the hill on the West Bank and north of Kitchener's Island and with a lovely view of Aswan (take a camel or walk up the hill), these tombs date from the 23rd century BC and are the final resting place for the many noblemen who ran this trading outpost. A few of these tombs are open to the public. The most interesting ones include the tombs of:

- Heqaib (#35)
- Khounes (#34)
- Mekhu and Sabni (#25 and 26)
- Serenput I (#36)
- Serenput II (#31)

❑ **Mausoleum of the Aga Khan:** You can't miss this mausoleum as you look up the hill of the West Bank toward St. Simeon's Monastery – it's on the left. A recent structure (Mohammed Shah Aga Khan, who was the leader of the Ismaili sect of Islam, died in 1957), this attractive domed granite and sandstone tomb, modeled after the Fatimid tombs of Cairo, is currently closed to the public.

ASWAN DAM AND LAKE NASSAR

Any visit to Aswan would be incomplete without touring the massive Aswan Dam. Designed by the Germans and constructed by the Soviet Union, this controversial dam was completed in 1971. Ostensibly designed to generate electricity, control unpredictable annual flooding, provide year-round irrigation, and develop fisheries, the dam also displaced thousands of Nubians as well as created new ecological and health problems along the river which were unanticipated by concrete gravity dam, designers who were more familiar with building such structures in temperate rather than tropical climates. Nonetheless, the dam has been functioning for nearly 30 years and the cost-benefits at present tend to favor advocates of cheap electricity and irrigation, although the ecological and health problems remain very real – a lesson in what not to do when building such dams.

Once you drive across the spillway and arrive at the viewing area, there's really not much to see or even photograph – just a lot of water and an occasional boat on Lake Nassar. Consequently, don't plan to spend much of your day here – you can do the dam and lake in less than two hours, preferably early in the morning or late in the afternoon. Cruise boats do operate on the lake but the view doesn't get much better, and the river cruises are much more interesting. However, to approach Abu Simbel from the lake is supposedly quite an experience. At the same time, there are several Nubian monuments that were rescued during the construction of the dam and relocated to higher ground; most of these monuments can only be reached by cruise boats.

The sprawling Aswan Dam is one of those been-there-done-that type of attractions which you may soon forget.

ABU SIMBEL

Many visitors come to Aswan for one purpose – visit Abu Simbel, which is located 175 miles south of Aswan. This is where the two massive temples (the Great Temple of Ramses II and the Temple of Nefertari) were moved to higher ground when the Aswan High Dam was being built. A four-year international project, it was one of the world's major engineering feats that seems to rival the building of the great pyramids! While the temples themselves are very interesting, and visitors marvel at how such massive structures could be relocated, there's another side to these temples which you could easily miss if you only looked at the outside structures and visited the various chambers of the temples. Whatever you do, make sure you walk through the dome enclosure concealed behind and on top of the two temples. There you will be able to see the incredible engineering work that continues to this day to preserve these two temples. Indeed, many visitors find these engineering works as interesting as the temples below!

You can reach Abu Simbel by road, air, or boat. The road to Abu Simbel, which was closed for a couple of years due to security issues, is once again open to the public. The trip by car or bus takes about 3½ hours each way. The 30-minute Egypt Air flight to Abu Simbel, which regularly leaves Aswan, is the most convenient way to visit this site. If you fly, the trip to and from Abu Simbel only takes a half day. You'll probably only visit the site for one or two hours and then be ready to return to Aswan. Seven hours of driving through the desert for a one- to two-hour visit is not our idea of good time! There are few hotels here and most visitors fly in and out within a two hour or so period (your plane stays on the ground with your luggage while you visit the site).

ENJOYING YOUR STAY

In addition to visiting monuments, museums, and gardens, consider doing the following during your stay in Aswan:

❑ **Camel ride:** If you visit the West Bank, take a camel ride to or from St. Simeon's Monastery and/or the Tombs of the Nobles. It's great fun and the views of Aswan and river from the top of your camel are spectacular.

❑ **Felucca ride:** Aswan is one of the best places to take a *felucca* ride. The surrounding scenery is beautiful and the river very pleasant. Hire a *felucca* by the hour to tour the islands and sail up and down the river. Two hours on the water will probably be plenty. Be sure to bargain hard for your boat which should run about L£20-25 per hour for the whole boat (add L£2-3 per person if you have a group of 12 or more people).

❑ **Sunsets:** Aswan has beautiful sunsets. One of the best places to enjoy the sunset is the terrace on the south side of the Old Cataract Hotel. Pull up a table, order a drink, and look out over the Nile and West Bank as the sun slowly sets on Aswan's Necropolis. This may be the same place Winston Churchill, Agatha Christie, Theodore Roosevelt, and/or Howard Carter of Tutankhamun fame enjoyed their sunsets over the Nile. It's the perfect ending to what may have been a perfect cruise down the Nile.

❑ **Sound and light show at Philae:** Three sound and light shows take place each night at the Temple of Philae. Check with your hotel or guide on the exact times for various languages. At least one show is in English each night (usually the first show on Wednesdays, Fridays, and Saturdays and the second show on Mondays and Thursdays).

❑ **Bars, discos, nightclubs, and cultural shows:** The major hotels have bars which are tame by most standards. The Old Cataract, Oberoi, Isis, Kalabsha, Amon Island, and Ramses Hotels also have nightclubs – yes, you'll often get another belly dancer! Some hotels also put on cultural shows. Check with the Aswan Cultural Center (Corniche, Tel. 313-390) for their program of events, which include Nubian folkloric dances, which usually take place in the evenings during the winter months.

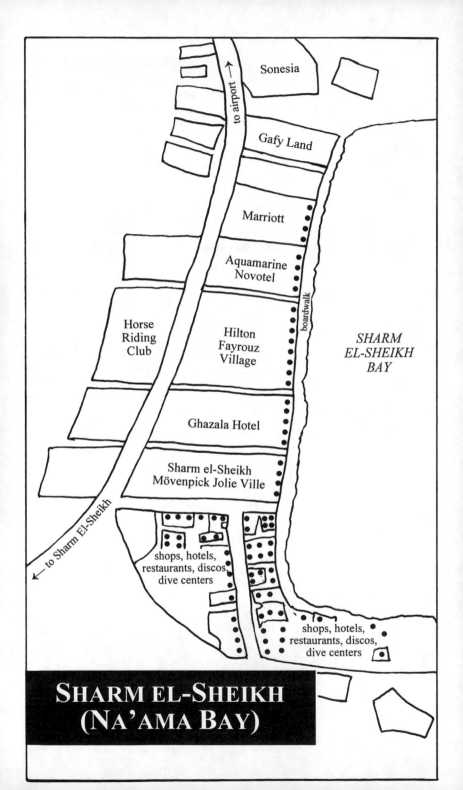

SHARM EL-SHEIKH (NA'AMA BAY)

9

Sharm el-Sheikh
and the Sinai

A FTER EXPLORING CAIRO, ALEXANDRIA, AND the Nile Valley, Sharm el-Sheikh and the Sinai are unexpected surprises. Located at the tip of the Sinai Peninsula and facing the Red Sea, Sharm el-Sheikh is one of Egypt's most popular resort destinations for both Egyptians and foreigners who often refer to it as the center of the "Red Sea Riveria," the area that runs the length of the east coast of the Sinai Peninsula, from Taba in the north to Sharm el-Sheikh in the south. Indeed, Sharm el-Sheikh represents Egypt's plunge into major international resort tourism, complete with well managed five-star resorts offering the best in sports, entertainment, dining, and shopping. Other areas that dot the Sinai Peninsula also offer some interesting surprises.

Tourism in Sharm el-Sheikh and other parts of the Sinai Peninsula is relatively recent. Following Israel's seizure of the Sinai Peninsula in the 1967 Six Day War, Sharm become a favorite outpost for Israelis, who also saw the potential for developing tourism in this ideal location. However, Israel returned Sharm el-Sheikh, along with the rest of the Sinai Peninsula, to Egypt as a result of the Camp David negotiations in the 1980s. Since the mid 1990s, Sharm has taken off as a major resort destination as millions of dollars in foreign investment have gone into developing a first-class tourist infrastructure. Today, Sharm el-Sheikh is one of Egypt's great success stories. Major hotels and resorts, such as the Ritz-Carlton, have opened properties within the past year. And more and more resorts continue to be built in anticipation of more and more tourists discovering the sun and fun charms of Sharm.

THE CHARMS OF SHARM

Each year thousands of Italians, Swiss, French, Spanish, Greek, British, Russian, Japanese, and American tourists come to Sharm el-Sheikh to enjoy the pleasant climate, beaches, water sports, skin diving, shopping, dining, and nightlife. It's an especially popular destination with Italians, who are responsible for the resort's many nice open-air Italian restaurants that face Na'ama Bay. For most visitors, this is a relatively inexpensive resort destination with lots to see and do, from water and beach activities to day trips into the desert. Although many new hotels and resorts are being built in Sharm el-Sheikh to accommodate the growing number of tourists, many properties are fully booked during the popular resort months of September to March. Be sure to make reservations well in advance during those months.

❑ Sharm el-Sheikh represents Egypt's plunge into major international resort tourism. It represents one of Egypt's great success stories.

❑ Many properties are fully booked during the popular resort months of September to March.

❑ Sharm offers spectacular diving opportunities – reputed to be the best in the world.

❑ The main shopping area is in the southern section of Na'ama Bay.

❑ Most shops stay open until midnight – the ultimate place in Egypt for late night shopping – given the night owl nature Sharm's tourist crowd.

While the resort is especially popular for its spectacular diving opportunities – reputed to be the best in the world – it's also one of the better places to shop in Egypt. There's lots of shopping in main resort area of Na'ama Bay. Shopping in Sharm can be both fun and rewarding despite its stereotyped resort character. Numerous shops line the southern section of Na'ama Bay which especially comes alive late in the evening. Indeed, most shops stay open until midnight because of the crowds that like to stay up late dining, drinking, and dancing until way beyond midnight – the streets finally quiet down after 3am! Unlike the many tourist trinket shops, with their in-your-face retailers that line the streets of the Upper Nile, in Sharm el-Sheikh the merchants are very laid back and offer more quality merchandise than found in other Egyptian cities. In fact, shopping in Sharm may become one of the major highlights of visiting this resort community.

INTO THE DESERT

Located 320 miles southeast of Cairo, Sharm el-Sheikh is conveniently reached within 55 minutes by daily Egypt Air service. On most days one flight goes to Sharm el-Sheikh. On some busy days there may be up to three flights servicing Sharm. You can also drive to Sharm from Cairo which will take about seven hours.

Since Sharm el-Sheikh is increasingly becoming a very popular destination for international travelers, many flights, including charters, fly directly into Sharm. At present 15 to 20 international flights arrive each day.

As soon as you fly into Sharm el-Sheikh, you'll notice the difference in typography between the Upper Nile and the Sinai Peninsula. Large expanses of sandy desert punctuated with rugged dry mountains characterize much of the Sinai Peninsula. Except for an occasional oasis, this is a very dry peninsula where the only vegetation seems to have been planted and irrigated by resort complexes that hug the coastal areas facing the Red Sea and the Gulf of Aqaba.

While there is not a lot to see and do in the Sinai outside the major resort cities, any visit to the Sinai should include a visit to the Monastery of St. Catherine which is located approximately 150 miles northwest of Sharm el-Sheikh. If you're planning to visit Israel, you also may want to drive from St. Catherine to Taba, which is Egypt's northeastern border town next to the Israeli resort of Eilat as well as Jordan's port and resort town of Aqaba. Not far from the convergence of these three cities, just south of Aqaba, lies Saudi Arabia.

GETTING TO KNOW YOU

Sharm el-Sheikh consists of several beach and town areas that are spread over a 20-kilometer coastal area. Most visitors head for **Na'ama Bay** which is the major resort area. Here you'll find most four- and five-star resorts as well as the top restaurants, entertainment, shopping, and diving centers. Sharm el-Sheikh City is located about 4½ miles from Na'ama Bay. It has a few hotels, restaurants, supermarkets, banks, a post office, and the

Egypt Air office. Since Sharm el-Sheikh is a decidedly upscale resort area, backpackers tend to head 50 miles north for the beach resort of Dahab where they find accommodations, restaurants, and entertainment more within their budgets. The crowd in Sharm loves to have a good time, be it on the beach, scuba diving, shopping, gambling, or disco dancing until 4am.

Unlike other areas in Egypt, you may want to rent a car in Sharm el-Sheikh. While taxis are available, they can be very expensive and inconvenient. For car rentals, try these agencies: **Budget** (Tel. 601-610), **Hertz** (Tel. 600-100), and **Europcar** (Tel. 600-686 and 600-266).

SHOPPING SHARM

The shops in Sharm el-Sheikh tend to be more upscale than those found elsewhere in Egypt. This in part reflects Sharm's wealthier clientele – European tourists who shop for quality goods. Consequently, you won't find a lot of the tourist kitsch here that you might find in Luxor. But you will find many shops offering the T-shirts and souvenirs normally associated with beach resorts.

Na'ama Bay's pleasant downtown area includes several sidewalk cafes, diving centers, and small supermarkets along with jewelry, rug, and handicraft shops. This whole area becomes very crowded late at night, especially from 8pm to midnight. Since shops close at midnight, this is the ultimate place in Egypt for late night shopping!

Shops are found along the main streets as well as in small malls, centers, and lanes. Half the fun of shopping here is discovering unique shops tucked away off the main thorough-fare. Some of our favorite shops in Sharm include the following:

❑ **Aqua Marine Jewelry:** *Na'ama Bay, Tiran Hotel.* Offers a nice collection of gold jewelry and precious stones. Factory located in Cairo.

❑ **Lost Treasure Galley:** *Na'ama Bay, Sharm Mall, Tel. 670-407.* This shop is a good place to shop for jewelry and gift items. It includes a nice selection of jewelry, loose stones, amber, inlaid boxes, chest sets, alabaster, and plates.

❑ **Karkade Shops:** *Na'ama Bay, Sharm Mall, Tel. 602-855.* This small but colorful and charming spice shop ("natural pharmacy") offers an excellent selection of spices, herbs, oils, creams, and perfumes for medicinal purposes.

❑ **Bashayer:** *Na'ama Bay, El Sharm Mall, Tel. 600-808.* This is a branch shop of a major arts and crafts shop in Cairo (58 Mosadek Street, Dokki, Giza, Tel. 336-1006) which also has another branch in Abu Dhabi. Includes an attractive collection of brass pots, Siwe textiles, pillows, bags, and stuffed toys.

❑ **Baraka Carpets:** *Na'ama Bay, El Sharm Mall, Tel. 181-597.* Offers a nice colorful selection of old and new wool kilims, Bedouin (Siwe) carpets, silk patchwork, applique, and wall hangings. Many of the items are made in Luxor.

❑ **Stella di Sharm:** *Na'ama Bay, Shamandura Mall, Tel. 600-414.* This small but popular shop includes silver, rings, and cartouches as well as coral from Tunisia and turquoise from Egypt.

❑ **Bedouin:** *Na'ama Bay, The Old City Walk, Sanafir Hotel, Tel. 600-197, ext. 570.* Somewhat difficult to find because it is located off the main street along a small lane, this shop includes a good collection of Bedouin tribal jewelry and handicrafts. Everything is handmade by Bedouins in the Sinai and elsewhere in Egypt.

ACCOMMODATIONS

Some of the best hotels and resorts in all of Egypt, as well as the Middle East, are found in Sharm el-Sheikh.

❑ **The Ritz-Carlton:** *Om-El Seed, (P.O. Box 72) Sharm el-Sheikh, South Sinai, Egypt, Tel. (2062) 661-919 or Fax (2062) 661-920. Website: www.ritzcarlton.com.* A new standard of luxury just opened in Sharm El Sheikh in December 1999. The Ritz-Carlton resort offers 307 guestrooms, including 48 suites, in low-rise two-level buildings. Each room has a private terrace with a choice of overlooking the sea or the lush landscaped gardens and unique desert oasis of pools, waterfalls, bridges and the 'lazy river.' The Ritz-Carlton Club is comprised of 25 rooms and 5 suites and offers a special measure of privacy, amenities, elegance, and service. Five complimentary food presentations daily are made available to Club guests. The guestroom bathrooms are large and luxurious and provide a separate shower enclosure, tub and a toilet enclosure. The Café offers all-day dining with lavish buffet presentations for breakfast and dinner. Choices include Californian, European, and Middle Eastern specialties. A la carte menus are available for breakfast, lunch and dinner. La Luna, an Italian restaurant, has an award-winning Italian chef who presents cuisines from various regions of Italy. Blue Ginger presents the flavors and spices of the Far East in this Red Sea specialty restaurant; the Singaporean Chef presents a blend of Malaysian, Singaporean, Korean, Chinese, Thai and Japanese cuisines. The *teppanyaki* table is a focal point amidst the Chinese lanterns and black marble pools. Fayrouz serves Lebanese dishes in a sumptuous setting. Several additional restaurants are available for snacks and poolside dining. The Ritz-Carlton is known for its attention and dedication to service. If you want to be truly pampered, you just can't do better in Sharm el-Sheikh than the Ritz-Carlton. The hotel will arrange tours to St. Catherine Monastery as well as other area sights. Shopping Arcade; Fitness Facilities; Spa; Business Services; Conference and Banquet Facilities.

❑ **Sharm El Sheikh Marriott Beach Resort:** *Na'ama Bay, Sharm el-Sheikh, South Sinai, Egypt, Tel. (2062) 600-190, Fax (2062) 600-188 or toll-free from the U.S. & Canada 800-228-9290.* Located on the Sinai Peninsula along the shores of the Red Sea, with its own private beach, the Sharm El Sheikh Marriott is one of the area's newest resorts. The two-story white facade sparkles in the sun against the blue of the sea. A spacious and light-filled atrium welcomes guests. The 206 guestrooms situated on two floors are spacious, comfortable and filled with light and offer all the expected amenities. Most rooms open onto the large pool or the beach. The Buffet Restaurant serves breakfast and dinner buffets. Kona Kai features Japanese *teppanyaki* table cooking and Polynesian specialties. Parmizziano Italian Restaurant serves authentic Italian dishes. The Beach BBQ and Fresh Seafood Market's selections are accompanied by a dance show and other live entertainment. There is a small shopping arcade off the lobby. Fitness facilities and water sports include water skiing, windsurfing, parasailing, snorkeling, and scuba diving – a world-renowned sport in this area. Complimentary airport shuttle bus.

❑ **Hilton Sharm El Sheikh Fayrouz Resort:** *Na'ama Bay, Sharm el-Sheikh, South Sinai, Egypt, Tel. (2062) 600-137, Fax (2062) 601-040, or toll-free from the U.S. & Canada (800) 445-8667.* The Hilton Fayrouz Resort commands the most central position on Na'ama Bay and boasts the longest sandy beach along with beautiful gardens. The 150 guest-rooms of the original resort plus the 60 new rooms of the extension which opened in July of 1999 all provide a private terrace and expected amenities. The Wadi Restaurant serves buffet style meals; the Fish Restaurant offers a la carte dinner; the Italian Beach Restaurant serves lunch and dinner; the Pirate Bar offers a light menu all day. A special event is a Starlight Dinner in the desert offered once weekly. Fitness Center and wide range of activities including a dive center, a branch center offering glass bottom boat, private yacht, kayak, waterskiing, parasailing and snorkeling trips. There are also desert safaris, camel safaris and excursions to all major points of interest.

❏ **Hilton Sharm Waterfalls Resort:** *Na'ama Bay, Sharm el-Sheikh, South Sinai, Egypt, Tel. (2062) 600-136, Fax (2062) 601-040, or toll-free from the U.S. or Canada (800) 445-8667.* Hilton Sharm Waterfalls Resort is situated on Ras Um El Sid cliff and is configured in a U-shape with all guestrooms overlooking the sea. The hotel is the first of its kind having a panoramic funicular connecting the lobby area to the main swimming pool along with water cascades. The 252 spacious guest rooms – each with a private terrace – offer expected amenities. The Main Dining Room and Terrace serves buffet style meals; the Fish Restaurant is located on the beach; There is an Italian and a Thai restaurant serving their respective specialties. The Starlight Dinner takes place in the desert one night each week. Fitness Center; Dive Center; extensive leisure activities; kids' playground and club; Meeting Facilities.

❏ **Hilton Sharm Dreams Resort:** *Na'ama Bay, Sharm el-Sheikh, South Sinai, Egypt, Tel. (2062) 603-040, Fax (2062) 602-828, or toll-free from the U.S. or Canada (800) 445-8667.* Hilton Sharm Dreams commands a central position on Na'ama Bay and boasts beautiful swimming pools and gardens. The 334 guest rooms offer private terraces and expected amenities. The Main Dining Room and Terrace serves buffet style meals. Other restaurants include a Seafood Restaurant, Italian Restaurant, Tex-Mex Restaurant and Terrace, Open air snack bar and BBQ area. A Starlight Dinner is offered once a week. Shops on premises; Disco-theque; Fitness Center plus a wide range of activities; Spa; Dive Center; Tennis Courts; Squash and Volleyball Courts; Billiards; kids' playground and club; Meeting Facility.

❏ **Mövenpick Jolie Ville Resort & Casino:** *Na'ama Bay, Sharm el-Sheikh, South Sinai, Egypt, Tel. (2062) 600-100, Fax (2062) 600-111.* Directly on the beach, the 356 guest rooms (10 are suites) are spacious and inviting and are located in 42 modern bungalows. Bleached woods and light-hued stone floor tiles give a visual coolness to sun-filled rooms with the expected amenities. Choose from La Fleur Restaurant; Orangerie; Pool Terrace Seagull's Pub; The Pavillion, or 64 Bar Barbecue and Beach Bar on the beach. Fitness Facilities; Dive Center and water sports including parasailing, water-skiing, wind surfing, catamaran, and snorkeling. Conference Rooms.

RESTAURANTS

Sharm el-Sheikh offers a good selection of restaurants, most of which are found in the hotels or in open-air settings along the boardwalk in Na'ama Bay where people-watching also is a favorite dining activity. Reflecting the resort's European clientele, many hotels have beachfront Italian and Continental restaurants. Seafood dishes are especially popular. You'll also find McDonald's, Pizza Hut, Pizza Express, and a Hard Rock Café in Sharm. Some of the best restaurants include:

❏ **La Luna:** *Ritz-Carlton, 661-919. Open nightly 6:30pm to 10:30pm.* This well appointed Italian restaurant, in the tradition of grand Italian palaces, is served by the hotel's award-winning Italian chef. Offers authentic cuisine from various regions of Italy. Includes a wine room.

❏ **Blue Ginger:** *Ritz-Carlton, 661-919. Open nightly 6:30pm to 10:30pm.* The Singaporean chef offers a wide range of Asian specialties that blend Malaysian, Singaporean, Korean, Chinese, Thai, and Japanese cuisine. The 12-seat *teppanyaki* table is a focal point amidst the Chinese lanterns and black marble pools.

❏ **Fayrouz:** *Ritz-Carlton, 661-919. Open nightly 6:30pm to 10:30pm.* This cozy Lebanese restaurant, with gold leaf ceilings, silk wall coverings, and black marble waterfall, offers native Lebanese and Middle Eastern cuisine accompanied by regional wines. Includes nightly Lebanese instrumental music and a bellydancer performance. Guests can relax after dinner on the patio to smoke the traditional *shisha* pipe.

❑ **Kokai:** *Ghazala Hotel, Na'ama Bay, Tel. 600-150.* This popular Polynesian-Japanese-Chinese specialty restaurant serves excellent dishes with a flair: watch the chefs prepare dishes at the *teppanyaki* grill tables. Good location along the boardwalk.

❑ **De Franco:** *Ghazala Hotel, Na'ama Bay, Tel. 600-150. Open for lunch and dinner.* This popular Italian restaurant serves everything from soups and pizzas to fine pasta dishes. Its popular pizzas are baked in wood-heated clay-brick ovens. Dine outside on the terrace by candlelight, but get there before 6:30pm if you want a seat.

❑ **Kona Kai:** *Marriott Beach Resort, Na'ama Bay, Tel. 600-190. Open nightly 7 to 11pm.* Serves excellent Japanese teppanyaki dishes.

❑ **Liwa:** *Sofitel Sharm al-Sheikh Coralia, Na'ama Bay, Tel. 600-080.* Serves an excellent dinner buffet with an heavy emphasis on seafood.

❑ **Tam Tam:** *Ghazala Hotel, Na'ama Bay, Tel. 600-150. Open for lunch and dinner.* If you're looking for authentic Egyptian and Arabic food in a resort town that favors Italian, Continental, and Asian restaurants, this is the place to dine. Offers excellent and inexpensive Egyptian dishes. The open-air second floor dining area offers excellent views of the crowds below.

❑ **La Fleur:** *Jolie Ville Mövenpick Hotel, Tel. 600-100.* This elegant and pleasant French restaurant offers a daily special in addition to its a la carte menu.

BEYOND SHARM

If you have time, consider taking a day trip to St. Catherine Monastery, which is located 150 miles northwest of Sharm el-Sheikh. For many visitors to the Sinai Peninsula, this is truly one of the highlights of this area. Constructed in the 6th century AD, the monastery remains one of the most important Greek Orthodox religious centers. Located at the foot of Mount Sinai, St. Catherine is rich in history which it displays well in its basilica (Church of the Transfiguration), Chapel of the Burning Bush, the Skull House, and the Library. But the real focal point is the basilica with its beautiful mosaic of the Transfiguration of Jesus and its incredible collection of fine icons (be sure to bring your flashlight in order to see the icons near the dark entrance to the basilica). The Library, which requires a special entrance fee of L£20, is well worth visiting because of its unique manuscripts. While most monks are of Greek descent, English-speaking visitors will be fortunate to encounter the only American monk (from Boston) who can explain the basilica as well as take them on a tour of the Library. Even though these monks pray several hours each day, they do keep up with modern society. After all, this is a very successful monastery that seems to be well endowed for its many construction projects. Indeed, these ostensibly tradition-laden monks drive cars and trucks, and the American monk is wired to the world with a computer and an email address!

If you decide to go farther north to Israel (Eilat), you can cross the border at Taba, which is a two-hour drive from St. Catherine. Along the way you'll see lots of Bedoiuns and camels alongside the road. Just south of Taba you'll encounter a great deal of new construction for hotels and residences. The Taba area is fast becoming another major resort area in the Sinai Peninsula. However, except for the Hilton Hotel in Taba, there's not much to do here. Most of the action is on the Israeli side in the resort of Eilat. For more information on Eilat and Israel, see our separate volume, *The Treasures and Pleasures of Israel and Jordan: Best of the Best*.

ENJOYING YOUR STAY

If you enjoy resorts, Sharm el-Sheikh will not disappoint you. There's lots to see and do both day and night in Sharm. Many visitors come here because of Sharm's incredible reefs and outstanding **diving** opportunities. The whole area, with its many certified diving schools, is well organized for diving. Several companies offer diving tours which go to the popular site near Sharm, Tiran. Some companies, such as the Camel Drive Club (Tel. 600-700 or Fax 600-601), offer one-week diving cruises on the Red Sea.

Other **water sports** include waterskiing, windsurfing, banana boating, parasailing, and snorkeling. Most of the major hotels along the boardwalk in Na'ama Bay can assist you with such activities.

If you are interested in exploring the desert, several tour companies in Sharm sponsor **desert excursions** with profes-sional desert guides. Most of these excursions are day trips with visits to Bedouin camps, green oases, and the Coloured Canyon.

Sharm el-Sheikh also has the only **golf** course on the Sinai Peninsula, the Sharm el-Sheikh Golf Resort (Airport Road, Tel. 600-635).

If you like bars, discos, loud music, and dancing, Sharm has it all and it goes on all night, starting around 11pm and continuing until 3 or 4am. Check out the action at the **Pirates Bar** (Fayrouz Hilton, Tel. 600-137); **Bus Stop** (Sanafir Village Hotel, Tel. 600-197); **Cactus Disco** (Mövenpick Hotel Jolie Ville, Tel. 600-100); **Cyber Disco** (Fayrouz Hilton, Tel. 600-137); **The Spot** (Ghazala Hotel, Tel. 600-150); **Stars Music Bar** (Hyatt Regency, Tel. 601-234); and **Salsa** (Cataract Resort, Tel. 601-820).

And gamblers have the choice of two **casinos**: Coral Bay Hotel (Tel. 601-610) and the Mövenpick Hotel Jolie Ville (Tel. 600-100).

Index

CAIRO

LUXOR AND BEYOND

SHARM EL-SHEIKH AND THE SINAI PENINSULA

The Authors

WINSTON CHURCHILL PUT IT BEST – *"My needs are very simple – I simply want the best of everything."* Indeed, his attitude on life is well and alive amongst many of today's travelers. With limited time, careful budgeting, and a sense of adventure, many people seek both quality and value as they search for the best of the best.

Ron and Caryl Krannich, Ph.Ds, discovered this fact of travel life 17 years ago when they were living and working in Thailand as consultants with the Office of the Prime Minister. Former university professors and specialists on Southeast Asia, they discovered what they really loved to do – shop for quality arts, antiques, and home decorative items – was not well represented in most travel guides that primarily focused on sightseeing, hotels, and restaurants. While some guidebooks included a small section on shopping, they only listed types of products and names and addresses of shops, many of which were of questionable quality. And budget guides simply avoided quality shopping altogether, as if shopping was a travel sin!

The Krannichs knew there was much more to travel than what was represented in most travel guides. Avid collectors of Asian, South Pacific, Middle Eastern, and Latin American arts, antiques, and home decorative items, they learned long ago that one of the best ways to experience another culture and meet its talented artists and craftspeople was by shopping for local products. Not only would they learn a great deal about the culture and society, they also acquired some wonderful products, met many interesting and talented individuals, and helped support the continuing development of local arts and crafts.

But they quickly learned shopping in Asia was very different from shopping in North America and Europe. In the West, merchants nicely display items, identify prices, and periodically run sales. At the same time, shoppers in the West can easily do comparative shopping, watch for sales, and trust quality and delivery; they even have consumer protection! Americans and Europeans in Asia face a shopping culture based on different principles. Like a fish out of water, they make many mistakes: don't know how to bargain, fail to communicate effectively with tailors, avoid purchasing large items because they don't understand shipping, and are frequent victims of scams and rip-offs, especially in the case of gems and jewelry. To shop a country right, travelers need to know how to find quality products, bargain for the best prices, avoid scams, and ship their purchases with ease. What they most need is a combination travel and how-to book that focuses on the best of the best.

In 1987 the Krannichs inaugurated their first shopping guide to Asia – *Shopping in Exotic Places* – a guide to quality shopping in Hong Kong, South Korea, Thailand, Indonesia, and Singapore. Receiving rave reviews from leading travel publications and professionals, the book quickly found an enthusiastic audience amongst other avid travel-shoppers. It broke new ground as a combination travel and how-to book. No longer would shopping be confined to just naming products and identifying names and addresses of shops. It also included advice on how to pack for a shopping trip (take two suitcases, one filled with bubble-wrap), comparative shopping, bargaining skills, and shopping rules. Shopping was serious stuff requiring serious treatment of the subject by individuals who understood what they were doing. The Krannichs subsequently expanded the series to include separate volumes on Hong Kong, Thailand, Indonesia, Singapore and Malaysia, Australia and Papua New Guinea, the South Pacific, and the Caribbean.

Beginning in 1996, the series took on a new look as well as an expanded focus. Known as the Impact Guides and appropriately titled *The Treasures and Pleasures of . . . Best of the Best*, new editions covered Hong Kong, Thailand, Indonesia, Singapore, Malaysia, Paris and the French Riviera, and the Caribbean. In 1997 and 1999 new volumes appeared on Italy,

Hong Kong, and China. New volumes for 2000 and 2001 covered India, Australia, Thailand, Hong Kong, Singapore and Bali, Egypt, Israel and Jordan, Rio and São Paulo, Morocco, Vietnam, Indonesia, and the Philippines.

Beginning in October 2000, the Impact Guides became the major content for the new travel-shopping website appropriately called *i*ShopAroundTheWorld:

www.ishoparoundtheworld.com

While the primary focus remains shopping for quality products, the books and website also include useful information on the best hotels, restaurants, and sightseeing. As the authors note, *"Our users are discerning travelers who seek the best of the best. They are looking for a very special travel experience which is not well represented in other travel guides."*

The Krannichs passion for traveling and shopping is well represented in their home which is uniquely designed around their Asian, South Pacific, Middle East, North African, and Latin American art collections and which has been featured on CNN. *"We're fortunate in being able to create a living environment which pulls together so many wonderful travel memories and quality products,"* say the Krannichs. *"We learned long ago to seek out quality products and buy the best we could afford at the time. Quality lasts and is appreciated for years to come. Many of our readers share our passion for quality shopping abroad."* Their books also are popular with designers, antique dealers, and importers who use them to source products and suppliers.

While the Impact Guides keep the Krannichs busy traveling to exotic places, their travel series is an avocation rather than a vocation. The Krannichs also are noted authors of more than 30 career books, some of which deal with how to find international and travel jobs. The Krannichs also operate one of the world's largest career resource centers. Their works are available in most bookstores or through the publisher's online bookstore: *www.impactpublications.com*

If you have any questions or comments for the authors, please direct them to the publisher:

Ron and Caryl Krannich
IMPACT PUBLICATIONS
9104 Manassas Drive, Suite N
Manassas Park, VA 20111-5211 USA
Fax 703-335-9486
Email: *krannich@impactpublications.com*

Feedback and Recommendations

WE WELCOME FEEDBACK AND RECOMMEN-dations from our readers and users. If you have encountered a particular shop or travel experi-ence, both good or bad, that you feel should be included in future editions of this book or on *www.ishoparoundtheworld.com*, please send your comments by email, fax, or mail to:

Ron and Caryl Krannich
IMPACT PUBLICATIONS
9104 Manassas Drive, Suite N
Manassas Park, VA 20111-5211 USA
Fax 703-335-9486
Email: *krannich@impactpublications.com*

_____

_____

_____

_____

_____

_____

_____

_____

More Treasures and Pleasures

THE FOLLOWING TRAVEL GUIDES CAN BE ordered directly from the publisher. Complete the following form (or list the titles), include your name and address, enclose payment, and send your order to:

IMPACT PUBLICATIONS
9104 Manassas Drive, Suite N
Manassas Park, VA 20111-5211 (USA)
Tel. 1-800-361-1055 (orders only)
703/361-7300 (information) Fax 703/335-9486
Email: *egypt@impactpublications.com*
Online bookstores: ***www.impactpublications.com*** or
www.ishoparoundtheworld.com

All prices are in U.S. dollars. Orders from individuals should be prepaid by check, moneyorder, or credit card (we accept Visa, MasterCard, American Express, and Discover). We accept credit card orders by telephone, fax, e-mail, and online (visit Impact's two online travel bookstores). If your order must be shipped outside the U.S., please include an additional US$1.50 per title for surface mail or the appropriate air mail rate for books weighting 24 ounces each. Orders usually ship within 48 hours. For more information on the authors, travel resources, and international shopping, visit ***www.impactpublications.com*** and ***www.ishoparoundtheworld.com*** on the World Wide Web.

Qty.	TITLES	Price	TOTAL
___	Travel Planning on the Internet	$19.95	_____
___	Treasures and Pleasures of Australia	$17.95	_____
___	Treasures and Pleasures of the Caribbean	$16.95	_____
___	Treasures and Pleasures of China	$14.95	_____
___	Treasures and Pleasures of Egypt	$16.95	_____
___	Treasures and Pleasures of Hong Kong	$16.95	_____

__ Treasures and Pleasures of India	$16.95	_____
__ Treasures and Pleasures of Indonesia	$14.95	_____
__ Treasures and Pleasures of Israel & Jordan	$16.95	_____
__ Treasures and Pleasures of Italy	$14.95	_____
__ Treasures and Pleasures of Morocco	$16.95	_____
__ Treasures and Pleasures of Paris and the French Riviera	$14.95	_____
__ Treasures and Pleasures of Rio/São Paulo	$13.95	_____
__ Treasures and Pleasures of Singapore/Bali	$16.95	_____
__ Treasures and Pleasures of Thailand	$16.95	_____
__ Treasures and Pleasures of Vietnam	$16.95	_____

SUBTOTAL ------------ $ _____

■ Virginia residents add 4.5% sales tax $ _____

■ Shipping/handling ($5.00 for the first
  title and $1.50 for each additional book) $ _____

■ Additional amount if shipping outside U.S. $ _____

TOTAL ENCLOSED ---------- $ _____

SHIP TO:

Name _____

Address _____

_____

_____

Phone Number: _____

PAYMENT METHOD:

❑ I enclose check/moneyorder for $ _____
   made payable to IMPACT PUBLICATIONS.

❑ Please charge $ _____ to my credit card:

❑ Visa ❑ MasterCard ❑ American Express ❑ Discover

Card # _____

Expiration date: _____/_____

Signature _____

Rave Reviews About The Impact Guides:

Travel and Leisure: *"An excellent, exhaustive and fascinating look at shopping."*

Travel-Holiday: *"Books in the series help travelers recognize quality and gain insight to local customs."*

Washington Post: *"You learn more about a place you are visiting when Impact is pointing the way. The Impact Guides are particularly good in evaluating local arts and handicrafts while providing a historical or cultural context."*

▶ *The Treasures and Pleasures of China: Best of the Best.* 1999. 317 pages. ISBN 1-57023-077-3

▶ *The Treasures and Pleasures of the Caribbean.* 1996. 371 pages. ISBN 1-57023-046-3

▶ *The Treasures and Pleasures of Indonesia.* 1996. 243 pages. ISBN 1-57023-045-5

▶ *The Treasures and Pleasures of Italy.* 1997. 271 pages. ISBN 1-57023-058-7

▶ *The Treasures and Pleasures of Paris and the French Riviera.* 1996. 263 pages. ISBN 1-57023-057-9

▶ *The Treasures and Pleasures of Singapore and Malaysia.* 1996. 282 pages. ISBN 1-57023-044-7

Authors: Drs. Ron and Caryl Krannich are two of America's leading travel and career writers with more than 40 books to their credit. They have authored 10 books in the Impact Guides series, including volumes on Hong Kong, Singapore, Malaysia, Indonesia, Italy, and France.

Order Toll-free! 1-800/361-1055

Start Your Next Trip On the Internet!

Travel Planning On the Internet: The Click and Easy™ Guide
Ron and Caryl Krannich, Ph.Ds

The Internet has fast become the traveler's best friend. You can quickly go online for airline tickets, hotel reservations, car rentals, restaurants, shopping, visa applications, tours, newspapers, translations, travel gear, tips, and information on your favorite destinations – nearly everything you ever wanted to know about the wonderful world of travel. Here's the book that pulls it all together. Identifying over 2,000 key websites dealing with all aspects of travel, *Travel Planning on the Internet* is your passport to a whole new world of travel. Along with *www.ishoparoundtheworld.com*, use this invaluable guide to plan your next trip or explore new travel options 24 hours a day. Even use it while traveling for locating restaurants, shops, tours, travel tips, and more! New for 2001. $19.95 plus shipping.

TO ORDER: Use the form on pages 231-232 or order online: *www.impactpublications.com* or *www.ishoparoundtheworld.com*

Meet Talented Artisans of Israel and Jordan

The Treasures and Pleasures of Israel and Jordan: Best of the Best
Ron and Caryl Krannich, Ph.Ds

While they often appear worlds apart politically, these two countries and cultures share one thing in common – talented artists and craftsmen who produce wonderful treasures for discerning travel-shoppers. Here's the book that identifies the best of shopping and traveling in two of the world's most fascinating places. Examining the treasures and pleasures of Jerusalem, Tel Aviv, and Eilat in Israel and Amman, Jerash, and Petra in Jordan, this new Impact Guide reveals what to buy, where to shop, and how to acquire your treasures with ease – from bargaining to shipping. It also includes the best in accommodations, restaurants, and sightseeing. Discover top quality jewelry, ceramics, antiques, religious objects, and leather goods. Develop new shopping skills for getting great bargains in shops, markets, and souks. June 2001. $16.95 plus shipping.

TO ORDER: Use the form on pages 231-232 or order online: *www.impactpublications.com* or *www.ishoparoundtheworld.com*

Discover the Unique Treasures of Morocco

The Treasures and Pleasures of Morocco: Best of the Best
Ron and Caryl Krannich, Ph.Ds

Discover the unique treasures and pleasures of this exotic North African country. Includes the business, government, and resort centers of Casablanca, Rabat, Tangier, and Agadir; the exotic shopping paradises of Fez, Marrakech, and Essaouria; the fascinating southern desert cities of Erfoud, Ouarzazate, and Taroudant; and a gorgeous countryside toured by car. Uncover terrific ceramics, jewelry, leather goods, arts, crafts, and antiques found in the many souks and shops of Morocco's intriguing medinas. Locate the best hotels, restaurants, and sightseeing. Learn how to bargain for 30 to 70 percent discounts; the best ways to avoid pesky touts and commissioned tour guides; the secrets to shipping your treasures home with ease; and much more. May 2001. $16.95 plus shipping.

TO ORDER: Use the form on pages 231-232 or order online: *www.impactpublications.com* or *www.ishoparoundtheworld.com*

Travel the World for Treasures!

Welcome to *i*ShopAroundTheWorld, an Internet site that brings together the best of the best in shopping and traveling around the world. If you enjoy shopping, be sure to visit our one-stop-shop for great advice, resources, discussion, and linkages to make your next trip a very special adventure. Discover how to:

- Prepare for a shopping adventure
- Find quality shops and products
- Bargain for the best prices
- Identify local shopping rules
- Order custom-made goods
- Handle touts and tour guides
- Avoid shopping and travel scams
- Pack and ship goods with ease
- Select the best hotels and restaurants
- Use the Internet to travel and shop
- Find inexpensive airfares and cruises
- Travel independently or with tours
- Hire cars, drivers, and guides
- Schedule times and places
- Choose the best sightseeing
- Enjoy terrific entertainment

…and meet talented, interesting, and friendly people in some of the world's most fascinating destinations. Join our community as we travel to the intriguing worlds of artisans, craftspeople, and shopkeepers in search of fine jewelry, clothing, antiques, furniture, arts, handicrafts, textiles, and numerous other treasures to grace your home and enhance your wardrobe. Best of all, shop and travel online before and after your next trip!

www.ishoparoundtheworld.com